Language Arts Pre-K-3
Reading • Writing • Spelling • Phonics • Speak

A Total Language Arts Curriculum
36 Steps to Independent Reading Ability

Instructor's Manual
A-Z

for **Off We Go** and *Raceway Book*

Author
Sue Dickson

Contributing Author
Jeanette Cason

Modern Curriculum Press, an imprint of Pearson Learning
299 Jefferson Road, P.O. Box 480, Parsippany, NJ 07054
1-800-321-3106 / www.pearsonlearning.com

ISBN:1-56704-618-5

Printed in the United States of America

D E F G H I J K L M N–HG–05 04 03 02 01

Table of Contents

A Total Language Arts Curriculum

SING, SPELL, READ & WRITE - WHAT IS IT?

Colorful, creative, exciting, enjoyable, and effective are only a few of the adjectives used by teachers, parents, and administrators in describing *Sue Dickson's* sound approach to teaching reading. *Sing, Spell, Read & Write* is a systematic, total Language Arts program that provides correlated lessons in six subjects: Reading, Writing, Phonics, Spelling, Comprehension, and Grammar. Assessments and Achievement Tests are also included.

With *Sing, Spell, Read & Write's* 36-step method and materials, you can be sure your student will reach independent reading ability quickly and happily. The **Home Tutoring Kit** you are using was voted #1 in three consecutive national polls of parents teaching their children at home.*

SUCCESS FOR THE CHILD

What makes *Sing, Spell, Read & Write* so psychologically and academically effective is the method requires total participation. The child must respond to each step in the program. While playing Sound-O, singing the Phonics Songs, leading the ABC Echoes, "riding" the Ferris Wheel, "popping" the Balloons, and moving the car around the Raceway, it is impossible to remain passive. Every activity in the program is an enjoyable event for the child where learning becomes synonymous with doing, making a reality of the old Chinese proverb:

> I hear and I forget.
> I see and I remember.
> I do and I understand.

There is no better way of building wholesome personalities than through the progressive accumulation of success, and success has been built into the program. Nothing is demanded of students that they cannot do. They progress through the program at their own speed. An eagerness to learn seems to increase each time their car is moved forward one space on the Raceway charting their progress. Further, since many of the game activities are based on chance, there are many opportunities to win.

We thank you for choosing *Sing, Spell, Read and Write*. We are certain you will find it effective and enjoyable in teaching your child to read, write and spell.

* Practical Homeschooling Magazine Poll

   3

A Total Language Arts Curriculum

Dear Instructor,

You are about to begin a most wonderful adventure: teaching someone to read, write and spell. You will be using a step-by-step approach that is easy to follow. A Raceway Chart will help you track your student's progress through the 36 steps to independent reading ability.

The following will be used:

- 6 recorded cassettes or the CD
- 5 games
- 2 Curriculum Books: **Off We Go** and **Raceway Book**
- **Assessment Book**
- 17 **Phonetic Storybook Readers** (with 1,000 pages of stories, poems, and rhyming tales)
- Raceway Chart and car
- A to Z Phonics Song Placemat
- Sing-along & point Phonics Song Charts in the Raceway Book
- Treasure Chest with prizes
- Dry erase marker and felt eraser for My Little Writing "Slate" on back cover.

During 27 years in the classroom, I experienced many trends in reading instruction, but I found the only way to have my students achieve **independent reading ability** quickly was to correlate instruction for Phonics, Reading, Writing, Spelling, Comprehension, and Grammar into one unified approach. When I wrote the Phonics songs and added games "to put a sparkle" into Phonics lessons, I saw a major surge in student performance. When I added the Phonetic Storybook Readers to connect the Phonics, Writing, and Spelling Lessons with Literature/Comprehension, all the pieces clicked together, and scores rose dramatically.

The **Sing, Spell, Read and Write** Curriculum you are going to be using is a research based, complete and balanced Language Arts Program that does much more than meet new state Language Arts Guidelines. You will find that it is fun and will capture the attention of your student(s). "What children like, they pay attention to. What they pay attention to, they learn."

You'll want to check your kit to be sure you have everything shown on page 5, and then you'll be ready to start your student on the "raceway to literacy!"

Have a great time singing, spelling, reading and writing. I look forward to hearing of your success.

Sue Dickson

Sue Dickson
Author/Teacher

CONTENTS

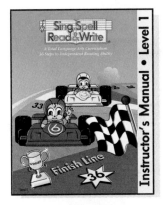

Instructor's Manual

Dry Erase Marker and Felt Eraser

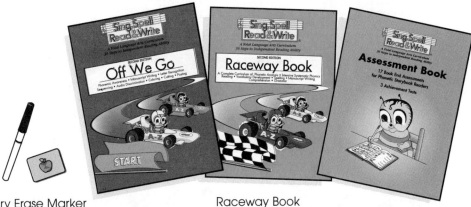

Off We Go

Raceway Book

Assessment Book

17 Phonetic Storybook Readers

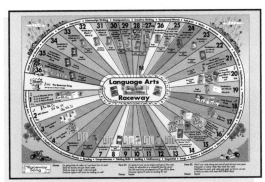

Raceway Chart and Car for refrigerator (11"x17")

Placemat (11"x17") and Dry Erase "Slate"

CD & 6 Sing-Along Cassettes

Treasure Chest & Prizes

GAMES

A to Z Pick-A-Sound

Word-O

Letter Cluster Pick-A-Sound

A to Z Sound-O

Letter Cluster Sound-O

Trip 1

Trip 2

GETTING READY

Directions and Suggested Script by Sue Dickson

Show your student the **Raceway Chart** and **static cling car** and say:

- "We're going to move your car around this **Raceway Chart two times** as you learn how to read, write, and spell."

- "On the **first trip** around the **Raceway Chart**, your car will be moved forward (from wedge to wedge) as we keep an eye on the white "inside track" with letters **Aa** to **Zz**. (point to it). **Aa** is the letter we will learn first, (today!), so we'll place your car in the center of the blue wedge just out from letter **Aa**. We will be using the **Off We Go** student book, (show it). You will learn about a letter of the alphabet each day and move your car forward when you complete the 4 pages in **Off We Go** for that letter."

- "On the **second trip** around the Raceway, we'll be moving your car forward from wedge to wedge looking at the **outside edge of the track** and doing what it says to do by each number from #1 to #36."

- "Now it's time to get your CD/cassette player ready and listen to the **Raceway Song** (Directions follow on next page).

RACEWAY SONG

Directions:
Raceway Song, on CD or Cassette #1 will help your student set the goal of getting to Step 36 on the *Raceway Chart.* After listening to the song several times, you may want to have your student sing along and use the suggested hand motions indicated in parentheses below.

Chorus: I'm going thirty-six miles so I can learn how to read. (steering)

Thirty-six lessons are just what I need. (thumbs up)

Thirty-six stops to read, write and spell. (holding hands together and up to indicate OK! YES!)

Everyone rejoice I'll soon be reading so well! (clapping)

Verse 1:   I'm going to tune up my engine and get on the road, (turn on key)

I know an education is a wonderful load. (carrying load on back)

The hills and turns are pleasant so I'll go 'til I'm done. (turn steering wheel and sway)

Everyone rejoice I'll soon be reading for fun! (clapping)

REPEAT CHORUS

Verse 2:   So won't you come along one and all and set your own pace. (motions to come with you)

Everyone's a winner when they finish this race! (clapping hands above head)

We'll learn to read, and write and spell, as fast as we can. (hold up finger for #1 winner)

In thirty-six miles we'll read ANYTHING, man! (hold hands up with fingers outstretched)

REPEAT CHORUS

SING ALONG WITH THIS GOAL SETTING SONG AT THE START OF LESSONS.

Sing Spell Read & Write.

INTRODUCTION AND INSTRUCTION

Next, show your student the **A to Z Phonics Song Placemat** and ask:

A to Z Phonics Song Placemat

Instructor:	"Do you see anything on this placemat that you think will help you learn to read?"
Student:	"Yes, those letters and pictures."
Instructor:	"Why do you think we have to know about **letters** to get ready to read?" (Elicit the following answer, even if it takes some discussion):
Student:	"Because **everything we will ever read is made up of letters!**"
Instructor:	"That's right! **Everything!** Whether it is a little child's book or a great big grown-up's book (or even the newspaper!) **all reading is made up of just these (26) letters of the ABC's (or Alphabet)!** It seems almost a miracle, doesn't it?"
Student:	"I already know the ABC's."
Instructor:	"That's great."

You may want to have your student sing the **Alphabet Song** to the tune of "Twinkle, Twinkle Little Star," being sure to point along to the letters on the back cover of **Off We Go** as you sing. Slow down singing as you point to L-M-N-O-P! Some students think it is one letter! One point per letter: L-M-N-O-P! Almost all children know this song and the **names** of the letters, but just in case they don't, you want to "cover all bases," so sing it, **ALWAYS POINTING TO THE ALPHABET LETTERS AS YOU DO**. Also, randomly point to the letters and ask the child to tell you the *name* of the letter, until all letters can be readily identified by **name**.

Then continue...

Instructor:	"I am so happy that you know the **names** of the letters! But did you know there is something *more important* than the letter **names**? Did you know that each letter has a **sound**? We're going to learn the sound of each letter, all the way from A to Z! This will help you learn to read and write, and we're going to start TODAY! Let's begin! We have the **A to Z Phonics Song Placemat** with pictures and letters to help us learn the **sounds** of all the letters, and we have a song (on a CD/cassette). We also have a game. It's going to be lots of fun!" Point to first section (yellow) on the placemat and read: **"When we learn these sounds you'll see, ready to read then we will be. . ."**

8

Next, point to the section for **Aa** (with the picture of the apple), and say:

Instructor: Let's look at big letter **A** (point), and little letter **a** (point) on the next section of the placemat. There is a picture above the letters (**Aa**). What is this picture?"

Student: "An apple."

Instructor: "Yes! Now let's **start** to say **apple**, s t r e t c h i n g the word very slowly, and listen to the VERY BEGINNING of the word to hear the **sound** of letter **a**. Let's try."

Student: "ă......pple." (stretch the ă)

Instructor: "Yes! Big letter **A** (point) says ă and little letter **a** (point) says ă, and it is the beginning of the word ăpple. Can you hear it? Now echo after me." IN RAPID SUCCESSION: "Ă" (pointing to capital A) "ă" (point to little a) "ăpple" (pointing to the picture of the apple)

Student: "Ă, ă, ăpple." (with Instructor pointing)

1) First, to capital letter **A,**
2) then to small letter **a**, and
3) then to the **picture of the apple**.

Instructor: "That's right! Let's go on. Let's look at the next letters and picture (for **B**). How do we find (or discover) the **sound** of **B**?"

Student: "We look at the picture."

Instructor: "Right! What is it?"

Student: "Ball!"

Instructor: "Yes, ball. Let's try to **start** to say ball and not finish it."

Student: "Buh!"

Instructor: "Oops! That's almost right but I hear "uh" for umbrella on the end of your sound! (buh)! Do you know it never rains in Letter Land, so we don't want that "uh" for umbrella when we say the letter sounds! Instead, try to get just a little explosion on your lips at the beginning of ball." (think "bh" or "bi"as you say it!)

Student: "Bh!"

Instructor: "That's right. Do you hear the difference? Listen. **Buh! — Bh!** or **Bĭ**."

1) First point to capital letter **B**,
2) then to small letter **b**, and
3) then to the **picture of the ball**.

Suggested Script Continued

Instructor: "Let's see whether you can echo after me as we go across the rows of letters and pictures saying the sound of the big letter (capital/upper case) and the small letter (lower case) and then naming the picture. Ready? Here we go!"

INSTRUCTOR:			STUDENT ECHOES:		
Ă !	ă!	apple	Ă !	ă!	apple
Bh!	bh!	ball	Bh!	bh!	ball
Ck!	ck!	cat (not "cuh")	Ck!	ck!	cat
Dh!	dh!	doll (not "duh")	Dh!	dh!	doll
Ĕh!	ĕh!	egg	Ĕh!	ĕh!	egg
Ff !	ff !	fan (not "fuh")	Ff !	ff !	fan
Gh!	gh!	goat (not "guh")	Gh!	gh!	goat
Hh!	hh!	hand (not "huh")	Hh!	hh!	hand
Ĭ!	ĭ!	inchworm	Ĭ!	ĭ!	inchworm
J!	J!	jam (not "juh")	J!	j!	jam
K!	k!	kite	K!	k!	kite
L!	l!	lamb	L!	l!	lamb
M!	m!	monkey	M!	m!	monkey
N!	n!	noodles	N!	n!	noodles
Ŏ!	ŏ!	octopus	Ŏ!	ŏ!	octopus
P!	p!	poodles	P!	p!	poodles
Q!	q!	quilt	Q!	q!	quilt
R!	r!	rail	R!	r!	rail
S!	s!	sun	S!	s!	sun
T!	t!	tail	T!	t!	tail
Ŭ!	ŭ!	umbrella	Ŭ!	ŭ!	umbrella
V!	v!	vase	V!	v!	vase
W!	w!	wagon	W!	w!	wagon
X!(ks)	x!(ks)	box *	X !(ks)!	x!(ks)!	box
Y!	y!	yarn	Y!	y!	yarn
Z!	z!	zoo	Z!	z!	zoo

✶NOTE: *For letter **Xx** give this brief explanation:*

Instructor: "There is something special about letter **X**. At the beginning of a word, Mr. **X** often steals another letter sound (as in **x**ylophone, the **z** sound). And sometimes it says the letter **name** as in **X-ray**. Do you hear the **X**? X-ray? So we will learn the *sound* **X** makes at the **END OF A WORD**. It says **ks** (like saying "kiss" quickly and quietly). Say fo**x** (**ks**), bo**x** (**ks**), mi**x** (**ks**), a**x** (**ks**), wa**x** (**ks**). So in the song we will sing/say: `**Ks, ks,** bo**x** (**ks**).` Now, we have a song that will help us learn all the letter sounds. It starts -- '***When we learn these sounds you'll see, ready to read then we will be.***' LISTEN AND WATCH."

(Continued on next page)

Suggested Script Continued

 Play A to Z Phonics Song, on CD or Cassette #1, and point along to the letters and pictures, demonstrating the song for your student.

Instructor: "Now, let's try to sing it together all the way through. We will study thoroughly one letter each day, but we can have fun singing and pointing to **all** of the letters starting now! Remember to say the sounds without adding "**uh**" for umbrella."

Play the **A to Z Phonics Song** again and point along to letters and pictures as your student sings along. Don't expect perfection. It will be refined as you study each letter more thoroughly.

Before introducing your student to the *Off We Go* book, you will want to read pp. 12-21 in this Manual.

Ă...ă...apple

B...b...ball

D...d...doll

C...c...cat

OFF WE GO

INTRODUCTION

Off We Go is the first curriculum book you will use with your student. It is designed to be used during the **first 6 weeks** of first grade, but may be used with second or third grade students who need a new or remedial approach to beginning Language Arts skills. It has also been successfully used with Special Education students, however, the pace has to be somewhat slower than outlined.

EDUCATIONAL CONTENT

Off We Go includes lessons in:
- Letter Recognition
- Phonemic Awareness/Phonics
- Manuscript Writing
- Alphabet Sequencing

For each of the twenty-six letters of the alphabet there are four activity pages:
- a Key Word Picture/Phonics Song Coloring Page (phonemic awareness)
- a Manuscript Writing Page (learning to write)
- a Cut and Paste Page (auditory discrimination)
- a Follow the Dots Page (alphabet sequencing)

THAT VERY IMPORTANT FIRST DAY

There are four activity pages for letter **Aa** (**OWG**, pp. 3, 4, 5, 6). The pages do not have to be completed at one sitting, but all four pages should be completed before the day is through. This is very important, as the establishing of specified goals, good work habits, and a systematic approach to learning are important educational goals of this program. When your student completes the four pages for letter **A,** move his/her car forward one space on the Raceway as a reward for completing the work. Point to the Raceway Chart and say, "The next goal is to learn about letter **B,** which will be introduced tomorrow.

MAKE YOUR STUDENT AWARE OF GOALS IMMEDIATELY

Your student should be aware that he/she has learned about the letter **A** that says **Ă, ă**, apple, and **Ă, ă, alligator**, etc., on that first day. Tell him/her the goal is to learn about each of the twenty-six letters of the alphabet until all are known. (Approximately six weeks.) The student should know the reason for learning about letters is this knowledge will help him/her in learning to read and write. Aren't all signs, books, and magazines filled with **ABC's** that say something?

OFF WE GO

OVERVIEW FOR INSTRUCTOR

Goals

To learn/practice/master:

- Letter Sounds and Letter Names
- Phonemic Awareness
- Manuscript Writing
- Auditory Discrimination
- A to Z Alphabet Sequence

Suggested Pacing

26 days (1 letter per day)

Materials

1. CD or Cassette #1
2. *Off We Go*

Phonics Song(s)/Games

The Raceway Song, CD or Cassette #1
A to Z Phonics Song, CD or Cassette #1
Name That Word Game, Directions/Manual p. 15
A to Z Sound-O Game, Directions/Manual p. 19
A to Z Pick-A-Sound Game, Directions/Manual p. 20

Getting Ready To Write

Teach your student how to:

- hold a pencil
- write his/her name with upper and lower case letters
- remove pages from *Off We Go*

1. Demonstrate the correct way to hold a pencil as shown. Check student's grip. Also, show student correct arm position on the page, coming straight up from the **bottom** of the page, **not from the side of the page**.

2. Write a sample of your student's first and last name. Have him/her practice writing on the lines provided. (Be sure to check directions for proper letter formation found on bottom of writing pages in *Off We Go*.)

3. Show your student that the pages of this book are perforated for easy removal (**beginning with p. 3**) by pulling gently at the top of each page. It's easier to do the lessons (which call for using scissors, glue, pencils, and crayons) if you remove the four lesson pages each day and put the book away.

p. 2

Activity Pages

Phonics Song Coloring Pages

Phonemic Awareness/Phonics
pp. 3, 7, 11, 15, 19, etc., (every fourth page)

For each letter of the alphabet there is a **Phonics Song Coloring Page** which provides a **key word picture** for each letter sound.

p. 3

PROCEDURE

1. Turn to the **Phonics Song Coloring Page**, (p. 3), and have your student identify the picture as **apple**, and say "apple."

2. Have him/her say "apple" again very slowly, s t r e t c h i n g out the "ă" sound at the beginning. Ă..ă...apple.

3. Next, have student start to say **apple**, but not finish it: ă, ă, ă! Direct your student to look at the letters below the picture of the apple and teach: **"All three forms of the letter A/a/a stand for the sound ă."**

4. Point to the letter form (a) in the middle and tell your student this is the letter form we often see in books and on signs, but will not learn to write that form of the letter. However, we do need to recognize it.

5. Point to the other letters below the picture, and tell your student **these are the letters he/she will be using to learn to read and write (Aa),** and they all say ă as in apple.

Have student point to:

- capital **A** and say Ă
- lower case letter **a** and say ă
- the picture of the apple and say "**apple**" (See illustration)

   Instructor: "Ă, ă, ăpple" (Pointing from corner to corner and then to the picture of the apple.)

   Student: "Ă, ă, ăpple" (Pointing from corner to corner and then to the picture of the apple.) Repeat this procedure several times, then have your student color the apple.

6. Follow this same procedure to teach the sounds of each of the 26 letters. Listen to the **A to Z Phonics Song** (CD or Cassette #1), to hear the correct sound for each letter.

NOTE: Be very careful to say and teach sounds of consonants without an ŭ sound after each one! For example, it's **s, s, sun,** not **sŭ, sŭ, sun!** It's **m, m,** (humming) **monkey,** not **mŭ, mŭ, monkey!** This is **EXTREMELY** important! Listen to the recording of the **ABC Echoes** to hear the correct sound for each letter.

(Continued on next page)

7. Have your student sing the **A to Z Phonics Song** (pointing along to letters and pictures on the placemat) daily at the start of each lesson.

8. Have him/her color the **Phonics Song Coloring Page** after singing the song.

NOTE: If you have wall space, remove the **Phonics Song Coloring Pages** from *Off We Go* as your student colors them, and hang them in sequence. The student can point along to these letters and pictures while singing the **A to Z Phonics Song**.

Name That Word Game

Phonemic Awareness: The conscious awareness of the sounds in spoken words.

One of the prerequisites for learning to read is for students to become aware that words are made up of individual sounds. You can readily accomplish teaching this by playing **Name That Word** in the following way: Ask your child to identify the words you say, "stretching" them as:

Instructor:	"ssss - uuuu - nnn. What word is that? Name that word!"
Student:	"sun"
Instructor:	"mmmm - aaaa - nnn. What word is that?"
Student:	"man"

Continue to play **Name that Word** throughout the first weeks while using *Off We Go*. By the end of the third week you should ask, "Do you know what letter you hear at the **beginning** of the word **mm - aa - nn**. What letter do you hear on the **end**?" etc.

Manuscript Writing

Learning to Write
pp. 4, 8, 12, 16, 20, etc. (every fourth page)

For each letter of the alphabet there is a **Manuscript Writing** page.

At the bottom of each **Manuscript Writing** page in *Off We Go* there are directions for the formation of the letters. **It is important to use the "script" provided**. The teaching of manuscript writing using this method is designed to do away with difficulties such as:

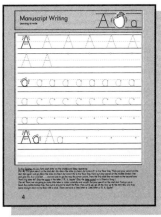

p. 4

- FLIPPING OF LETTERS (Reversals).

- INABILITY TO TELL THE DIFFERENCE BETWEEN SIMILAR LETTERS, ESPECIALLY LITTLE LETTERS **d** and **b**, **p** and **q**.

- INABILITY TO CHANGE TO CURSIVE WRITING (Script).

(Manuscript Writing Continued)

Avoiding Confusion

One popular method of teaching writing has students form all letters from "balls and sticks". This can be confusing. The muscle movement is indeed simple, because every letter is formed from either straight lines or complete circles, or both. However, the brain is confused when a child is taught, "Letter **b** is formed by making a straight line here and a ball down here, and letter **d** is formed by making a straight line down here with a ball over here." It is certainly easy to see why a child may find it difficult to remember which one is which.

d   b

p   q

Another popular method teaches lower case letters on a slant with lots of "tails" and "curve ups." These letter forms are *never seen in any readers, library books, or standardized tests*, thus forcing the child to learn one form of letters for **writing**, and another form for **reading**.

Some students become confused when they are taught to write this form of **a** and then are expected to read books with this form of **a**; when they are taught to write this **g** and are expected to read this **g**. When books have the letter **j** look like letter **i**, without its identifying hook at the bottom, kids stumble. Take a look at Exhibits **A**, **B**, **C** and **D**, taken from beginning reading books used in schools, and try to see it from the child's perspective.

	Exhibit A		Exhibit B		Exhibit C	Exhibit D
(I)	**(a)**	**(t)**	**(a)**	**(g)**	**(kitten)**	**("give me the five fish,")**
It is a big tin lid. I will jump in.			I can go.		*kitten* *little*	"give mē the fīve fish," the *dog* said.
(j)					**(little)**	**(the dog said.)**

You will find the method for teaching manuscript writing presented in *this* program:

- Has the student recognize just one alphabet form for both reading and writing. Writing and reading letter forms are identical.

- Has fewer touchdowns, helping the student transition easily to cursive writing.

- Provides teaching techniques to assist the student in remembering which letter is which: "first little **c**, then little **d**".

WHAT WE SAY GUIDES THE WAY in teaching manuscript writing. Oral, visual, and kinesthetic avenues to the brain will be utilized in learning to write with the **Sing, Spell, Read & Write** method. So repeat, repeat, repeat the script provided at the bottom of each writing page as you teach each manuscript letter.

p. 16

OFF WE GO

Instructor Tip ✓ The following illustrations provide an example of how your student's writing paper should be slanted, depending on whether he/she is right or left handed. **The arm should rest on the paper, coming up from the bottom,** not around from the side.

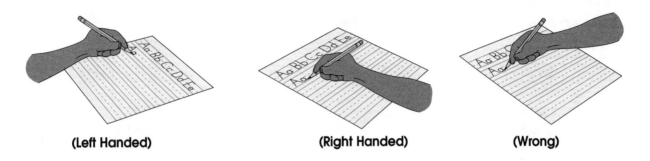

(Left Handed)   **(Right Handed)**   **(Wrong)**

My Little Writing Slate

Manuscript Writing Practice
The back cover of **Off We Go** has an erasable writing slate for manuscript writing practice. Your student will use the dry-erase marker and miniature felt eraser when tracing over the letters, practicing correct letter formation.

back cover

Cut and Paste

Auditory Discrimination
pp. 5, 9, 13, 17, etc., (every fourth page)
For each letter of the alphabet, there is a **Cut and Paste** page which provides practice in auditory discrimination (hearing the differences in the beginning sounds of words).

PROCEDURE

Have student:

- Turn to the **Cut and Paste** page (p. 5).
- Identify each picture at the bottom of page.
- Repeat the beginning sound of each picture twice when naming it (examples: **ă, ă, ă**x; **ă, ă, ă**stronaut; **f, f, f**lower).
- Tell whether each picture begins with the same beginning sound as the key picture on the page.
- Cross out the pictures that do not begin with the key sound.
- Color, cut, and paste (in the spaces provided) the pictures that begin with the key sound.
- Write the small letter (as shown) on the line provided to complete the key word (apples).

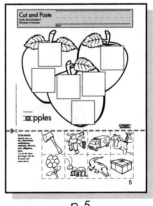

p. 5

Sing Spell Read & Write

OFF WE GO

Follow the Dots

Alphabet Sequence

pp. 6, 10, 14, 18, 22, etc., (every fourth page)

For each letter of the alphabet there is a **Follow the Dots** page providing a **mystery item** to identify and color.

PROCEDURE

Have student:

- Turn to the **Follow the Dots** page (p. 6).

- Connect the dots going from capital **A** to lower case **a.**

- Write the first letter of the mystery item on the line (**a**crobats).

- Color the picture.

p. 6

Off We Go
Daily Lesson Plan

- Sing *Raceway Song* – *(1 time) 2 minutes*
- Sing *A to Z Phonics Song* – *(several times) 3 minutes*
- Complete 4 pages in *Off We Go* – *1 hour*
- Move car around "inside track" of *Raceway Chart*
- Play *A to Z Sound-O Game* – *15 minutes*
- Play *A to Z Pick-A-Sound Game* – *15 minutes*
- Storytime Literature – *15 minutes*

When your child completes the last page in **Off We Go,** hold up his/her hand, lead the family in giving three cheers, and select a prize from the Treasure Chest. Move the car to Step 1 on the **Raceway Chart**, ready to start the second race, and present the **Raceway Book.** The real adventure is about to begin!

YOU'RE OFF! HAVE A GREAT TIME!

OFF WE GO

A to Z Sound-O Game

TO BE PLAYED FROM STEPS 1-36

Goal
To play a game which will give the student practice in recall of letter sounds as taught in the *A to Z Phonics Song*.

Preparation
1. Cut apart **Teacher Caller Card** found in the package of 5 *A to Z Sound-O Cards.*

2. Place the **Teacher Caller Cards** in the round plastic container labeled *A to Z Sound-O.*

Directions
1. Give each player a card and some see-through game markers.

2. Have player place the side with *blue capital letters* face up.

3. Tell player to put a marker on the **X** with Gus-the-Bug in the center of the card. This is a free space.

4. Draw a Caller from the container and call that letter's **name**, **sound**, and **the key word picture learned in the A to Z Phonics Song** for each, as:

   "Cover the letter **A** that has the sound **ă**, as in **ă**pple."
   "Cover the letter **E** that says **ĕ**, as in **ĕ**gg."
   "Cover the letter **O** that says **ŏ**, as in **ŏ**ctopus," etc.

   Assure player that **each** card has **every** sound being called;
   "Keep looking -- it's there somewhere!"

5. Tell player to call out "Sound-O!" when he/she gets a straight line vertically, horizontally, or diagonally.

6. Have fun! And don't forget to allow your winner to select a prize from the Treasure Chest!

7. Follow these same directions for Side 2, with lower case red letters after the student has mastered Side 1.

8. Play often and have fun!

> **Important:** Keep *A to Z Phonics Song Placemat* in view while playing, as this should be an enjoyable <u>practice</u>, **not a test**. When your child no longer needs to check the pictures on the placemat, it is an indication that the letters and sounds have been mastered.

OFF WE GO

A to Z Pick-A-Sound Game

TO BE PLAYED FROM STEPS 1-36

Goal

To play a game which will give your student practice in identifying letter sounds as taught in the **A to Z Phonics Song.**

A to Z Pick-A-Sound is played with the **yellow** deck of cards. Two to five players may take part. The object is to make pairs from cards in each player's hand. The game ends when any player is completely out of cards. The player with the most pairs is the winner.

Directions

1. Place the yellow Merry-Go-Round container in the center of the table. Shuffle the deck of cards and deal one card at a time until each player has five cards. Place the rest of the cards face down in a pile inside the Merry-Go-Round container.

2. All players should then sort their cards, placing any pairs they have face-up on the table in front of them.

3. The player to the left of the dealer should begin the game by calling any player by name and asking for a card. *"Mary, do you have the letter **m** that says **m-m-m**onkey?"* The player making the request **must hold that card** in his/her possession.

4. If Mary has the **Mm** card, she must give it to that player who will put the pair down. That player will get another turn, calling on another person for a sound. However, if Mary does not have the **Mm** card, she must call, *"Pick-A-Sound from the Merry-Go-Round."*

5. The player must then pick the top card from the pile of cards inside the Merry-Go-Round, and add that card to those in his/her hand. If the player picks the card with the sound called for, he/she makes a pair and takes another turn. When the player can no longer make a pair, the person on the left then becomes the next player. When a player pairs all the cards in his/her hand, the game is over. The player with the most paired cards is the winner. The winner gets to choose a prize from the Treasure Chest.

Important: Keep **A to Z Phonics Song Placemat** in view when playing so this will be a fun practice, **not a test.** When student no longer has to check pictures, it is an indication that the letters and sounds have been mastered.

OFF WE GO

STORYTIME LITERATURE SUGGESTIONS

Letter	Book	Author
Aa	There's an **A**lligator Under My Bed	Mercer Mayer
Bb	The **B**ike Lesson	Stan & Jan Berenstain
Cc	The **C**at in the Hat	Dr. Seuss
Dd	Go, **D**og, Go!	P.D. Eastman
Ee	Green **E**ggs & Ham	Dr. Seuss
Ff	One **F**ish Two **F**ish Red **F**ish Blue **F**ish	Dr. Seuss
Gg	Three Billy **G**oats **G**ruff	Fairy Tale
Hh	**H**orton **H**atches the Egg	Dr. Seuss
Ii	**I**f You Give a Mouse a Cookie	Laura Joffe Numeroff
Jj	**J**ack and the Beanstalk	Fairy Tale
Kk	Three Little **K**ittens	Nursery Rhyme
Ll	A **L**etter to Amy	Ezra Jack Keats
Mm	If You Give a **M**oose a **M**uffin	Laura Joffe Numeroff
Nn	The Best **N**est	P.D. Eastman
Oo	Ten Apples Up **O**n Top	Theo Le Sieg
Pp	A **P**ickle for a Nickel	Lilian Moore
Qq	The **Q**uilt Story	Tony Johnston & Tomie dePaola
Rr	Peter **R**abbit / **R**umplestilskin	Beatrix Potter / Fairy Tale
Ss	**S**oldiers and **S**ailors	Carla Greene
Tt	Big **T**racks, Little **T**racks	Franklyn Mansfield Branley
Uu	The **U**gly Duckling	Fairy Tale
Vv	The **V**elveteen Rabbit	Margery Williams
Ww	Make **W**ay for Ducklings	Robert Mc Closkey
Xx	O**x**-Cart Man	Donald Hall
Yy	Are **Y**ou My Mother?	P.D. Eastman
Zz	**Z**in, **Z**in, **Z**in or Violin	Loyd Moss

The storybooks listed on pp. 21-22 are recommended for reading aloud to your student while working in *Off We Go* or *Raceway Book*. Reading these books to your child will help him/her develop a love for literature. Check your public library for these books.

Sing, Spell Read & Write.

STORYTIME LITERATURE SUGGESTIONS

Step 4
Little Engine That Could — by Watty Piper

Step 6
Go, Dog, Go! — by P.D. Eastman
The Cat in the Hat — by Dr. Seuss
Puss-in-Boots — by Paul Galdone
Koko's Kitten — by Francine Patterson

Step 8
The Little Red Hen — by Margot Zemach
Green Eggs and Ham — by Dr. Seuss
Horton Hatches the Egg — by Dr. Seuss
Chicken Little — Fairy Tale

Step 10
I'll Teach My Dog 100 Words — by Michael Frith

Step 12
Go, Dog, Go! — by P.D. Eastman
Officer Buckle and Gloria — by Peggy Rathmann

Step 14
The Grouchy Ladybug — by Eric Carle
Quick as a Cricket — by Audry Wood
The Ugly Duckling — Treasury of Virtues*

Step 15
Amelia Bedelia — by Peggy Parish
Who Will be My Friends? — by Syd Hoff
A Chair for My Mother — by Vera B. Williams

Step 19
Brown Bear, Brown Bear,
What Do You See? — by Bill Martin, Jr.
The Velveteen Rabbit — Treasury of Virtues*

Step 20B
The Tale of Peter Rabbit — by Beatrix Potter
The Tortoise and the Hare — Treasury of Virtues*
The Selfish Giant — Treasury of Virtues*

Step 21A
Ten Apples Up On Top! — by Theo LeSieg
Are You My Mother? — by P.D. Eastman
One Fish, Two Fish,
    Red Fish, Blue Fish — by Dr. Seuss
Pinocchio — Fairy Tale
Jack and the Beanstalk — Fairy Tale

Step 21B
Curious George Flies a Kite — by H.A. Rey
Amelia Bedelia and the Baby — by Peggy Parish

Step 21D
Listening Walk — by Paul Showers

Step 22A
Nate the Great and the Lost List — by Sharmat

Step 22B
Gingerbread Man — by Karen Schmidt
The Emperor's New Clothes — Treasury of Virtues*

Step 22D
Caps for Sale — by Esphyr Slobodkina
Harry the Dirty Dog — by Gene Zion
A Fly Went By — by Mike McClintock

Step 23
Play Ball, Amelia Bedelia — by Peggy Parish

Step 24A
Berenstain Bears Go
Out for the Team — by Stan & Jan Berenstain

Step 24C
Josefina's Story Quilt — by Eleanor Coerr

The Gift — Treasury of Virtues*
The Quilt Story — by Tony Johnston &
                    Tomie de Paola
Ox-Cart Man — by Donald Hall

Step 25A
Ferdinand the Bull — by Munro Leaf
The Lion and the Mouse — Treasury of Virtues*

Step 25B
Bambi — by Walt Disney
The Lion and the Little Red Bird — by Elisa Kleven

Step 25C
Cinderella — Fairy Tale
Stone Soup — Treasury of Virtues*

Step 26A
Three Little Pigs — Fairy Tale
The Pied Piper of Hamelin — Fairy Tale
Little Rabbit's Loose Tooth — by Lucy Bate
Johnny Appleseed — Treasury of Virtues

Step 26B
Arthur Meets the President — by Marc Brown

Step 27
Rapunzel — Fairy Tale
Rumpelstiltskin — Fairy Tale

Step 28A
The Little House — by Virginia Burton
Harry and the Lady Next Door — by Gene Zion
The Tortoise and the Hare — Treasury of Virtues*
Arthur's Valentine — by Marc Brown

Step 28B
Father Bear Comes Home — by Minarik
The Biggest Bear — Lynd Ward
The Woodcutter — Treasury of Virtues*

Step 28C
The Fisherman and his Wife — Treasury of Virtues*
The Pearl — by Helme Heine
My Buddy — by Audrey Osofsky

Step 29
The Bell of Atri — Treasury of Virtues*
I Have A Sister, My Sister is Deaf — by Jeanne Peterson

Step 30A
Cloudy With a Chance
    of Meatballs — by Judi Barett

Step 30B
Happy Birthday Moon — by Frank Asch
The Prince and the Pea — Fairy Tale
Wait Till the Moon is Full — by Margaret Wise Brown

Step 31
The Polar Express — by Chris Van Allsburg

Step 32
The Very Hungry Caterpillar — by Eric Carle
The Ugly Duckling — Fairy Tale
The Best Nest — by P.D. Eastman
The Big Snow — by Berta and Elmer Hader

Step 33
The Very Busy Spider — by Eric Carle
Many Moons — by James Thurber

Step 34B
Little Toot — by Hardie Gramatky

Step 35
Hiawatha — by Henry W. Longfellow
Many Nations — by Joseph Bruchac

* Available through ILS of N.A., Inc. 1-800-321-8322

OVERVIEW FOR INSTRUCTOR

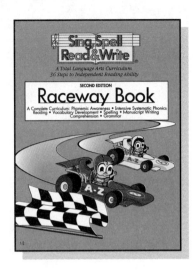

Contents

The **Raceway Book** provides correlated lessons in Reading, Manuscript Writing, Phonics, Comprehension, Grammar, and Spelling arranged in a sequence of graduated difficulty for 36 Raceway Steps. The steps are shown on the **Raceway Chart** found on page 3 of the **Raceway Book,** and on the **Raceway Chart** for the refrigerator. These charts provide motivation and a record of accomplishment for the child as he/she moves the car forward while progressing through the program.

Grade Levels for *Raceway Book* Skills

The **Raceway Book** is designed for first grade, however, it may be used at the 2nd or 3rd grade level when students need beginning Reading and Language Arts skills. In first grade, it provides a BASIC FUNDAMENTAL APPROACH to beginning Phonics, Reading, Writing, Spelling, Grammar, and Comprehension. In grades two and three it provides a remedial approach. (The WINNING Program, also by Sue Dickson, is recommended for students 4th grade to adult who need beginning literacy skills.)

Pacing Your Student

We have included our suggested pacing for each step in this Manual, but **your** pacing should "fit" **your** child. We encourage you to move as quickly as possible through the lessons, but your daily schedule should take into account your child's attention span. Each lesson has varied activities (singing, games, writing, spelling, reading, storytime, etc.) to capture and keep your child's attention. Some lessons are longer than others, however, an **hour** to an **hour and a half** per day is appropriate for your Language Arts lessons.

Aiming for Step 36

Instructors who really want to help a child become an *independent reader* should aim for Step 36 and **keep going until the child gets there**. This is why:

- When you help a child learn the skills to Step 18, (halfway around the Raceway), he/she will know ALL THE SOUNDS ONE NEEDS TO KNOW IN ORDER TO READ ENGLISH. (That is certainly something to aim for!)

- However, when you help the child learn the skills to the **completion** of the Raceway, that is, to Step 36, he/she will also know THE ODDITIES OF THE ENGLISH LANGUAGE. That information is necessary to become an independent reader.

A to Z Phonics Song

p. 4

Goal

To sing **A to Z Phonics Song**, pointing to letters and pictures in *Raceway Book* for mastery check-off.

Suggested Pacing

1 day

Materials

1. *Raceway Book,* p. 4
2. A to Z Sound-O Game
3. A to Z Pick-A-Sound Game
4. A to Z Phonics Song, CD or Cassette #1

PROCEDURE

Instructor:

- Have student sing the **A to Z Phonics Song**, pointing to letters and pictures in the **Raceway Book**.
- Initial and date box provided at bottom of p. 4 to indicate mastery.

INITIAL + DATE
CAN SING

Move
Raceway Car
to Step **2**

ABC Echoes

Goals

To say the correct sound for each letter (without looking at the pictures for the *A to Z Phonics Song*)

To write the letters from A to Z

Suggested Pacing

1 day

Materials

1. *Raceway Book*, pp. 5-10
2. **ABC Echoes**, CD or Cassette #1
3. A to Z Sound–O Game
4. A to Z Pick-A-Sound Game

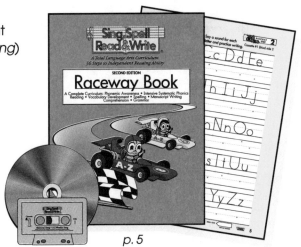

p. 5

PROCEDURE

Instructor:

- Have student listen to **ABC Echoes**.
- Next, have student point to letters A to Z, one by one, in **Raceway Book** p. 5 and echo sounds as demonstrated on CD or cassette.
- Practice until student is able to lead **ABC Echoes** without hesitation.
- Have student write letters A to Z on p. 5.
- Initial and date box provided at bottom of p. 5 to indicate mastery.
- Have student complete **Raceway Book** pp. 6-10 independently.

Phonics Song(s)/Games

Each day's lesson should begin with one or two previously learned phonics songs and end with a phonics game.

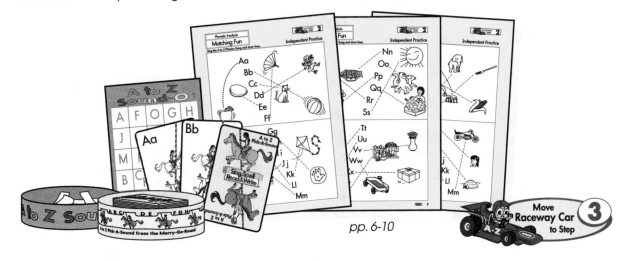

pp. 6-10

Move **Raceway Car** to Step **3**

Short Vowel Song

Goal
To learn **short vowel** sounds

Suggested Pacing
1 day

Materials
1. *Raceway Book*, p. 11
2. **Short Vowel Song**, CD or Cassette #1

p. 11

PROCEDURE

Tell student:

- There are five letters of the alphabet more important than any others: **Aa, Ee, Ii, Oo, Uu**.
- The letters **Aa, Ee, Ii, Oo**, and **Uu** are known as **vowels**.
- These vowel sounds were learned when he/she sang the **A to Z Phonics Song**, but they are so important we have a special song for them.

Have student:

- Cut out the five **short vowel cards** on p. 11 in **Raceway Book**.
- Spread out cards on table (in front of student).
- Play and sing the **Short Vowel Song,** holding up the correct short vowel card, one by one, while singing along with the CD or cassette.

Instructor: When the student can sing the **Short Vowel Song** and hold up appropriate cards, initial and date the box provided at bottom of p. 11 to indicate mastery.

Phonics Song(s)/Games

Each day's lesson should begin with one or two previously learned phonics songs and end with a phonics game. A new song is introduced in this Step.

Move
Raceway Car
to Step **4**

RACEWAY STEP 4

Ferris Wheel Song

Goal
To slide together (blend) letter sounds in preparation for reading words

Suggested Pacing
6 days ★■○△ "consonant tickets" (b, t, etc.)
6 days 🔔🏠⚑ "blends tickets" (bl, st, etc.)

Materials
1. **Ferris Wheel Song**, CD or Cassette #2
2. **Ferris Wheel Blends Song**, CD or Cassette #2
3. *Raceway Book*, pp. 12-26

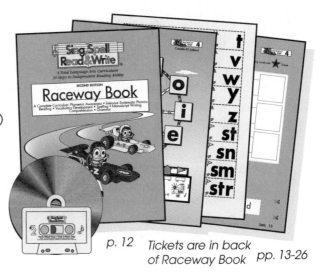

p. 12   *Tickets are in back of Raceway Book*   pp. 13-26

PROCEDURE

Note: For Step 4, there are 14 pages in the **Raceway Book,** pp. 13-26 (Cut and Paste, and Beginning Blends) for your student to complete while practicing/mastering the Ferris Wheel Step.

Instructor:

- Remove page of "tickets" from back of **Raceway Book** and separate at perforations. Be careful to keep **c** and **k** tickets joined on the fold as shown.

- Sort "tickets" into 7 stacks according to symbols. There are 5 tickets for each symbol:

- Stack "tickets" in each group from #1 to #5 following the numeral inside each symbol.

- Point to the vowels around the **Ferris Wheel Chart**, in **Raceway Book** p. 12. Have student tell you the short vowel sounds already learned for each.

- Sing with your student the **Short Vowel Song**, pointing from lower left **a** to **u** at the top.

- Pick up Star Ticket #1 with an arrow. Help student hold ticket in left hand as shown, covering thumb print with his/her thumb. Use it to point to each vowel starting at lower left **a** and going clockwise, and sing the sounds of the vowels up the scale five notes and back down the scale five notes. (Listen to this on your CD or cassette.)

- Pick up Star Ticket #2 (letter **b**) and ask for the sound of **b**. Tell the student, "We are going to practice putting two sounds together by 'Riding the Ferris Wheel' and we will be making **beginning parts of words** as we ride and sing this song." Upon completion of this Step, your student will be able to read and spell hundreds of words!

(Continued on next page)

Making Words With the Ferris Wheel

Instructor: (holding **b** ticket) "What is the sound of **b**?"

Student: "**Bh**!"

Instructor: "What is the sound of **a**?" (pointing to letter **a** on Ferris Wheel)

Student: "**ă**"

Instructor: (Holding **b** ticket to left of the **a** on Ferris Wheel) "Let's say the sound of **b** first, then slide to the **ă** sound. Ready? Watch! **Bh**...**ă**! Now put them together!"

Student: "**Bă**!"

Instructor: "Great! Can you think of a word that begins **bă**?"

Student: "**Bat**!"

Instructor: "Yes, and what do you hear after **bă** in bat?"

Student: "**T**!"

Instructor: "Can you write "**bă**t?" (allow student to write it)

Instructor: "Great! See we're reading and spelling already! Do you know another word that begins, **bă**?"

Student: "**Bag**!" (or bad)

Instructor: "Yes, and what do you hear at the end of **bă**g?" (or bad)

Student: "**G**," (or d), etc.

Continue in this manner with different tickets to let your student begin to see and understand the "sound-symbol-word-reading-writing" relationship. **It is important to have a time in each day's lesson for "making words" in this way.**

- **c** and **k** have the same sound so they are on opposite sides of the same ticket. Your student must flip the ticket over to have **c** appear with **a, o**, and **u**, (and **k** with **e** and **i**) going around the Ferris Wheel with your tickets. (This is because the **c** gives the **ss** sound before **e** and **i**, as in **cent** and **circus**, but don't go into this with the student now.) **Just remember, k goes with e and i. (c goes with all the other vowels.)**

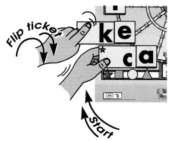

Now we're ready to sing the Ferris Wheel Song!

Instructor:

- Tell student there is a song that will help him/her practice sliding the first two letters together for the beginnings of hundreds of words.

- Tell student to notice the symbols on the tickets, and have him/her point to the row of corresponding symbols which are printed across the Ferris Wheel Chart. Say: "This is the order in which the tickets will be used when we sing the **Ferris Wheel Song.**"

- Sing along with the **Ferris Wheel Song**, practicing daily with ★ ■ ○ △ tickets until the student can blend beginning consonant and short vowel sounds. (Mastery of this skill is very important. Have student stay at the "carnival" and keep "riding the Ferris Wheel" until he/she can blend sounds easily to make beginnings of words.)

Ferris Wheel Song

Sing: "Round and round and up and down
The Ferris Wheel we go
Round and round and up and down
Come on now don't be slow.
Have your ticket in your hand,
The ride will soon begin.
Do your best, your very best
Go round and round again!

(Vowels only) ă, ĕ, ĭ, ŏ, ŭ, ŭ, ŏ, ĭ, ĕ, ă, – *use pointing arrow ticket*
bă, bĕ, bĭ, bŏ, bŭ, bŭ, bŏ, bĭ, bĕ, bă" – *use b ticket*
că, kĕ, kĭ, cŏ, cŭ, cŭ, cŏ, kĭ, kĕ, că – use c & k ticket

(*Flip ticket so **k** is with **e** and **i**)

- Upon your student's successful demonstration in blending the "tickets" of each symbol, **initial and date the symbols as shown below. You will spend approximately 6 days with the** ★ ■ ○ △ **"tickets".**

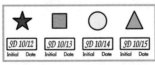

Raceway Book: Phonetic Analysis

Cut and Paste, *pp. 13-16, 21-22, 25-26*

- Discuss each page with your student and have him/her write correct answers. Next, have student complete the cutting, pasting, drawing, and coloring independently.

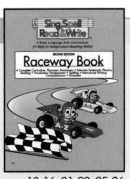

pp. 13-16, 21-22, 25-26

Introduce Consonant Blends

Suggested Pacing: 6 days. Teach your student how to blend consonants (tickets with 🔔 🏠 🚩 symbols). Next, use the blends tickets (dr, fl, st, etc.) and sing around the Ferris Wheel again with the CD or cassette.

Making Words With the Ferris Wheel Blends Tickets

Each day after singing the **Ferris Wheel Song**, have your student use the **Ferris Wheel Chart** and **tickets** for "making words":

Instructor:	(Holding **dr** ticket before **a** on the chart) "What do we sing for these letters?"
Student:	"dră"
Instructor:	"Can you add a **g**?" (say letter name)
Student:	"drăg"
Instructor:	(Holding **dr** ticket before **e** on the chart) "What do we sing for these letters?" "Can you add **ss**?" (say letter names)
Student:	"dress"
Instructor:	(Holding **dr** ticket before **i** on the chart) "What do we sing for these letters?" "Can you add a **p**?" (say letter name)
Student:	"drip"
Instructor:	(Holding **dr** ticket before **o** on the chart) "What do we sing for these letters?"
Student:	"dro"
Instructor:	"Can you add a **p**?" (say letter name)
Student:	"drop"
Instructor:	(Holding **dr** ticket before **u** on the chart) "Can you add an **m**?" (say letter name)
Student:	"drum"

Holding "tr" ticket before "u" on the chart:

Instructor:	"What do we sing for these letters?""
Student:	"tru"
Instructor:	"Can you add **ck**?" (say letter names)
Student:	"truck"
Instructor:	"Since both **c** and **k** have the same sound, we use both letters at the end of a word. Put the tall one (**k**) on the end to 'hold the letters together'." **sta**ck

Continue using the Ferris Wheel Chart and tickets each day in this way. Your child will "discover" hundreds of words. It has been estimated that 62% of the English language is made up of short vowel words and syllables.

- **Initial and date the boxes in the Raceway Book upon your student's successful demonstration in blending the "tickets" of each symbol.**

Raceway Book: Phonetic Analysis

Beginning Blends Tickets, pp. 17-20, 23-24

- Write the beginning sound and color the pictures.

Move Raceway Car to Step **5**

Sing Spell Read & Write.

Read, Write and Spell

Short a Words

Goals
To read, write and spell **short a** words
To use **short a** words in oral sentences

Suggested Pacing
2 days

Material
Raceway Book, pp. 27-28

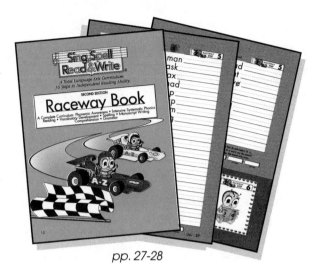

pp. 27-28

PROCEDURE

Use **Raceway Book**, pp. 27-28 to introduce this lesson. Point to the letter **a** and the key picture of the apple at the top of the page and proceed:

Instructor:	"Can you tell me why this page has an apple at the top?"
Student:	"Because there is an **a** that says ă as in apple in each word."
Instructor:	"Yes! We are ready to read **short a** words. Look at the first word on the chart. I am going to cover the last letter showing, ...**ma**. Now, what did we say on the Ferris Wheel when we saw these letters?" (Connecting this with the previous Raceway Step.)
Student:	"**Mă**"
Instructor:	"Right! Now let's add the last letter sound. What is it? **p**! Put it all together now, **ma...p**! Our street is on the map."

Always have the student use each word in a sentence after decoding it, so he/she will not only be able to identify the word, but also will know its full meaning. Beginners will not know what a sentence is, so you must tell them to "say something using that word." If they say "Cat -- The tan cat" -- you have a perfect opportunity to teach that a sentence must tell completely about something. For example: "The tan cat was doing **what**, Jimmy? Was the tan cat sitting on the fence or eating his food?" Gradually, the student will become an expert in knowing what a complete sentence is as you provide this guidance.

Next:
- Have your student orally read to you all words in *Raceway Book*, p. 27. Tell him/her there are some longer words (which have four letters) on this Step. For these words he/she must decode the first three letters, and then add the final sound.
- Tell your student that for words ending with **ss**, **zz**, **ll**, etc., say the sound only once. (Remind student that **c** and **k** both have the same sound, so we say the sound just once when letters **c** and **k** come together at the end of a word.)
- Explain that **e** on the end of "hav**e**" is silent, so we put a strike mark through it. Teach **s** taking the **z** sound in **has** and **as**. Teach that the article **a** sounds like ŭ as in umbrella. A "cage" over a word means that some letter is stealing another letter's sound. h̅a̅s̅ s=z
- The student must practice until he/she can read, write, and spell the **short a** words on pp. 27 and 28.

(Continued on next page)

- It sometimes helps the student in the **oral spelling** of the longer (4-letter) words to draw four horizontal lines on a card and have the student (1) say the word, (2) sound it out pointing to the lines and then (3) spell it. h e l p

- Have student practice until he/she can read the words fluently. "Practice makes perfect." He/she must also say each word in a sentence, and then spell it. When your student can do this, initial and date boxes at the bottom of the page and move the Raceway car to the next Step.

NOTE: You may elect to have your student illustrate some of the words on folded paper to make a picture dictionary (see sample illustration).

Phonics Song(s)/Games

Each day's lesson should begin with one or two previously learned phonics songs and end with a phonics game.

The "Onesy, Twosy, Threesy" Technique for Word Identification

It has been estimated that some children need to see a word from 12-25 times before they are able to recognize it instantly. To provide practice, use the "Onesy, Twosy, Threesy" technique:

- The student reads word #1. (map)

- Then the student reads words #1 and #2. (map, van)

- Next, the student goes back to the top of the list and reads #1, #2, and #3. (map, van, bad)

- Next, the student goes back to the top of the list and reads #1, #2, #3, and #4. (map, van, bad, hat)

- Continue in same manner for word #5, etc., to the end of the row.

Read, Write, and
1. map
2. van
3. bad
4. hat

p. 27

By the time the child reaches #20 at the bottom of the page, he/she has usually mastered the list. The instructor will put his/her *first initial* in the box. When your student has mastered #21-40, add your last initial and the date in the box.

Instructor Tip ✔

Sometimes students have trouble telling the difference between **b**'s and **d**'s. He/she knows **b** goes "**bh**" and **d** goes "**dh**," but doesn't know *which* is *which*. You can help the student with this tip: Write a very large **b** and a very large **d** on a page. Tell him/her to point in the direction that you write across the page. Say: "If you come to the *straight line first*, **put your lips in a straight line** which is the way they must be to say **bh**! If you come to the *round part first*, **put lips in a round circle** which is the way they must be to say **dh**!"

 →bat
→dad

Move
Raceway Car
to Step 6

Reading

PHONETIC STORYBOOK READER 1, *The Apple Book*

Goals

To read Phonetic Storybook Reader 1,
The Apple Book

To practice Grammar Skills

To take Book End Assessment

Suggested Pacing

3 days

Materials

1. Phonetic Storybook Reader 1, *The Apple Book*, pp. 2-64

2. *Raceway Book*, pp. 29-35

3. Assessment Book: Assessment for Phonetic Storybook Reader 1

PROCEDURE

- In **Phonetic Storybook Reader 1**, have student read the vocabulary on pp. 2-3, pointing to each word.

- Introduce the Rulebreaker Words, (words with a letter that steals another letter's sound. These are shown in a "cage". Example: **has** (**s** is stealing the **z** sound.)

- Have student read the first story, **Al and Nat**, pp. 5-22. **If a word is read incorrectly, the correct response from you should be:**

Instructor: "Not bat, (or whatever the word was called), look at the first sound again."

Student: "Cat"

Never tell the student a word. Say, "Sound it again," or remind the child the word may be a rule-breaker, but let him/her do the decoding. **Do not suggest looking at the picture for a clue. That is what caused the problem many children have today where they look-and-guess "bucket" to be "pail" and "birthday" to be "party," etc. We want accurate decoding and reading, not looking and guessing.**

Have student:

- Read each story two or three times for fluency, after the initial reading with you asking the comprehension questions (see next page).

- Complete **Raceway Book** pp. 29-35.

- Complete **Assessment** for Storybook Reader 1. See Manual pp. 37-39.

Phonics Song(s)/Games

Each day's lesson should begin with one or two previously learned phonics songs and end with a phonics game.

Comprehension Questions

An Instructor's "script" is provided for each story to reinforce comprehension during reading. In addition, sometimes ask your student to tell you in his/her own words what happened after reading a page.

When your student is able to read the Phonetic Storybook Reader with fluency, administer the Book End Assessment found in the Assessment Book.

Phonetic Storybook Reader 1

Comprehension Questions
Al and Nat
Story 1 • pp. 5-22

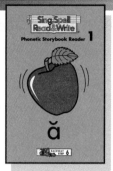

Have student read orally the designated pages.
Ask the following questions:

After reading pp. 5-7:
- Who are the two characters? (*Story Detail*)
  Al and Nat
- Which one is the dog? (*Picture Clue*) Nat
- What did Al have to eat? (*Story Detail*) Jam

After reading pp. 8-10:
- Name some things Al had in his toy chest.
  (*Story Detail*) Bag, bat, blocks, bear, books, hat
- Which toys begin with the "**b**" sound?
  (*Classification*) Bat, blocks, bear, books

After reading pp. 11-13:
- How did Nat get his hat? (*Story Detail*)
  Al tapped the hat.
- What other toy does Al have? (*Story Detail*)
  A fan

After reading pp. 14-17:
- How do you think Al and Nat feel about
  each other? (*Inference/Drawing Conclusion*)
  They like each other.

- What does a real van need to make it go?
  (*Personal Experience*) Gas
- Why does the gas man have a rag?
  (*Picture Clue*) He's washing the windows.

After reading pp. 18-22:
- What did Al have that needed something to
  make it go? (*Inference/Drawing Conclusion*)
  A van
- What does Al have to make his van go?
  (*Picture Clue*) Nat
- Look on pp. 20-21 and name in order the things
  the van passed. (*Sequence*) Map, bat, fan, hat
- Read aloud the page that tells us how Nat and
  Al felt toward each other. (*Story Detail*) p. 22
- Tell me a word on p. 22 that means the same as
  friend. (*Vocabulary Expansion - Synonyms*) Pal

Complete pp. 29-30 in Raceway Book.
See directions below.

Raceway Book: Grammar/Comprehension

Singular and Plural, *p. 29*
- Tell student some words mean "more than one" and
  are called *plurals*. Write words **cats** and **hats** and ask
  whether these words mean "one" or "more than one."

- Instructor: Write 10 words from the **short a** vocabulary list,
  Raceway Book p. 27 that can be made plural by adding
  an **s**. Next, have student add an **s** to the end of each word
  to make it mean more than one, and use the word orally in
  a sentence.

- Have student circle the correct word in each box on p. 29.

Matching, *p. 30*
Tell student to match the sentences with the pictures.

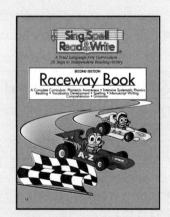

pp. 29-30

Comprehension Questions
Dad, Pam, and Sam
Story 2 • pp. 24-42

Have student read orally the designated pages.
Ask the following questions:

After reading pp. 24-27:
- Who are the three characters in the story? *(Story Detail)* Dad, Pam, and Sam
- Which one is not a person? *(Classification)* Sam
- Who do you think Sam belongs to? Why do you think this? *(Context Clue)* Either Pam or Dad

After reading pp. 28-29:
- Who do you think the ham is for? Why do you think this? *(Predicting)* Sam, because Dad is showing the ham to Sam.

After reading pp. 30-33:
- How can we tell Sam is happy to be fed? *(Picture Clue)* He wags his tail and looks happy.
- Did Sam enjoy his ham? How do you know? *(Context Clue/Picture Clue)* Yes, he ate it all.
- Do you think Sam lives on a farm? Why not? *(Analyzing/Drawing Conclusion)* No. Tall buildings are outside the window.

After reading pp. 34-37:
- On pp. 34-35, name the four things Dad has. *(Story Detail)* Cap, hat, rag, and wax

- Which two items are used for the same job? *(Classification)* Rag and wax
- Why is Dad unhappy with Sam? *(Picture Clue)* He jumped up on his freshly waxed car.
- How do you think Sam feels? *(Story Detail/Inference/Drawing Conclusion)* Sad

After reading pp. 38-39:
- Why do you think Sam ran? *(Predicting)* He knew Dad was mad at him.
- Where is Pam? *(Picture Clue)* Under a tree

After reading pp. 40-42:
- Why would Sam jump in Pam's lap? *(Inference/Drawing Conclusion)* He needs a friend.
- What does Sam do in Pam's lap? *(Story Detail)* Sam takes a nap.
- What is the problem in this story? *(Analyzing)* Sam got into trouble with Dad.
- How was it solved? *(Analyzing)* Sam ran off to get comfort from Pam.

Complete pp. 31-33 in Raceway Book.
See directions below.

Raceway Book: Grammar/Comprehension

Capital Letters, *p. 31*
Tell student the first word in a sentence always starts with a capital letter. Student will write the sentences on p.31 and start the first word with a capital letter.

Writing Sentences, *p. 32*
Tell student to put an index finger space between each word in each sentence when writing.

Picture Clues, *p. 33*
Tell student to choose the word that completes the sentence and write it.

pp. 31-33

Comprehension Questions
Nat, a Man, and Sam
Story 3 • pp. 44-64

Have student read orally the designated pages.
Ask the following questions:

After reading pp. 44-45:
- Who are the three characters in this story?
(Story Detail) Nat, a Man and Sam
- Can cats and dogs be friends?
(Personal Experience) Yes

After reading pp. 46-49:
- Where did the man go for a picnic?
(Picture Clue) The beach
- What did he take with him for the picnic?
(Story Detail) A bag of food
- What time of day do you think it is?
(Inference/ Drawing Conclusion)
Probably afternoon

After reading pp. 50-53:
- Why would Nat wag his tail?
(Inference/ Drawing Conclusion)
He's probably very happy. Dogs like the beach.
- Why did Sam tag Nat?
(Inference/Drawing Conclusion)
He wants to play.
- Think of some words that describe Sam's behavior. *(Analyzing)*
Playful, curious, mischievous

After reading pp. 54-57:
- What did Sam want Nat to do?
(Inference/ Drawing Conclusion)
Run and chase/play tag
- How do you think the man feels on pp. 56-57?
(Picture Clue) Shocked/surprised/upset

After reading pp. 58-63:
- What happened to the picnic food?
(Story Detail) Sand is all over it.
- Which word describes Nat and Sam?
(Story Detail) Bad
- What is a word that would describe the man?
(Drawing Conclusion) Mad
- Why do you think the man came to the beach?
(Predicting Outcome) To eat and rest
- What did the man bring with him to help him relax? *(Picture Clue)* Radio/blanket
- Tell me a good title for this story. *(Main Idea)*
"A Man at the Beach" or "A Tough Time at the Beach"

Complete pp. 34-35 in Raceway Book.
See directions below.

Raceway Book: Grammar/Comprehension

Names of People, p. 34
Tell student that names of people are always written with a capital letter. Give an example: **Nat, Dan.** Next, student will write names with capital letters on p. 34.

Read and Draw, p. 35 (top half)
Student will:
- Read each sentence.
- Draw a picture to illustrate it.

Matching Fun, p. 35 (bottom half)
- Match words with pictures.

pp. 34-35

Assessing Your Student

**Administer Book End Assessment for Phonetic Storybook Reader 1.
Directions and Answer Key on next 2 pages.**

Assessment Book
17 Book End Assessments
for Phonetic Storybook Readers
3 Achievement Tests

Overview

There are 17 Book End Assessments, one for each Storybook Reader. The Assessments are to be used after student completes each Storybook Reader.
The following areas are assessed:

- Word Identification
- Sentence Comprehension
- Word Comprehension
- Story Comprehension

The following types of questions are included:

- Story Detail
- Story Sequence
- Classifying
- Inference/Drawing Conclusions
- Cause and Effect
- Context Clues
- Main Idea
- Fantasy and Realism
- Predicting

Getting Started

In order to allow a beginning student to become familiar with the testing formats, directions, and tasks, the Assessments for Storybooks 1, 2, and 3 should be administered in an instructor-directed setting. This will allow you to closely supervise and help the student until he/she becomes comfortable. For Assessments 1, 2, and 3:

- Have student read each item aloud.
- Answer questions with discussion.
- Have student mark Assessment items/answers with your supervision.
- Have student understand and correct mistakes.

If student marks an item incorrectly, go over it, discuss it, and allow time to erase and correct it. *The purpose is to teach the child how to take a test* before taking one independently. When your student completes the Assessment for Phonetic Storybook Reader 3, the skill of *taking a test* will have been learned.

Introducing the Assessment

Remove Assessment from the Assessment Book, staple the pages, and fill out the information on the cover. *Before you administer each Assessment, tell your student to:*

- Think hard and "Don't get tricked!"
- Stay on task.
- Read all possible answers before choosing one. Only one is correct.
- Look back to the story passage to find any answers you don't remember.
- Put a little check by the questions you aren't sure about and come back to them (thus teaching student the process of elimination).

Scoring and Interpreting Results

An Answer Key for each Book End Assessment is included in this Manual. Each Assessment has a Student Record Sheet on the front cover for recording scores. Transfer the scores for each section of the Assessment to the appropriate lines on the Student Record Sheet and convert them to percentage scores. If student scores below 70% in any area, he/she should repeat the lessons before going on.

Move
Raceway Car
to Step **7**

Sing Spell
Read & Write

Raceway Step 6

Book End Assessment
Phonetic Storybook Reader 1

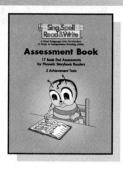

Word Recognition

Short a Words

Instructor: Direct student to "Put your finger on box #1. Now circle the word in the box that I call... 'fan.' Put your finger on box #2. Now circle the word 'tag,' etc." The words the instructor should call are listed below. Say each word distinctly with emphasis upon initial and final consonants.

1. fan	2. tag	3. at	4. Nat	5. and
6. map	7. van	8. pass	9. and	10. fan
11. fat	12. rag	13. man	14. hand	15. last
16. Al	17. lap	18. ham	19. had	20. Pam

Record scores in the space provided on the front cover of the Student Assessment Record and calculate the Percentage of Mastery Score as indicated.

Word Comprehension

Short a Words

Directions: Tell student to point to box #1 again and listen to what you say:

Instructor: *Underline the word that...*

1. tells what you use in baseball. bat
2. is a member of your family. Dad
3. is another name for a friend. pal
4. tells what Dad uses to polish the car. wax
5. means "happy." glad
6. is a man's name. Sam
7. tells something Mom or Dad cooks in. pan
8. means a short sleep. nap
9. tells what we bring the groceries home in. bag
10. is a good kind of meat. ham
11. tells what a dog does with his tail. wag
12. tastes good on toast. jam
13. means naughty. bad
14. tells what we find at the seashore. sand
15. means quick. fast
16. tells what you did when you wanted to get somewhere in a hurry. ran
17. tells what you say to a bad cat. scat
18. means angry. mad
19. tells what you would do to a good dog. pat
20. tells what you put in your car to make it run. gas

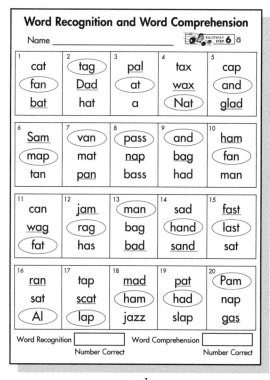

Word Recognition and Word Comprehension

Name _____ RACEWAY STEP 6 ă

1	2	3	4	5
cat	tag	pal	tax	cap
fan	Dad	at	wax	and
bat	hat	a	Nat	glad

6	7	8	9	10
Sam	van	pass	and	ham
map	mat	nap	bag	fan
tan	pan	bass	had	man

11	12	13	14	15
can	jam	man	sad	fast
wag	rag	bag	hand	last
fat	has	bad	sand	sat

16	17	18	19	20
ran	tap	mad	pat	Pam
sat	scat	ham	had	nap
Al	lap	jazz	slap	gas

Word Recognition _____   Word Comprehension _____
Number Correct   Number Correct

p. 1

Record scores in the space provided on the front cover of the Student Assessment Record and calculate the Percentage of Mastery Score as indicated.

Picture-Word Matching Fun

Picture-Word Matching Fun pages serve as a check of reading comprehension. Have student read the words and draw a line to the correct illustration. Record scores in the space provided on the front cover of the Student Assessment Record and calculate the Percentage of Mastery Score as indicated.

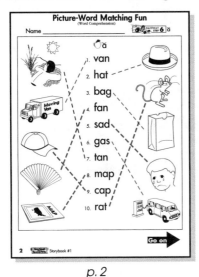

p. 2

p. 3

Story Comprehension Matching Fun

Story Comprehension Matching Fun pages serve as a check of reading comprehension. Have child read the sentences on the left side of each page and then draw a line to the picture which illustrates what he/she read. The sentences and pictures are taken from stories which the child read in Phonetic Storybook Reader 1, *The Apple Book*. Record scores in the space provided on the front cover of the Student Assessment Record and calculate the Percentage of Mastery Score as indicated.

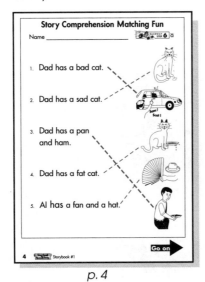

p. 4

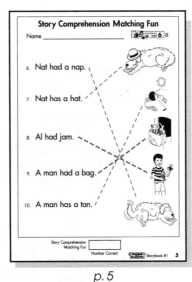

p. 5

Missing Letter Fun, p. 6

Have student look at the pictures and write the missing letter. Record scores in the space provided on the front cover of the Student Assessment Record and calculate the Percentage of Mastery Score as indicated.

1. rag	2. pan	3. ant	4. cat	5. lamp
6. glass	7. hand	8. mask	9. tack	10. flag

Read, Write and Spell

Short e Words

Goals

To read, write, and spell **short e** words

To use **short e** words in oral sentences

To practice Grammar Skills

Suggested Pacing

2 days

Materials

Raceway Book, pp. 36-37

pp. 36-37

PROCEDURE

Instructor:

- Use **Raceway Book**, pp. 36-37 to introduce this lesson.
  Refer to shaded sections pp. 31-32 in Manual for directions.

- Teach **Grammar Chalkboard Lessons** shown below.

Phonics Song(s)/Games

Each day's lesson should begin with one or two previously learned phonics songs and end with a phonics game.

Grammar Chalkboard Lessons

PLURALS

Write the plural form of each word.

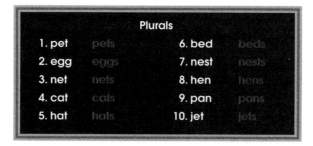

Plurals			
1. pet	pets	6. bed	beds
2. egg	eggs	7. nest	nests
3. net	nets	8. hen	hens
4. cat	cats	9. pan	pans
5. hat	hats	10. jet	jets

PLURALS

Choose the correct word for each sentence.

Plurals
1. Pam has 2 ___legs___ . (leg, legs)
2. Peg had a red ___hat___ . (hat, hats)
3. Ken had 3 ___bats___ . (bat, bats)
4. The nest has an ___egg___ . (egg, eggs)

Move
Raceway Car
to Step **8**

Reading

PHONETIC STORYBOOK READER 2, *The Egg Book*

Goals

To read Phonetic Storybook Reader 2, *The Egg Book*

To practice Grammar Skills

To take Book End Assessment

Suggested Pacing

3 days

Materials

1. Phonetic Storybook Reader 2, *The Egg Book*, pp. 2-32
2. *Raceway Book*, pp. 38-44
3. Assessment Book: Assessment for Phonetic Storybook Reader 2

PROCEDURE

Have student:

- Read vocabulary pp. 2-6 in **Storybook Reader 2**.
- Read **Peg, Ken, and Sal**, pp. 7-32. See PROCEDURE on p. 33 in Manual.
- Complete **Raceway Book** pp. 38-44.

Instructor:

- Teach **Grammar Chalkboard Lessons**/Manual p.43.
- Administer **Assessment**/Manual p. 44.

Phonics Song(s)/Games

Each day's lesson should begin with one or two previously learned phonics songs and end with a phonics game.

Phonetic Storybook Reader 2

Comprehension Questions

Peg, Ken, and Sal

pp. 7-32

Have student read orally the designated pages. Ask the following questions:

After reading pp. 7-9:

- Who is Sal? (Story Detail) A pet hen
- Is it unusual to have a hen for a pet? (Personal Experience) Yes
- Where does Sal live? (Story Detail) In a hen pen

After reading pp. 10-13:

- What are words that mean the same as *hen*? (Vocabulary Expansion) Mother chicken

- What does a hen like to eat? (Personal Experience) Corn, grain, and wheat
- How many eggs does Sal have in her nest? (Story Detail) Ten
- Why would Sal sit and sit on her eggs? (Predicting/Personal Experience) To keep them warm so they'll hatch into baby chickens

(Continued on next page)

After reading pp. 14-17:

- Why would Ken and Peg keep Sal in a pen? (Personal Experience/Predicting) So she wouldn't go away and to protect her from dogs

- What do Ken and Peg have in the can? (Picture Clue) Red paint

- What happened to the can of paint? (Story Detail) It fell.

After reading pp. 18-19:

- What do Peg and Ken yell? (Story Detail) "Help! Help!"

- What is a word that means a *sound*? (Vocabulary Expansion) "Bam!"

After reading pp. 20-23:

- What word on p. 22 describes what Ken and Peg have? (Vocabulary Expansion) A mess

- How does Sal run? (Comparison/Analogy) Fast

- What two words describe Sal? (Story Detail) Mad and wet

After reading pp. 24-25:

- Why would they go to Dad for help? (Inference/Drawing Conclusion) He was nearby and they needed a grownup to help.

- Why did Dad tell Peg to get a rag and pan? (Predicting) To clean up the mess

After reading pp. 26-27:

- How does Dad help? (Context Clue) He cleans the hen's neck and left leg.

- What does this sentence mean: "A neck has less red mess"? (Context Clue) Dad cleaned some of the red paint off the hen's neck.

After reading pp. 28-29:

- Did Sal sit on her eggs before or after they were cleaned? (Sequence) Either

After reading pp. 30-32:

- What did Dad, Ken, and Peg do next? *(Story Detail)* They mended the bent pen.

- Why would we say Dad can tap best? *(Picture Clue)* His nail is going in straight.

- What is the problem in the story? *(Analyzing)* Having an accident, spilling paint, and bending the fence

- How is it solved? *(Analyzing)* By asking for help from Dad, and all of them working together
Complete pp. 38-44 in Raceway Book. See directions below.

Raceway Book: Grammar/Comprehension

Make Words and Draw, p. 38
Fill in the missing letter to complete the word and draw a picture.

Singular and Plural, p. 39
Plurals mean more than one, and you usually add an **s** to the end of the word to make a plural. Example: hat-hats. Circle the correct word in each box.

Picture Clues, p. 40
Choose the word that completes the sentence and matches the picture.

Scrambled Sentences, p. 41
Tell student a sentence is a group of words that makes sense and expresses a complete thought. On p. 41 there are some groups of words that do not make sense. Have student rearrange the words to form a sentence that has a complete thought and makes sense. Give your student a reminder to begin each sentence with a capital letter and end it with a period.

Rhyming Words, pp. 42-43
Words that end in the same vowel and consonant sound are called rhyming words. **Cat** and **fat** rhyme because they end in the same vowel and consonant sound. Use some examples of

pp. 38-44

words that rhyme, such as **Sam** and **ham** and ask why they rhyme. Then use some examples of words that do not rhyme, as **set** and **bat**. Ask why these words *don't* rhyme. Continue in this manner until student understands rhyming words. Student will circle the two rhyming words on p. 49.

Favorite Character, p. 44
Have student draw a picture of a favorite character from Phonetic Storybook Reader 2.

Grammar Chalkboard Lessons

SCRAMBLED SENTENCES

Write the scrambled sentences shown below and have student unscramble them to make sentences. Remind him/her to begin each sentence with a capital letter and put a period at the end.

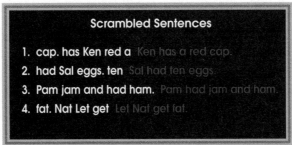

Scrambled Sentences

1. cap. has Ken red a   Ken has a red cap.
2. had Sal eggs. ten   Sal had ten eggs.
3. Pam jam and had ham.   Pam had jam and ham.
4. fat. Nat Let get   Let Nat get fat.

RHYMING WORDS

Write the pairs of words below. Have the student write *yes* if the words rhyme and *no* if they do not.

Rhyming Words

1. get - bet   yes
2. sat - hat   yes
3. get - bed   no
4. rag - tag   yes
5. ham - Sam   yes
6. fat - bat   yes
7. red - let   no
8. map - sat   no

Assessment Book

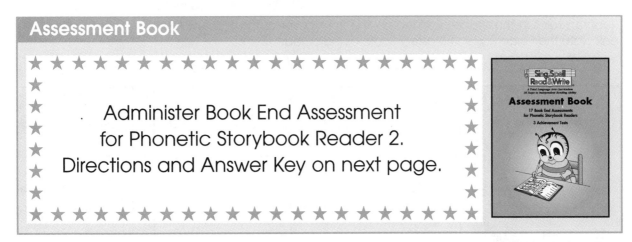

Administer Book End Assessment for Phonetic Storybook Reader 2. Directions and Answer Key on next page.

Move Raceway Car to Step **9**

Sing Spell Read & Write

Raceway Step 8

Book End Assessment
Phonetic Storybook Reader 2

Word Recognition: Short e Words

Instructor: Direct student to "Put your finger on box #1. Now circle the word in the box that I call... 'ten.' Put your finger on box #2. Now circle the word 'pet,' etc." Say each word below distinctly with emphasis upon initial and final consonants.

1. ten	2. pet	3. leg	4. red	5. less
6. egg	7. sent	8. held	9. bent	10. end
11. yell	12. next	13. get	14. help	15. went
16. end	17. best	18. mend	19. wet	20. fed

Record scores in the space provided on the front cover of the Student Assessment Record and calculate the Percentage of Mastery Score as indicated.

Word Comprehension: Short e Words

Directions: Tell student to put a finger on box #1 again and listen to what you say: *p. 1*

Instructor: *Underline the word that...*

1. tells what you are when you go swimming. wet
2. tells what color the light is that means stop. red
3. tells something that says "cluck-cluck". hen
4. means a kind of airplane. jet
5. tells what it looks like when you don't pick up your room. mess
6. a boy's name. Ken
7. tells what you use when you write with ink. pen
8. tells what Mom likes you to do for her. help
9. tells what we do when the ball game gets exciting. yell
10. tells where you go to sleep. bed
11. tells what Humpty Dumpty did. fell
12. tells where a bird lives. nest
13. tells something you walk with. leg
14. tells what part of your body holds your head up. neck
15. tells what some people eat for breakfast. eggs
16. tells what you need to do when you are tired. rest
17. a girl's name. Peg
18. a number. ten
19. a word Mom likes to hear us say. yes
20. tells how we are when we're healthy. well

Record scores in the space provided on the front cover of the Student Assessment Record and calculate the Percentage of Mastery Score as indicated.

Picture-Word Matching Fun

p. 2

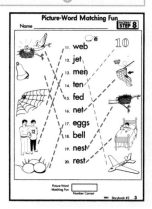

p. 3

Story Comprehension Matching Fun

p. 4

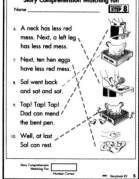

p. 5

Missing Letter Fun, p. 6

1. bed	2. ham	3. tent	4. hen	5. map
6. egg	7. leg	8. desk	9. can	10. pen

RACEWAY STEP 9

Read, Write and Spell

Short i Words

Goals

To read, write, and spell **short i** words

To use **short i** words in oral sentences

To practice Grammar Skills

Suggested Pacing

2 days

Material

Raceway Book, pp. 45-46

pp. 45-46

PROCEDURE

Instructor:

- Use **Raceway Book** pp. 45-46 to introduce this lesson.
  Refer to shaded sections, pp. 31-32 in this Manual for directions.
- Teach **Grammar Chalkboard Lessons** shown below.

Phonics Song(s)/Games

Each day's lesson should begin with one or two previously learned phonics songs and end with a phonics game.

Grammar Chalkboard Lessons

SENTENCES

Unscramble the sentences.

Sentences
1. Tim give gift. Dad will a   Tim will give Dad a gift.
2. can swim. Bill   Bill can swim.
3. Sis yell. will and Peg   Sis and Peg will yell.
4. bit his lip. Jim   Jim bit his lip.

CAPITALIZATION

Choose the correct word for each sentence.

Capitalization
1. Give ___Tim___ a mitt. (tim, Tim)
2. Pass ___Ann___ the ham. (Ann, ann)
3. Ed and ___Peg___ have a mess. (peg, Peg)
4. Dad sent ___Ken___ a pet. (Ken, ken)

Move Raceway Car to Step **10**

Reading

PHONETIC STORYBOOK READER 3, *The Inchworm Book*

Goals
To read Phonetic Storybook Reader 3, *The Inchworm Book*
To practice Grammar Skills
To take Book End Assessment

Suggested Pacing
3 days

Materials

1. Phonetic Storybook Reader 3,
   The Inchworm Book, pp. 2-32
2. *Raceway Book,* pp. 47-50
3. Assessment Book: Assessment for **Storybook Reader 3**

PROCEDURE

Have student:

- Read vocabulary pp. 2-5 in **Storybook Reader 3**.
- Read stories **Jim**, pp. 7-19, **Sis and Biff**, pp. 20-32. See PROCEDURE on p. 33 in Manual.
- Complete **Raceway Book** pp. 47-50.

Instructor:

- Teach **Grammar Chalkboard Lessons**/Manual p. 48.
- Read **Comprehension Hints**/Manual p. 50.
- Administer **Assessment**/Manual p. 49.
- Introduce **Written Spelling Tests**/Manual p. 51.

Phonics Song(s)/Games

Each day's lesson should begin with one or two previously learned phonics songs and end with a phonics game.

Written Spelling Test Introduction

See p. 51 in this Manual for directions.

Phonetic Storybook Reader 3

Comprehension Questions
Jim
Story 1 • pp. 7-19

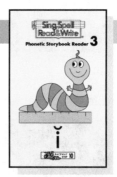

Have student read orally the designated pages, Ask the following questions:

After reading pp. 7-11:

- Who is the main character in this story? (Context Clue) Jim
- How old is Jim? *(Story Detail)* Six

- What do you think makes him feel big? *(Inference/Drawing Conclusion)* Jim is bigger than his sister and it's his birthday.

(Continued on next page)

After reading pp. 12-13:
- Who will help Jim bat? *(Story Detail)* Dad
- What do you think Dad will do to teach Jim how to bat? *(Picture Clue/Predicting)* Dad will show him how to hold and swing the bat.

After reading pp. 14-17:
- Why do you wear a mitt to catch a ball? *(Personal Experience)*
So you won't hurt your hand
- Do you think Jim and Dad are good friends? Why? *(Inference/Drawing Conclusion)* Yes, because they're playing together.
- How does Ripp feel when Jim misses the ball? *(Story Detail)* Sad

- What is the word on p.17 that shows the ball is going fast? *(Picture Clue)* Whiz

After reading pp. 18-19:
- What does Jim do to show his happiness? *(Story Detail)* A quick jig
- What is a jig? *(Context Clue)* A dance
- What is the problem in this story? *(Analyzing)* Jim needed to learn how to hit the baseball.
- How was it solved? *(Analyzing)* His dad helped him.
- Could this story be true? *(Reality/Fantasy)* Yes
- What would be a good title for this story? *(Main Idea)* "Jim learns to bat", etc.

Comprehension Questions

Sis and Biff

Story 2 • pp. 20-32

Have student read orally the designated pages. Ask the following questions:

After reading pp. 20-21:
- Who are the main characters in this story? *(Story Detail)* Sis and Biff
- Where do you think Sis is? *(Context Clue/Picture Clue)* At the beach

After reading pp. 22-25:
- What do you think she will do with the sand? *(Predicting)* Make a castle (Answers vary)
- What is Sis going to do with the sand? *(Story Detail)* Make a sand hill

After reading pp. 26-27:
- Where is Biff? *(Story Detail)* In back of the hill
- What may happen to the hill? *(Predicting Outcome)* It might slide over or fall down.

After reading pp. 28-32:
- What happened to the hill? *(Story Detail)* It spilled over.

- Do you believe Sis was mad at Biff? *(Inference/Drawing Conclusion)* No
- If so, did Sis forgive Biff? What makes you think she did? *(Context Clue)*
1) Yes 2) She gave him milk.
- What did Sis put on Biff that babies wear? *(Story Detail)* A bib
- Name in sequence the events in this story. *(Sequencing/Summarizing)*
    1. Sis was playing at the beach.
    2. Sis mixed sand and played with toys.
    3. Sis made a sand hill.
    4. The hill fell over when Biff dug a hole in it.
    5. Sis and Biff had a snack.

Complete pp. 47-50 in Raceway Book. See directions on next page.

Raceway Book: Grammar/Comprehension

Picture Clues, *p. 47*
Choose the word that completes the sentence and matches the picture.

Write the Word, *p. 48*
Write the word that names the picture. If the student needs help to spell the word, he/she may look on pp. 45-46 to find the word.

Rhyming Words, *p. 49*
Words that end in the same vowel and consonant sound are called rhyming words. **Bag** and **sag** rhyme because they end in the same vowel and consonant sound. Use some examples of words that rhyme, such as **men** and **ten** and ask *why* they rhyme. Then use some examples of words that *do not* rhyme, as **set** and **bat**. Ask why these words *don't* rhyme. Continue in this manner until student understands rhyming words. Student will circle the two rhyming words on p. 49.

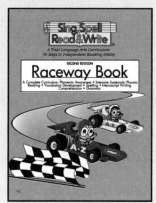

pp. 47-50

Favorite Character, *p. 50*
Have student draw a picture of a favorite character from *Phonetic Storybook Reader 3*.

Grammar Chalkboard Lessons

RHYMING WORDS REVIEW
Have student write *yes* if the words rhyme and *no* if they do not rhyme.

Rhyming Words			
1. lift - gift	yes	5. pig - dig	yes
2. tip - zip	yes	6. best - yes	no
3. ten - pat	no	7. rest - lip	no
4. fed - bed	yes	8. miss - kiss	yes

PLURALS REVIEW
Have student write the plural form of each word.

Plurals			
1. pig	pigs	6. rag	rags
2. mitt	mitts	7. cat	cats
3. jet	jets	8. bat	bats
4. hen	hens	9. bib	bibs
5. net	nets	10. pill	pills

Assessment Book

★ ★
Administer Book End Assessment
for Phonetic Storybook Reader 3.
Directions and Answer Key on next page.
★ ★

Move
Raceway Car
to Step **11**

Directions and Answer Key

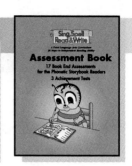

Book End Assessment
Phonetic Storybook Reader 3

Word Recognition: Short i Words

Instructor: Direct student to "Put your finger on box #1. Now circle the word in the box that I call... 'if.' Put your finger on box #2. Now circle the word 'miss,' etc." The words the instructor should call are listed below. Say each word distinctly with emphasis upon initial and final consonants.

1. if	2. miss	3. it	4. Sis	5. Jim
6. is	7. milk	8. hit	9. Ripp	10. give
11. did	12. will	13. tin	14. Jim	15. Biff
16. pig	17. fit	18. lift	19. spill	20. is

Record scores in the space provided on the front cover of the Student Assessment Record and calculate the Percentage of Mastery Score as indicated.

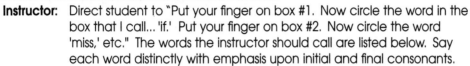

Word Comprehension: Short i Words

Directions: Tell student to point to box #1 again and listen to what you say:

Instructor: *Underline the word that...*

1. tells what you take of your soup when it's hot. sip
2. tells what your dog would do if you stepped on his tail. yip
3. tells the name of the cat in our storybook. Biff
4. is what you do to your gas tank at the gas station. fill
5. is a fat little animal. pig
6. tells something that might stick you. pin
7. tells what is fun to sleigh-ride down. hill
8. tells what you do with a football. kick
9. tells what the top of a can or jar is called. lid
10. tells what your clothes must do if they look nice on you. fit
11. tells what Biff likes to do in the sand. dig
12. means fast. quick
13. tells what the catcher wears on his hand when he/she plays baseball. mitt
14. is a girl's name. Jill
15. tells what you give Mom and Dad when you say good-night. kiss
16. means large. big
17. is something we get from cows. milk
18. tells the sound a car makes when it goes very, very fast. whiz
19. tells what you give your friend when you go to his/her birthday party. gift
20. tells what you are if you are not outdoors. in

Record scores in the space provided on the front cover of the Student Assessment Record and calculate the Percentage of Mastery Score as indicated.

Picture-Word Matching Fun

p. 2

p. 3

Story Comprehension Matching Fun

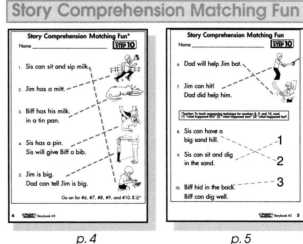

p. 4

p. 5

Missing Letter Fun, p. 6

1. fish	2. fin	3. hat	4. lid	5. dish
6. cap	7. net	8. web	9. ring	10. kit

Comprehension Hints

To improve comprehension, follow these helpful hints by checking/teaching the following:

1. Decoding

- Does the student know all the sounds necessary to decode and read all the words independently?
- Has the student mastered the vocabulary sufficiently (immediate word identification) so decoding does not interfere with fluency and comprehension?
- Does the student know the meaning of the words?

2. Observing Punctuation

Tell student to obey the "stop signs" of reading...punctuation marks.

(.) Periods - Teach student to stop at periods, and to start fresh at the next sentence. (Stop completely and shift gears before going on.)

(,) Commas - Teach student to pause for a comma. (Tap the brakes quickly.)

(?) Question Mark - Teach student to raise his/her voice at question marks to make it sound as if someone is asking a question. Practice asking questions.

(") Quotation Marks - Teach student to raise his/her voice when reading words that are between quotation marks to make it sound "alive" as if someone is talking.

(!) Exclamation Point - Teach student that an exclamation point is used after such words as "Help!" or "Hurrah!" or other exciting statements as "Fire! Fire!"

3. Grouping Words

- **Group Words Together in Clusters** - Beginning in *Phonetic Storybook Reader 3*, tell your student to "group words in clusters to make them sound like talking" rather than to "read smoothly". Practice grouping words in clusters the way we talk, as follows:

  the ball   the fox   the box   a cup   the bat   the bed

Remember to pronounce ***the*** and ***a*** as "**thŭ**" and "**ŭ**". This is called the schwa sound. Student should practice reading the words above until the two words sound almost as if they are one word.

Continue with grouping words :   The bat fell to the floor.   The boy had a cat.

Tell student:

- Writing is talk that has been put down in a "code" on paper.
- Reading is turning that "code" back into talking again.
- The best reading sounds like talking! Make your reading sound alive!
- If you are reading about a tiny mouse, make it sound like one!

4. Getting Background Information

There is an additional reason why young students (or people of any age) may have trouble understanding what they read, even when they know the words and can read with expression. They may not have any experience with what they are reading about. For example, if most adults were to read a technical book about Nuclear Engineering, they most certainly would have difficulty understanding it. Although they could read the words and perhaps even read with expression, they would need someone to explain what they read about to help them understand it. (This is different from someone teaching what the words are. It is a case of "reading to learn" rather than "learning to read." Obviously, "learning to read" must come first.)

(Continued on next page)

In Summary

To improve comprehension, work on:

- Decoding skills and word meanings
- Observing punctuation
- Grouping words and using expression
- Providing background Information

Only when the student is a *competent oral reader*, should he/she be encouraged to read silently.

Written Spelling Tests

Begin now to dictate 5 spelling words per day starting with ă words (Step 5, *Raceway Book*, p.27). Have the student circle the numeral next to the first five words (See example). These are the spelling words for the test. The following day the student will write each spelling word as you dictate slowly, emphasizing sounds (see illustration below). After each spelling test, have student circle the next five (or ten) words for the test the following day. **You should increase the number of words to 10 per day on Step 16,** as the student gains confidence in written spelling ability. **You will continue daily written spelling tests throughout the year going straight through the *Raceway Book*, at 10 words a day/50 words a week.**

p. 27

The procedure for the instructor for spelling dictation is:

1. Dictate a word
2. Sound-out the word
3. Use the word in a sentence

You, the instructor, **MUST ASSURE SUCCESS FOR THE STUDENT.** Your child will succeed if you think he/she can! Here's how to help:

Instructor: "The first word is hat. **h, a-a-a, t**" (Slowly, as student writes each letter, keep the sounds going.)

"My hat is big."

"h, a-a-a, t"

"h, a-a-a, t"

Establish this routine each time you dictate spelling words to the student. At Step 21, the student will begin writing the words in sentences.

Note: You may wish to cut handwriting paper in half to use for spelling tests.

sample spelling test

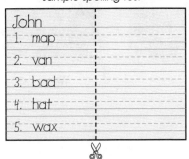

Read, Write and Spell

Short o Words

Goals

To read, write, and spell **short o** words

To use **short o** words in oral sentences

Suggested Pacing

2 days

Material

Raceway Book, pp. 51-52

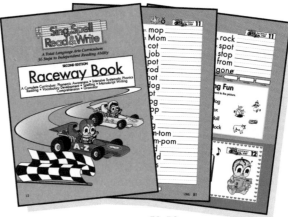

pp. 51-52

PROCEDURE

Instructor:

- Use **Raceway Book** pp. 51-52 to introduce this lesson.
  Refer to shaded sections pp. 31-32 in this Manual for directions.
- Teach **Grammar Chalkboard Lessons** shown below.

Phonics Song(s)/Games

Each day's lesson should begin with one or two previously learned phonics songs and end with a phonics game.

Written Spelling Tests

Dictate 5 words per day for a written spelling test. See p. 51 in this Manual for directions.

Grammar Chalkboard Lessons

PLURALS

Choose the correct word for each sentence.

Plurals
1. Sis will fill ten ___pans___ . (pan, pans)
2. Jim has a ___clock___ . (clock, clocks)
3. Mom held a ___pot___ . (pot, pots)
4. Bob will get six ___gifts___ . (gift, gifts)

RHYMING WORDS

Choose a word from the Word Bank to make rhyming pairs.

Rhyming Words			
1. sock	lock	6. red	bed
2. map	tap	7. pan	fan
3. let	set	8. fox	box
4. bag	rag	9. glad	sad
5. kiss	miss	10. last	fast

Word Bank: tap, rag, lock, set, miss, box, bed, fan, fast, sad

Move Raceway Car to Step 12

Reading

PHONETIC STORYBOOK READER 4, *The Octopus Book*

Goals

To read Phonetic Storybook Reader 4, *The Octopus Book*
To practice Grammar Skills
To take Book End Assessment

Suggested Pacing

3 days

Materials

1. Phonetic Storybook Reader 4, *The Octopus Book*, pp. 2-32
2. *Raceway Book*, pp. 53-57
3. Assessment Book: Assessment for Phonetic Storybook Reader 4

PROCEDURE

Have student:

- Read vocabulary pp. 2-5 in **Storybook Reader 4.**
- Read **Kim, Jill and Pep**, pp. 7-32. See PROCEDURE on p. 33 in Manual.
- Complete **Raceway Book** pp. 53-57.

Instructor:

- Teach **Grammar Chalkboard Lessons**/Manual p. 55.
- Administer **Assessment**/Manual p. 56.

Phonics Song(s)/Games

Each day's lesson should begin with one or two previously learned phonics songs and end with a phonics game.

Written Spelling Tests

Dictate 5 words per day for a written spelling test. See p. 51 in this Manual for directions.

Phonetic Storybook Reader 4

Comprehension Questions
Kim, Jill, and Pep
pp. 7-32

Have student read orally the designated pages. Ask the following questions:

After reading pp. 7-9:

- Who is the doll? *(Story Detail)* Kim
- Describe the way Kim is dressed. *(Story Detail)* She has a yellow dress with red dots and a red hat with a pom-pom on top.

After reading pp. 10-11:

- Tell me what Pep did. *(Summarizing)* He took the doll off the bed and ran outside.
- What do you think Pep will do with Kim? *(Predicting)* Leave her outside

(Continued on next page)

After reading pp. 12-13:

- Where did Pep put Kim? *(Story Detail)*
  In the big flower pot
- How fast did Pep run? *(Comparing/Analogy)*
  As fast as a fox
- Why would Jill look on the bed for Kim?
  (Analyzing) That's where she left her.

After reading pp. 14-15:

- How does Jill feel about not finding Kim?
  (Inference/Drawing Conclusion) She's upset.
- What does Mom suggest? *(Context Clue)*
  Go ask Todd
- Who do you think Todd is? *(Predicting)*
  Probably her brother
- What do we know that Jill does not know?
  (Analyzing) Pep hid Kim in the flower pot.
- Where do you look for lost toys in your house?
  (Personal Experience) In the toy box, under
  the bed, etc.

After reading pp. 16-19:

- Who is Todd? *(Picture Clue)* Jill's baby brother
- What does he have ten of? *(Story Detail)*
  Blocks
- Does Todd have Kim? *(Story Detail)* No

After reading pp. 20-21:

- What does Todd have with a red spot?
  (Story Detail) A rock

- What can the man do? *(Story Detail)* Jog

After reading pp. 22-23:

- When Jill sees Pep, what do you think she will
  do? *(Predicting)* Get Pep to lead her to Kim
- Let's look back and name ten things Todd
  had in his toy box. *(Story Detail)* A man, hen,
  top, tom-tom, bat, lock, rock, van, jet, hog,
  clock, odd sock, ox, and ten blocks

After reading pp. 24-27:

- What does Jill tell Pep to do? *(Story Detail)*
  Get Kim!
- Jill says Pep is a bad dog. Do you agree?
  Why? *(Opinion)* Answers will vary

After reading pp. 28-32:

- What is Pep's reward for bringing Kim back?
  (Context Clue) He gets to pick a toy from
  the box.
- What is the setting for this story? *(Analyzing)*
  Jill and Todd's house and yard
- Tell (in order) the most important events in this
  story. *(Sequence/Summarizing)* Jill's doll
  disappeared. She looked for the doll. Pep
  showed up with the doll's sash. Pep led them
  to the doll in the yard. They celebrated.

Complete pp. 53-57 in Raceway Book.
See directions below.

Raceway Book: Grammar/Comprehension

Rhyming Words, *p. 53*
Words that end in the same vowel and consonant sounds are
called rhyming words. Use examples like **big** and **wig** and explain
why they rhyme. Use examples **big** and **bag** and explain why they
do not rhyme. Student will circle the two words that rhyme on p. 53.

Picture Clues, *p. 54*
Tell student to choose the word that matches the picture and
completes the sentence.

Matching Fun, *p. 55*
Have student draw a line from the word to the
matching picture.

Picture Clues, *p. 56*
Tell student to choose the word that matches the picture and
completes the sentence.

Favorite Character, *p. 57*
Have student draw a picture of a favorite character from
Phonetic Storybook Reader 4.

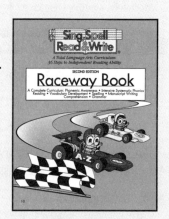

pp. 53-57

Grammar Chalkboard Lessons

CAPITALIZATION REVIEW

Student will write the sentences using capital letters correctly.

Capital Letters

1. tom has a hot rod.   Tom has a hot rod.
2. mom got Jill a doll.   Mom got Jill a doll.
3. the boss is on the job.   The boss is on the job.
4. bob sat on a rock.   Bob sat on a rock.

RHYMING WORDS REVIEW

Student will write the words and the corresponding rhyming word from the word bank.

Rhyming Words

1. Jill   hill   6. bet   met
2. not   hot   7. did   lid
3. log   jog   8. mat   pat
4. stop   mop   9. bent   sent
5. rock   lock   10. bass   pass

Word Bank: hot, mop, lock, hill, jog, met, pat, sent, lid, pass

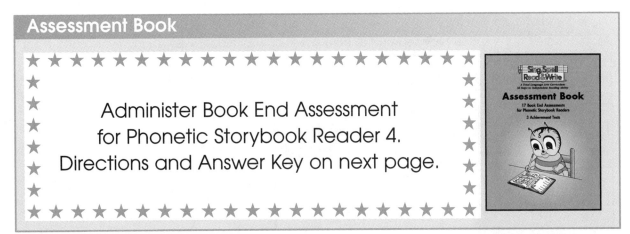

Assessment Book

★ ★ ★ ★ ★ ★ ★ ★ ★ ★ ★ ★ ★ ★ ★ ★ ★ ★ ★ ★

Administer Book End Assessment
for Phonetic Storybook Reader 4.
Directions and Answer Key on next page.

Move Raceway Car to Step **13**

Raceway Step 12

Book End Assessment
Phonetic Storybook Reader 4

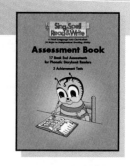

Word Recognition: Short o Words

Instructor: Direct student to "Put your finger on box #1. Now circle the word in the box that I call... 'fox.' Put your finger on box #2. Now circle the word 'box,' etc." The words the instructor should call are listed below. Say each word distinctly with emphasis upon initial and final consonants.

1. fox	2. box	3. nod	4. log	5. dog
6. hot	7. pot	8. hop	9. from	10. lot
11. Todd	12. on	13. sock	14. odd	15. rock
16. odd	17. spot	18. not	19. top	20. sock

Record scores in the space provided on the front cover of the Student Assessment Record and calculate the Percentage of Mastery Score as indicated.

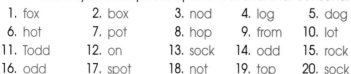

Word Recognition and Word Comprehension
p. 1

Word Comprehension: Short o Words

Directions: Tell student to point to box #1 again and listen to what you say:

Instructor: *Underline the word that...*

1. is what gets on your shirt when you spill something. spot
2. is another name for a very big pig. hog
3. is what a bunny does. hop
4. is how the weather is in the summertime. hot
5. is what Biff took and hid by the plant. doll
6. is the name of the best lady in the world. Mom
7. is what you might sleep on. cot
8. is what you do at a red light. stop
9. is what a bad person does when he/she steals from a house. rob
10. is the land where the big wizard is. Oz
11. is a kind of drum. tom-tom
12. is how much candy you would have if you had a whole bunch. lot
13. is what we burn in the fireplace. log
14. is the noise a balloon makes when someone sticks a pin in it. pop
15. tells what time it is. clock
16. is Jill's favorite toy. doll
17. would be what Mom tells us to do if we're fussy. stop
18. is what Mom does sometimes to get the baby to sleep. rock
19. is what your cereal comes in. box
20. is what you can build a lot of things with. blocks

Record scores in the space provided on the front cover of the Student Assessment Record and calculate the Percentage of Mastery Score as indicated.

Picture-Word Matching Fun

Picture-Word Matching Fun

1. hog	11. mop
2. top	12. cot
3. cob	13. hot dog
4. rob	14. rod
5. ox	15. jog
6. dot	16. mom
7. hop	17. tom-tom
8. fox	18. doll
9. box	19. sock
10. sob	20. blocks

p. 2   p. 3

Story Comprehension Matching Fun

Story Comprehension Matching Fun

1. Pep got on his cot. At last, Pep can rest.
2. Todd had a bat. Todd had a lock.
3. Todd had a tom-tom.
4. Jill has a doll. Jill's doll is Kim.

5. Jill set Kim on the doll bed.
6. Pep hid Kim in the big pot.
7. Jill went to get Kim. Kim was not in bed.
8. Pep got the doll from the pot.
9. Jill ran to Todd. Kim is not in the bed.
10. Todd did not have Kim.

p. 4   p. 5

Missing Letter Fun, p. 6

1. pot	2. dog	3. mitt	4. rocks	5. nest
6. log	7. pop	8. bag	9. six	10. jam

Read, Write and Spell

Short u Words

<u>Goals</u>

To read write, and spell **short u** words

To use **short u** words in oral sentences

To practice Grammar Skills

<u>Suggested Pacing</u>

2 days

<u>Material</u>

Raceway Book, pp. 58-59

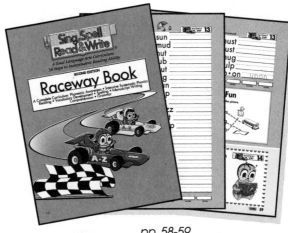

pp. 58-59

PROCEDURE

Instructor:

- Use ***Raceway Book***, pp. 58-59 to introduce this lesson. Follow procedure located in the shaded section, pp. 31-32 in this Manual for directions.
- Teach **Grammar Chalkboard Lessons** shown below.

Phonics Song(s)/Games

Each day's lesson should begin with one or two previously learned phonics songs and end with a phonics game.

Written Spelling Tests

Instructor will dictate 5 words per day for a written spelling test. See p. 51 in this Manual for directions.

Grammar Chalkboard Lessons

SENTENCES

Write sentences correctly.

Sentences
1. rug. Mom the will dust   Mom will dust the rug.
2. can swim. Gus and Max   Gus and Max can swim.
3. a duck. Gus has   Gus has a duck.
4. Gus is snug rug. in the   Gus is snug in the rug.

CAPITALIZATION

Write sentences correctly.

Capitalization
1. mom and gus live in a hut   Mom and Gus live in a hut.
2. dad and jim will bat   Dad and Jim will bat.
3. ken will see peg and sal   Ken will see Peg and Sal.
4. sam ran at pam and dan   Sam ran at Pam and Dan.

Move
Raceway Car
to Step **14**

Reading

PHONETIC STORYBOOK READER 5, *The Umbrella Book*

Goals

To read Phonetic Storybook Reader 5, *The Umbrella Book*

To get a head start on *Letter Cluster Phonics Song* (Step 16)

To practice Grammar Skills

To take Book End Assessment

Suggested Pacing

4 days

Materials

1. **Letter Cluster Phonics Song, Verses 1 and 2**, CD or Cassette #3
2. Phonetic Storybook Reader 5, *The Umbrella Book*, pp. 2-32
3. *Raceway Book*, pp. 60-64 and pp. 71-72 (for a head start on Step 16)
4. Assessment Book: Assessment for Phonetic Storybook Reader 5

PROCEDURE

Have student:

- Read vocabulary pp. 2-5 in **Storybook Reader 5**.
- Read **Gus**, pp. 7-32. See PROCEDURE on p. 33 in Manual.
- Complete **Raceway Book** pp. 60-64.

Instructor:

- Teach **Grammar Chalkboard Lessons**/Manual p. 61.
- Administer **Assessment**/Manual p. 62.

Getting a Head Start on Step 16

It is advantageous to begin preparing your student for Step 16 by singing Verses 1 and 2 of the **Letter Cluster Phonics Song** at this time. Introduce as follows: Turn in *Raceway Book* to pp. 71-72 to **Letter Cluster Phonics Song Charts**.

pp. 71-72 (Step 16)

Instructor: "These charts are to be mastered on Step 16, but we are going to start learning them now even though we're on Step 14. Each day we are going to learn 'letter cluster' sounds from these charts. We'll start with **o-r** today. I have taught you that letter **o** says **ŏ** as in **octopus**, and I have taught you that letter **r** says **rh** as in **rail**. Today we're going to learn *something new* about these two letters. Whenever you see letters **o** and **r** together, don't say **ŏ-rh** to sound out the word...it won't work! Whenever you see **o-r** say **or** as in **orbit**. (Echo the **or** sound.) Can you think of a word that starts with **or**?"

(Continued on next page)

Elicit:

orchestra -	The **or**chestra played beautiful music.
orchard -	Apple trees grow in the **or**chard.
organ -	She can play the **or**gan.
orphan -	The child was an **or**phan.
order -	The waitress took our **or**der.
orchid -	An **or**chid is a beautiful flower.
orbit -	An **or**bit is a circular pathway around the earth. The rocket was in **or**bit.

Talk about the word meanings and use the words in oral sentences as shown above. ***Do not expect your student to be able to read the words.*** Stick to the lesson: **o-r** says **or**, etc. Continue in this manner for **sh, ch, er, ir, ur**, and the remaining letter clusters on the charts. For letter cluster **th**, tell your student that letters **th** mean **"put your tongue to your teeth!"** Have student practice making the "**th**" sound. Say, "**th**ree, **th**ink, **th**rew," accenting the "unvoiced" **th** by blowing at the beginning of each word. Next, have your student put his/her fingers on the front of the neck with tongue on teeth again and say, "**th**is, **th**at, **th**ese, **th**ose," accenting the "voiced" **th** at the beginning of each word. Your student's fingers will feel a vibration.

Have your student sing the first two verses of the *Letter Cluster Phonics Song*. Play the song and **point to each letter cluster and key word picture**. (The very small words are for the benefit of the instructor only.)

Play CD or Cassette #3 and point along to charts each day.
Have your student join in singing when ready.

Phonics Song(s)/Games

Each day's lesson should begin with one or two previously learned phonics songs and end with a phonics game. A new song is introduced in this Step.

Written Spelling Tests

Dictate 5 words per day for a written spelling test. See p. 51 in this Manual for directions.

Phonetic Storybook Reader 5

Comprehension Questions
Gus
pp. 7-32

Have student read orally the designated pages.
Ask the following questions:

After reading pp. 8-9:
- Who is Gus? *(Story Detail)* A bug
- What is the word used for Gus' house? *(Context Clue)* A hut
- What is his hut? *(Story Detail)* A nut
- Does this house seem about the right size for a family of bugs? *(Analyzing)* Yes

After reading pp. 10-13:
- What does Gus have to eat and drink? *(Story Detail)* A ham sandwich and milk
- Read aloud the sentence that tells us Mom teaches Gus good manners. *(Reading For Understanding)* "His mom said not to gulp."

(Continued on next page)

- Why does Mom say, "It is not dull in the hut"?
  (Inference/Drawing Conclusion)
  Because there is so much going on.

After reading pp. 14-15:

- How many cups of mud did Gus dig?
  (Story Detail) Six
- Think of some words to describe Gus.
  (Vocabulary Expansion) Happy, busy, fun, etc.

After reading pp. 16-19:

- Read aloud the sentence that tells Gus has a friend. *(Context Clue)*
  "Gus has a pal. His pal is Max."
- Where do Gus and Max have fun?
  (Story Detail) In a cup
- Why should Max know how to swim? *(Analyzing)*
  He jumps up and into the mug of water.
- How is a mug like a cup? *(Classification)* They both hold liquids and have handles.

After reading pp. 20-23:

- What does Gus need help with? *(Context Clue)*
  Getting unstuck from the gum

- Does the butterfly see Gus hiding?
  (Predicting) Yes
- Who else gave Gus and Max a free ride?
  (Story Detail/Picture Clue) A duck

After reading pp. 24-27:

- What things do you think are the same size as Gus?
  (Analyzing) Answers may vary. A stone, flower...
- Why do you think Tom's pup can't run fast?
  (Predicting) He has little short legs.
- What did Dad use for a bathtub? *(Picture Clue)*
  A tree trunk

After reading pp. 28-32:

- What does the word *snug* mean?
  (Context Clue) "Tightly tucked in"
- Is this a true or make-believe story?
  (Reality/ Fantasy) Make-believe
- Why couldn't it be true? *(Analyze)* Answers will vary: A bug doesn't have clothes or play a guitar.

Complete pp. 60-64 in Raceway Book.
See directions below.

Raceway Book: Grammar/Comprehension

Picture Clues, *p. 60*
Choose the word that completes the sentence and matches the picture.

Compound Words and Syllabication, *p. 61*
Sometimes two words are put together to make a new word with a different meaning. These words are called *compound words*.

Write "sandbox". Have your student tell you the two words that make up the compound word. (**sand** and **box**)

Write other compound words (gumdrop, backpack, sunset, etc.). Have your student identify the two words that make up the compound word.

In the *Raceway Book* on p. 59, the word "up-on" has been divided. Tell student this is a compound word. "Up" is one syllable or part and "on" another syllable or part. Page 61 in the *Raceway Book* will give your student practice in making and dividing compound words into syllables. On p. 61 (bottom half), have your student write the two words that make the compound word and write the number of syllables each word has in the blank.

Picture Clues, *p. 62*
Choose the word that completes the sentence and matches the picture.

Capitals and Periods, *p. 63*
Remind the student that sentences always begin with a capital letter and end with punctuation; either a period or a question mark. Write these sentences and let the student tell you what is incorrect about the sentences.

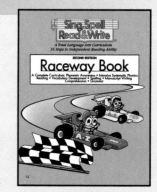

pp. 60-64

max can jump	Max can jump.
can Max jump	Can Max jump?
will gus run	Will Gus run?
gus will run	Gus will run.

Favorite Character, *p. 64*
Draw a picture of a favorite character from *Phonetic Storybook Reader 5*.

Sing-Spell Read&Write

Grammar Chalkboard Lessons

SPELLING REVIEW

Draw the pictures shown below. Have student write the word for each picture.

Spelling

1. _can_   4. _bed_
2. _fan_   5. _six_   6
3. _bat_   6. _box_

SENTENCE REVIEW

Have student write each sentence and choose a word from the Word Bank to complete it.

Sentences

1. Gus dug in the _mud_ .
2. The dog will _run_ .
3. Dad has a _truck_ .
4. Gus _sat_ on the rug.

Word Bank: run, sat, mud, truck

Assessment Book

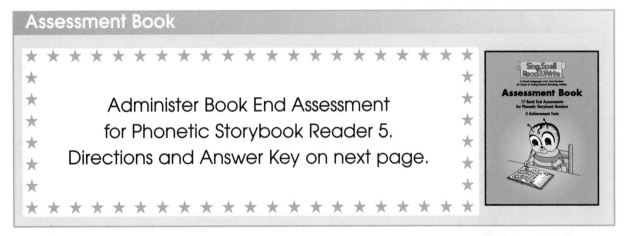

Administer Book End Assessment
for Phonetic Storybook Reader 5.
Directions and Answer Key on next page.

Move Raceway Car to Step **15**

Sing Spell Read & Write

Raceway Step 14

Book End Assessment
Phonetic Storybook Reader 5

Word Recognition: Short u Words

Instructor: Direct student to "Put your finger on box #1. Now circle the word in the box that I call... 'rub.' Put your finger on box #2. Now circle the word 'bug,' etc." Say each word below distinctly with emphasis upon initial and final consonants.

1. rub	2. bug	3. cup	4. mug	5. fun
6. us	7. bun	8. tug	9. pup	10. run
11. snug	12. dug	13. hut	14. nut	15. us
16. truck	17. cut	18. hum	19. must	20. puff

Record scores in the space provided on the front cover of the Student Assessment Record and calculate the Percentage of Mastery Score as indicated.

Word Comprehension: Short u Words

Directions: Tell student to point to box #1 again and listen to what you say:

Instructor: *Underline the word that...*

1. is what shines in the sky. sun
2. is something we can crack open and eat. nut
3. is the name of our little bug. Gus
4. means singing with your lips closed. hum
5. is what you do with a knife. cut
6. is where a kite goes. up
7. is what swims in the water. duck
8. is what Mom or Dad drink their coffee from. cup
9. is the noise that a bee makes. buzz
10. is a flower before it opens up. bud
11. is a musical instrument. drum
12. is something you might eat for breakfast. bun
13. is what has happened when you can't get your car out of the mud. stuck
14. is what dirt turns into when it gets wet. mud
15. is what we see on the floor when we haven't swept it. dust
16. is what you put over you when it rains. umbrella
17. is where you are when you take a bath. tub
18. is what we saw the cow do in "Hey Diddle Diddle". jump
19. is what says "quack". duck
20. is what the unhappy baby does. fuss

Record scores in the space provided on the front cover of the Student Assessment Record and calculate the Percentage of Mastery Score as indicated.

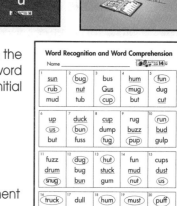
p. 1

Picture-Word Matching Fun

p. 2

p. 3

Story Comprehension Matching Fun

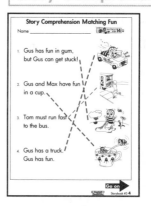
p. 4

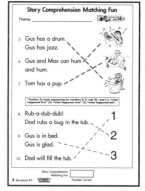
p. 5

Missing Letter Fun, p. 6

1. tub	2. jog	3. rod	4. gift	5. mug
6. wig	7. hut	8. fox	9. hug	10. yawn

RACEWAY STEP 15

Vocabulary and Reading

ă ĕ ĭ ŏ ŭ Words and Related Stories in Storybook Reader 6

Goals

To continue learning the *Letter Cluster Phonics Song*

To read, write, and orally spell longer *short vowel* words

To read Phonetic Storybook Reader 6, *The Truck Book*

To practice Grammar Skills

To take Book End Assessment

To take Achievement Test 1

Suggested Pacing

6 days

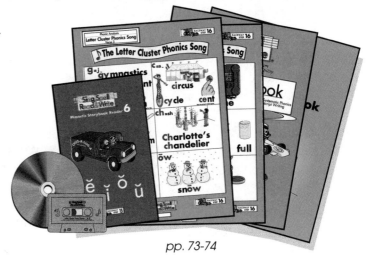

pp. 73-74

Materials

1. Letter Cluster Phonics Song, Verses 1-4, CD or Cassette #3
2. *Raceway Book*, pp. 65-70, 73-74
3. Phonetic Storybook Reader 6, *The Truck Book*, pp. 3-64
4. Assessment Book: Achievement Test #1, Assessment for *Phonetic Storybook Reader 6*

PROCEDURE

Instructor:

- Continue to sing with student **Letter Cluster Phonics Song**, Verses 1-2.
- Use **Letter Cluster Phonics Song Charts 3** and **4, Raceway Book** pp. 73-74, to introduce Verses 3 and 4.
- Have student read, write, and spell all words on pp. 65-66.
- Initial and date at bottom of pages to indicate mastery.

Have student:

- Read pp. 3-64 in **Storybook Reader 6**.
- Read each story two or three times for fluency.
- Complete **Raceway Book** pp. 67-70.

Instructor:

- Teach **Grammar Chalkboard Lessons**/Manual p. 68.
- Administer **Assessment**/Manual p. 69.
- Administer **Achievement Test 1**/Manual p. 70.

Phonics Song(s)/Games

Each day's lesson should begin with one or two previously learned phonics songs and end with a phonics game.

Written Spelling Tests

Dictate 5 words per day for a written spelling test. See p. 51 in this Manual for directions.

Phonetic Storybook Reader 6

Comprehension Questions
Jill Has a Spill
Story 1 • pp. 3-15

Jill ran fast.

Have student read orally the designated pages. Ask the following questions:

After reading pp. 4-7:
- Who has a problem? *(Context Clue)* Jill
- What happened to Jill? *(Story Detail/Cause & Effect)* She fell down and was hurt.

After reading pp. 8-15:
- Who will help her? *(Story Detail)* Mom

- Why is Jill glad at the end of the story? *(Inference/Drawing Conclusion)* Because Mom helped her.
- Who is the main character in this story? *(Main Character)* Jill

Comprehension Questions
The Red Truck
Story 2 • pp. 16-29

Ted has a truck. The truck is red. Ted gets gas in his truck. Ted fills it up. Ted's red truck runs fast.

Have student read orally the designated pages, and then ask him/her the following questions:

After reading p. 17:
- Do you think Ted will be the main character in this story? Why? *(Opinion/Predicting)* Yes, because he's the only one we see.

After reading pp. 18-19:
- Close your eyes and tell me three things the truck went past. *(Story Detail)* A frog, a log, a bell, a hill, etc.

After reading pp. 20-21:
- Look on p. 20 and tell me four words that rhyme. *(Story Detail)* Lock, sock, block, and lock

After reading pp. 22-25:
- Why is the popsicle melting? *(Cause & Effect)* It's warm.

After reading pp. 26-28:
- Name the animals on these pages. *(Story Detail/Classification)* A hen, a pig, and a cat

After reading p. 29:
- What sound did the truck make as it rolled down the steps? *(Story Detail)* Bump-te-bump-te-bump!
- What other name could you give this little truck? *(Picture Clue)* Dump truck

Complete p. 67 in Raceway Book. See directions below.

Raceway Book: Comprehension

Raceway Book

Scrambled Sentences, *p. 67*
Tell student a sentence is a group of words that expresses a complete thought and makes sense. A sentence tells *who* did something and *what* they did. Rearrange the words to make a sentence. Begin each sentence with a capital letter and end it with a period.

p. 67

Phonetic Storybook Reader 6

Comprehension Questions
West Camp
Story 3 • pp. 30-38

Have student read orally the designated pages.
Ask the following questions:

After reading p. 31:
- Look at the picture and tell me what kind of camp this is. Where is the camp? *(Predicting/Story Detail)* A western ranch in the west or cowboy ranch
- What is the name of the camp? How do you know? *(Story Detail/Picture Clue)* a) West Camp b) The sign says "West Camp."

After reading pp. 32-34:
- How does Bill feel about camp? *(Drawing Conclusion)* He thinks it's fun.
- Why is Bump! Bump! Bump! written in dark print? *(Analysis)* So you will say it with a loud voice when you read it.
- Do you think Bill and Rob will be angry at each other? *(Predicting)* No, they are playing.

After reading p. 35:
- Do Rob and Bill become friends? *(Context Clue)* Yes

- What did they mean when they said they could get a hill as big as West Camp? *(Figurative Language)* They meant they could make a very big hill.

After reading pp. 36-38:
- Why did Bill and Rob sift the sand? *(Story Detail)* To get the lumps out
- How do Rob and Bill feel about the hill? *(Drawing Conclusion)* Proud
- How did you know? *(Analysis)* They clapped.
- What does *grand* mean? *(Context Clue)* Terrific; great
- Why did Rob and Bill go back in the pond? *(Inference/Drawing Conclusion)* They were hot and wanted to get cool.
- What does this mean, "Last kid in is a wet hen." *(Figurative Language)* It's just a fun way of starting a race.

Complete p. 68 in Raceway Book.
See directions below.

Raceway Book: Grammar

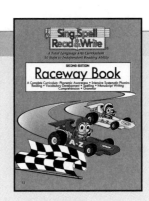

Alphabetical Order, *p. 68*
Tell student that words in alphabetical order are arranged so the first letter of the word follows the order of the alphabet. For example: **a**pple, **b**ag and **c**at are in A-B-C order because they begin with **a**, **b**, and **c**. Practice putting two words in A-B-C order by numbering 1,2 next to words found on p. 68.

p. 68

Phonetic Storybook Reader 6

Comprehension Questions

The Rust Rug

Story 4 • *Part 1*• pp. 39-49

Mom went to get a rug. Mom said to the man, "I must get a rug. I will pick a rust rug . . . not red, but rust." 40

"I have a rust rug," said the man. The man went to get the rust rug. 41

Have student read orally the designated pages. Ask the following questions:

After reading pp. 40-41:

● What is Mom shopping for? *(Story Detail)* A rug

● What color rug did she want? *(Story Detail)* Rust

● Why do you suppose she wanted a rust rug? *(Predicting)* It won't show dirt. It probably goes with her furniture.

After reading pp. 42-43:

● Look at the pages and name four things the man said was good about this rug. *(Story Detail)*

    1. It has the best back.
    2. It won't bend up and trip anyone.
    3. It will not get lumps.
    4. Dust will not stick to it.

After reading pp. 44-45:

● What else did the man say was good about this rug? *(Story Detail)* It will not stain. The fuzz is the best kind.

After reading pp. 46-47:

● Why did Mom ask if the rug cost a lot? *(Inference/Drawing Conclusion)* She has a certain amount of money she can spend.

● Why did the man name all the good things about the rust rug he showed Mom? *(Inference/ Drawing Conclusion)* He is a salesman and it's his job to tell about the rugs he sells.

After reading pp. 48-49:

● How will Mom get the rug home? *(Story Detail)* Dad will pick it up.

● What kind of salesman is this man? Why do you think this? *(Opinion)* He was helpful because he found the rug she wanted right away.

● What was Mom most concerned about in buying the rug? *(Context Clue)* The color and the price

● Who are the main characters in this story? *(Main Character)* Mom and the salesman

Comprehension Questions

Dad Gets the Rust Rug

Story 4 • *Part 2* • pp. 50-59

Have student read orally the designated pages, and then ask him/her the following questions:

Part 2: **Dad Gets the Rust Rug**

Dad went to get the rust rug. Dad went in his red van. 50

After reading pp. 50-51:

● Did Dad like the rug? Why? *(Context Clues/Opinion)* It didn't cost a lot and he thought it looked nice.

● Read the sentence that makes you know he likes the rug. *(Interpretation)* "It is a grand rug," said Dad.

After reading pp. 52-53:

● Who helped Dad with the rug? *(Story Detail)* Mom, Tim, and Bob

● How did Mom feel about her new rug? *(Inference/Drawing Conclusion)* Happy

● Read the sentence that makes you know. "At last I have a rust rug."

(Continued on next page)

After reading pp. 54-55:

- Why did Dad tack down the rug? *(Story Detail)* So it won't lift up and trip the kids.

- Would you find a desk, rug, and lamp in a house or a park? *(Classification)* In a house

After reading pp. 56-59:

- Let's look back in the story and name the rules in the right order. *(Sequence)*

  1 No snacks   2 No gum   3 No pops

- Do you think it is right for a family to have such rules? Why? *(Opinion)* Answers will vary.

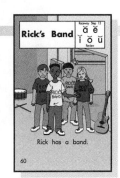

Comprehension Questions

Rick's Band

Story 5 • pp. 60-64

Have student read orally the designated pages, and then ask him/her the following questions:

After reading pp. 60-64:

- Who are the people in Rick's Band? *(Story Detail)* Rick, Don, Bob, and Jill

- Does everyone play an instrument? *(Context Clue)* No

- What do the others do? *(Story Detail)* Jill hums and Rick taps.

- What could **you** do in a band? *(Personal Experience)* Answers will vary.

- What could be another name for this story? *(Main Idea)* Answers will vary.

Complete pp. 69-70 in Raceway Book. See directions below.

Raceway Book: Grammar

Subject of a Sentence, *p. 69*

- The *subject* of a sentence is a word that tells **who** is doing something. It is usually a naming word like *boy, beach, park, Dad,* etc. Write some simple sentences and let your student tell you **who** is doing something.

  Examples: The man ran fast.
  A dog is in the pen.

Ask: Who ran fast? **man**
Ask: Who is in the pen? **dog**

- Continue in this manner until student understands what a subject is. On p. 69, have student draw a line under the subject in each sentence.

Periods and Question Marks, *p. 70*

- A period (.) is used at the end of a sentence that *tells*. A telling sentence does not need a response. An *asking* sentence *asks,* and needs a response. Words like **what, where, why, who,**

pp. 69-70

when, and **how** used at the beginning of a sentence ask a question.

- Give several examples of *telling* and *asking* sentences and have student tell you the kind of sentence and the mark that belongs at the end.

- Place a period or question mark and write **Telling** or **Asking** at the end of each sentence found on p. 70.

Grammar Chalkboard Lessons

A-B-C ORDER REVIEW

Student will place words in alphabetical order by numbering 1, 2.

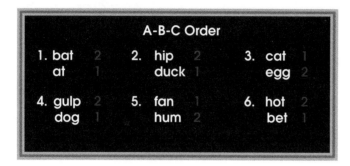

A-B-C Order

1. bat	2	2. hip	2	3. cat	1
at	1	duck	1	egg	2
4. gulp	2	5. fan	1	6. hot	2
dog	1	hum	2	bet	1

SUBJECT OF A SENTENCE

Have student write the sentences and underline the subject in each.

Subjects

1. Bill went to camp. Bill went to camp.
2. The man hit the rug. The man hit the rug.
3. Jill is glad. Jill is glad.
4. The dog ran. The dog ran.

Assessment Book

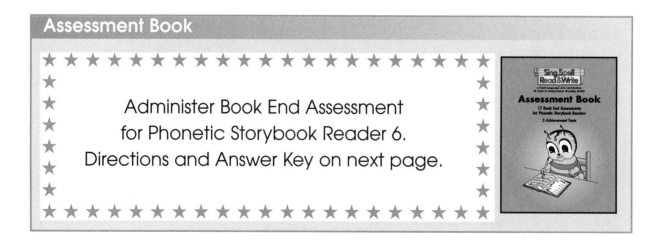

Administer Book End Assessment
for Phonetic Storybook Reader 6.
Directions and Answer Key on next page.

Move
Raceway Car
to Step
16

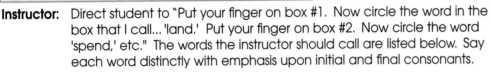

Raceway Step 15

Book End Assessment
Phonetic Storybook Reader 6

Instructor: Direct student to "Put your finger on box #1. Now circle the word in the box that I call... 'land.' Put your finger on box #2. Now circle the word 'spend,' etc." The words the instructor should call are listed below. Say each word distinctly with emphasis upon initial and final consonants.

1. land	2. spend	3. send	4. list	5. dots
6. just	7. melt	8. test	9. duck	10. hunt
11. grand	12. best	13. clock	14. bulb	15. fast
16. sift	17. must	18. pond	19. dump	20. from

Record scores in the space provided on the front cover of the Student Assessment Record and calculate the Percentage of Mastery Score as indicated.

Word Comprehension: ă ĕ ĭ ŏ ŭ Words

Directions: Tell your student to put his/her finger on box #1 again and listen to what you say:

Instructor: *Underline the word that (is)...*

1. a kind of light. lamp
2. something to eat. snack
3. something that you find at the beach. sand
4. means to pick up something. lift
5. what you do to remove dirt from the furniture. dust
6. a way to move. jump
7. something to drink. milk
8. something you use when camping. tent
9. a place to sit and do your work. desk
10. a part of a baby. hand
11. another word for a present. gift
12. a group of people who play musical instruments. band
13. something you could ride in. truck
14. something you wear around your waist. belt
15. a piece of information. fact
16. a word that means you don't feel good. sick
17. means to repair something. mend
18. something you may take when you are sick. pill
19. means a little bit wet. damp
20. an animal that is green and hops. frog

Record scores in the space provided on the front cover of the Student Assessment Record and calculate the Percentage of Mastery Score as indicated.

You will need to give student some new instructions before administering **Sentence Comprehension** and **Story Comprehension**.

1. Write as indicated (See Example A) and tell student to:
   A. Read the sentence
   B. Choose the answer
   C. Fill in the bubble under the correct answer

2. Teach student to say "blank" when he/she comes to a blank line in a sentence. This is especially important when the blank is at the beginning or in the middle of a sentence as in Example B.

Example A: Dad is a _____.
    pan   mat   map   man
    ○   ○   ○   ●

Example B: _____ had a rag and wax.
    cat   Dad   pal   Sal
    ○   ●   ○   ○

(Continued on next page)

3. Tell student that throughout the test he/she will see the words, "**Look back if you need help.**" Explain that this means your student may turn back to the story on the previous page or look up to the story at the top of the page to find the correct answer.

4. Tell student he/she will see an arrow and the words "**Go on**" at the bottom of some pages. This means to turn the page and go on.

Sentence Comprehension, pp. 2-6				
1. D	5. B	9. D	13. B	17. D
2. C	6. D	10. A	14. C	18. A
3. A	7. A	11. B	15. A	19. C
4. B	8. C	12. C	16. D	20. B

Story Comprehension, p. 7				
1. Rick	2. glad	3. 4	4. band	5. hum

Assessment Book

Achievement Test 1
for Raceway Steps 1-15

Achievement Test 1 may be used:
- As a post assessment to measure growth
- To determine mastery of skills

DIRECTIONS
- Remove **Achievement Test #1** from back of **Assessment Book**.
- Write student's name and other information on **Student Record Sheet**.
- Cut apart **Cue Cards** found on pp. 71-72 of this Manual. Give student Cue Card #1.

SECTION A: Letter Names and Sounds
- Seat student opposite the instructor.
- Say to student, "Tell me the **name** of this letter and the **sound** this letter makes."
- Each time the student gives an incorrect response (a miscue) strike a line through that item on the Student Record Sheet.
- If the student is unable to give the answer within five seconds, point to the next item and say, "Try this one." Mark the skipped item as a miscue on the Student Record Sheet.
- Record the number of CORRECT responses at the end of each column and enter the total for each Section.

SECTION B: Blends and Words
- In Section B, tell the student to blend the sounds together, just as he/she would do on the Ferris Wheel. Isolating the sounds "b" and "a" for "ba" would be a miscue. You may assist the student on the first item (only) of any column by saying, "Remember how we say this when we sing the A to Z Phonics Song (or Short Vowel Song or Ferris Wheel Song)?"

SECTION C: Vocabulary Words-Storybooks 1-6
- Allow the student five seconds to read each word.

SECTION D: Sentences-Storybooks 1-6
- Ask student to read each sentence. Allow student a maximum of five seconds for each word. After five seconds the examiner should read the word for the student and point to the next word. Encourage student to continue with the rest of the sentence. On Student Record Sheet strike a line through any skipped words, words supplied by the instructor, or any miscues.
- Count number of words skipped, omitted, supplied by the instructor, or mis-read as incorrect. Subtract that number from 36 and enter the number of CORRECT responses.

ACHIEVEMENT TEST #1
SECTION A: Letter Names and Sounds

Mm	D	s	o
Hh	R	p	e
Nn	T	w	a
Jj	L	b	u
Ff	V	k	i
Ll	Z	y	a

International Learning Systems of North America, Inc., 1000 112th Circle North, Suite 100, St. Petersburg, FL 33716, 1-800-321-8322

ACHIEVEMENT TEST #1
SECTION C: Vocabulary Words - Storybooks 1-6

went	camp	as	was
must	grand	the	to
bend	cannot	is	said
stick	flop	a	of
milk	swam	his	have

International Learning Systems of North America, Inc., 1000 112th Circle North, Suite 100, St. Petersburg, FL 33716, 1-800-321-8322

Cue Card #1 Steps 1-15

Cue Card #3 Steps 1-15

ACHIEVEMENT TEST #1
SECTION B: Blends and Words

ba	pi	ten	block
be	mo	job	dress
bi	fa	ran	trust
bo	ne	mug	flip
bu	mu	bit	strap

International Learning Systems of North America, Inc., 1000 112th Circle North, Suite 100, St. Petersburg, FL 33716, 1-800-321-8322

ACHIEVEMENT TEST #1
SECTION D: Sentences - Storybooks 1-6

1. A fat cat had ham.

2. Dad can mend the bent pen.

3. Biff has his milk in a tin pan.

4. Todd had a rock and a clock.

5. Gus is snug in the fuzz of his rug.

6. West Camp has a big pond.

International Learning Systems of North America, Inc., 1000 112th Circle North, Suite 100, St. Petersburg, FL 33716, 1-800-321-8322

Letter Cluster Phonics Song

Goal
To learn the **letter cluster sounds**

Suggested Pacing
10 days

Materials
1. *Raceway Book,* pp. 71-113
2. **Letter Cluster Phonics Song, Verses 1-4,**
   CD or Cassette #3
3. **Letter Cluster Sound-O Game** - Directions/Manual p. 77
4. **Letter Cluster Pick-A-Sound Game** - Directions/Manual p. 78
5. **Duck Pond** - Directions/Manual p. 78

PROCEDURE

Lesson Plans
Note: **Two weeks of suggested lesson plans for Step 16 are found on pp. 75-76 of this Manual.**

Phonics Song(s)/Games

Each day's lesson should begin with one or two previously learned phonics songs and end with a phonics game.

Written Spelling Tests

Beginning at Step 16, increase the number of words you dictate to 10 per day for a written spelling test.

pp. 71-74

Raceway Book: Phonics/Reading/Comprehension/Grammar

Letter Cluster Matching Fun, p. 75
Draw a line from the letter cluster to the picture.

Write and Draw, p. 76
Write the letter cluster that completes
each word. Draw a picture.

My Little Storybook #1:
Kim's Big Win, pp. 77-80
Make book, color, and read.

Fill in the Blank, p. 81
Write the letter cluster to complete the word.
Color the pictures.

Write and Draw, p. 82
Write the Letter Cluster that completes
each word. Draw a picture.

Matching, p. 83
Draw a line from the letter cluster to the picture.

Write and Draw, p. 84
Write the letter cluster that completes
each word. Draw each picture.

My Little Storybook #2:
Miss Duck's Big Picnic, pp. 85-88
Make book, color, and read.

Fill in the Blank, p. 89
Write the letter cluster to complete each word.
Color the pictures.

Write and Draw, p. 90
Write the letter cluster that completes each
word. Draw a picture.

Fill in the Blank, pp. 91-92
Write the letter cluster that completes each word.

My Little Storybook #3:
Miss Duck's Big Picnic: Part 2, pp. 93-96
Make book, color, and read.

Fill in the Blank, p. 97
Write the letter cluster that completes each
word. Color the pictures.

Letter Cluster Matching Fun, p. 98
Draw a line from the letter cluster to the picture.

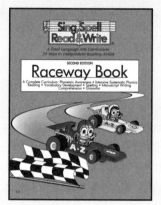

pp. 75-113

Letter Cluster Matching Fun, p. 99
Draw a line from the word to the picture.

Circle the Picture, p. 100
Trace the letters to finish each word.
Circle the picture that rhymes with the word.

My Little Storybook #4: *Jack's Jet, pp. 101-104*
Make book, color, and read.

Following Directions, p. 105
Draw a **box** around each picture with sound of **g**
as in **gem**. Draw a **circle** around each picture
with the sound of **g** as in **goat**.

Circle the Picture, p. 106
Trace the letters to finish each word. Name
the pictures next to each word. Circle the
picture that has the same letter cluster sound
as the letters you wrote.

Following Directions, p.107
Draw a **box** around each picture with the sound
of **c** as in **cent**. Draw a **circle** around each
picture with the sound of **c** as in **cat**.

Make Words, p. 108
Write the letter cluster that completes each word.

My Little Storybook #5: *Lost, pp. 109-112*
Make book, color, and read.

Make Words, p. 113
Write the letter cluster that completes each word.

Lesson Plans

WEEK	DAY	RACEWAY BOOK PAGES	LESSONS AND ACTIVITIES
1	1	*71-74*	• Sing *Letter Cluster Phonics Song,* Verses 1-4 (Concentrate on Verse 1)
			• Play *Letter Cluster Sound-O Game,* Side 1, blue (Instructor should point to letter cluster on charts in *Raceway Book* when calling out sounds.) Manual p.77
		75	• *Letter Cluster Matching Fun*
		76	• Write and Draw
		77-80	• *My Little Storybook #1: Kim's Big Win* (Make book and color)
	2		• Sing *Letter Cluster Phonics Song,* Verses 1-4 (Concentrate on Verse 1)
			• Play *Letter Cluster Sound-O Game,* Side 1, blue (Continue pointing to letter clusters on charts in *Raceway Book.*)
		81	• Fill in the Blank
		82	• Write and Draw
			• Read *My Little Storybook #1: Kim's Big Win*
	3		• Sing *Letter Cluster Phonics Song,* Verses 1-4 (Concentrate on Verse 2)
			• Play *Letter Cluster Sound-O Game,* Side 1, blue (Continue pointing to letter clusters on charts in *Raceway Book.*)
		83	• Matching
		84	• Write and Draw
		85-88	• *My Little Storybook #2: Miss Duck's Big Picnic* (Make book and color)
			• Grammar Chalkboard Lesson (Telling & Asking Sentences) Manual p. 77
	4		• Sing *Letter Cluster Phonics Song,* Verses 1-4 (Concentrate on Verse 2)
			• Play *Letter Cluster Sound-O Game,* Side 1, blue (Continue pointing to letter clusters on charts in *Raceway Book.*)
		89	• Fill in the Blank
		90	• Write and Draw
			• Read *My Little Storybook #2: Miss Duck's Big Picnic*
	5		• Sing *Letter Cluster Phonics Song,* Verses 1-4 (Concentrate on Verses 1 and 2)
			• Play *Letter Cluster Sound-O Game,* Side 1, blue (Point to letter clusters on charts)
		91	• Fill in the Blank
		92	• Fill in the Blank
		93-96	• *My Little Storybook #3: Miss Duck's Big Picnic Part 2* (Make book and color)
		97	• Fill in the Blank

Continue Spelling Tests *(vertical label, Week 1 column)*

Sing Spell Read & Write

Lesson Plans Continued

WEEK	DAY	RACEWAY BOOK PAGES	LESSONS AND ACTIVITIES
2	1	71-74	• Sing *Letter Cluster Phonics Song,* Verses 1-4 (Concentrate on Verses 3 and 4)
			• Play *Letter Cluster Sound-O Game,* Side 2, red (Point to letter clusters on charts)
		98	• Letter Cluster Matching Fun
		99	• Letter Cluster Matching Fun
			• Read *My Little Storybook #3: Miss Duck's Big Picnic Part 2*
			• Tear out Ducks for *Duck Pond* and fold on dotted lines to stand.
			• Grammar Chalkboard Lesson: Telling & Asking Sentences, Manual p. 77
Continue Spelling Tests	2		• Sing *Letter Cluster Phonics Song,* Verses 1-4 (Concentrate on Verses 3 and 4)
			• Play *Letter Cluster Sound-O Game,* Side 2, red
			• Play *Letter Cluster Pick-A-Sound Game,* Manual p. 78
			• *Visit the Duck Pond,* Manual p. 78
		100	• Circle the Picture
		100-104	• *My Little Storybook #4: Jack's Jet* (Make book and color)
	3		• Sing *Letter Cluster Phonics Song,* Verse 1-4 (Concentrate on Verses 3 and 4)
			• Play *Letter Cluster Sound-O Game,* Side 2, red
			• *Visit the Duck Pond*
		105	• Following Directions
		106	• Circle the Picture
			• Read *My Little Storybook #4: Jack's Jet*
	4		• Sing *Letter Cluster Phonics Song,* Verses 1-4 (Concentrate on Verses 3 and 4)
			• Play *Letter Cluster Sound-O Game,* Side 2, red
			• Play *Letter Cluster Pick-A-Sound Game*
			• *Visit the Duck Pond*
		107	• Following Directions
		108	• Make Words
		109-112	• *My Little Storybook #5: Lost* (Make book and color)
	5		• Sing *Letter Cluster Phonics Song,* Verses 1-4
			• Play *Letter Cluster Sound-O Game,* Side 2, red
			• Play *Letter Cluster Pick-A-Sound Game*
			• *Visit the Duck Pond*
		113	• Make Words
			• Read *My Little Storybook #5: Lost*

STEP 16

Grammar Chalkboard Lessons

Student will write sentences and use correct punctuation.

Telling and Asking Sentences
1. Will you come here ?
2. Dad has the rug .
3. Can the truck run fast ?
4. I will rest on the rug .

Telling and Asking Sentences
1. Do you like pops ?
2. We like pops .
3. Did we buy some snacks ?
4. Mom will buy snacks .

Letter Cluster Sound-O Game

TO BE PLAYED FROM STEPS 16-36

Goal
A Bingo-like game which will provide practice in recall of letter cluster sounds as learned in the *Letter Cluster Phonics Song*.

Preparation
- Cut apart *Caller Card* found in the package of 5 *Letter Cluster Sound-O Cards*.

- Place Caller Cards in the round plastic container labeled **Letter Cluster Sound-O**. The blue printed side is to be used with Side 1 of the Letter Cluster Sound-O Card to practice letter clusters taught in Verses 1-2 of the Letter Cluster Phonics Song. The red printed side is used with Side 2 to practice letter clusters learned in Verses 1-4.

Directions
1. Give your student a Letter Cluster Sound-O Card and game markers. Tell student to place the blue side of the card face-up and put a marker on Gus-the-Bug in the center of the card. This is a free space.

2. Instructor will draw a caller card from the container and use the blue printed side to read the exact script. The instructor will also go to the charts in the *Raceway Book* and point to the letter cluster(s) called. (When student no longer looks at charts, you know letter clusters have been mastered.)

3. Student may call "Sound-O" when he/she has a straight line vertically, horizontally, or diagonally covered with chips.

4. Follow these same directions for Side 2, red.

NOTE: Assure the player that every card has every sound called: "Keep looking. It's there somewhere."

Copyright © Sue Dickson, Sing Spell Read & Write® is a registered trademark of Pearson Education Inc.

Letter Cluster Pick-A-Sound Game

TO BE PLAYED FROM STEPS 16-36

Goal

To play a game which will give the student practice in letter cluster sounds as taught in the *Letter Cluster Phonics Song.*

This game is played with the blue deck of cards. Two to five players may take part. The object is to make pairs from cards in each player's hand. The game ends when any player is completely out of cards. The player with the most pairs is the winner.

Directions

1. Place the Merry-Go-Round in the center of the table. Shuffle the deck of cards and deal one card at a time until each player has five cards. Place the rest of the cards face down in a pile inside the Merry-Go-Round container.

2. All players should then sort their cards, placing any pairs they have face-up on the table in front of them.

3. The player to the left of the dealer should begin the game by calling any player by name and asking for a card. "Mary, do you have the card that says **or** for **orbit**?" The player making the request must hold that card in his/her hand.

4. If Mary has the "**or**" card, she must give it to that player who will put the pair down. That player will get another turn, calling on another player for a sound. However, if Mary does not have the **or** card, she must call: "Pick-a-Sound from the Merry-Go-Round."

5. The player must then pick the top card from the pile of cards inside the Merry-Go-Round, and add that card to those in his/her hand. If the player picks the card with the sound called for, he/she makes a pair and takes another turn. When the player can no longer make a pair, the person on the left then becomes the next player. When a player pairs all his/her cards the game is over. The player with the most paired cards is the winner.

6. Give prizes from the Treasure Chest to the winner.

Visit the Duck Pond

(located in back of Raceway Book)

Goal

To practice and test student's knowledge of all letter cluster sounds in a pleasant and enjoyable way.

Procedure

Have student
- cut out,
- fold to stand, and
- place ducks on the Duck Pond.

One by one, student should hold up a duck and say its letter cluster sound.

If the sound is correct, the student may remove the duck from the Duck Pond. Continue until all the ducks are out of the pond.

Ducks may be stored in a zip-lock bag.

Move Raceway Car to Step **17**

Pop the Balloons

Goals

To practice and test knowledge of all letter cluster sounds
To practice Grammar Skills

Suggested Pacing

1 day

Material

Raceway Book, p. 114

p. 114

PROCEDURE

Instructor:

- Ask your student to point to a letter cluster on any balloon on p. 114 and say its sound.
- If the correct sound is given, clap to indicate the balloon has been popped.
- Have your student practice this way until all balloons on the chart have been popped.
- Teach the sound of **wh** as **"hw"** and point out that many "question" words begin this way – **wh**ich, **wh**at, **wh**ere, **wh**y, **wh**en, etc.
- Balloons with the numeral 2 or 3 written on them have two or three sounds which must be called in order to "pop" them.
- When student can "pop" all the balloons without any help, or without referring to charts on pp. 71-74, initial and date the appropriate box at the bottom of p. 114.
- Teach **Grammar Chalkboard Lessons** shown below.

Phonics Song(s)/Games

Each day's lesson should begin with one or two previously learned phonics songs and end with a phonics game.

Written Spelling Tests

Dictate 10 words per day for a written spelling test. See p. 51 in this Manual for directions.

Grammar Chalkboard Lessons

A-B-C ORDER REVIEW

Student will place words in A-B-C order by numbering 1, 2.

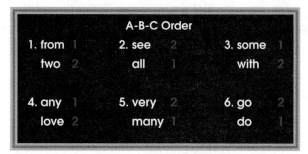

A-B-C Order

1. from	1	2. see	2	3. some	1
two	2	all	1	with	2
4. any	1	5. very	2	6. go	2
love	2	many	1	do	1

SUBJECT REVIEW

Have your student write the sentences and underline the subject.

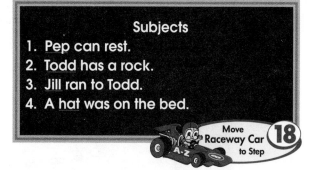

Subjects

1. <u>Pep</u> can rest.
2. <u>Todd</u> has a rock.
3. <u>Jill</u> ran to Todd.
4. A <u>hat</u> was on the bed.

Move Raceway Car to Step **18**

Sing Spell Read & Write

Long Vowel Song and ABC Echoes (all sounds)

Goals

To learn the **long vowel sounds**

To review the sounds of the letters A to Z (**All ABC Echoes**)

To practice Grammar Skills

Suggested Pacing

1 day

Materials

1. *Raceway Book*, p. 115

2. **Long Vowel Song**, CD or Cassette #4

3. **ABC Echoes (all sounds)**, CD or Cassette #4

p. 115

PROCEDURE

Long Vowel Song

- Review the short vowel sounds and "scoop" symbol (˘), then tell the student that he/she is going to learn something new about the vowels: **sometimes the vowels say their names.** (The name of the letter.)

Instructor:	"Ā says ā as in **a**pron. Do you hear the ā? **A**pron!" Point to the picture of the apron on p. 115.
Instructor:	"Ē says ē as in what?"
Student:	"**E**agle"
Instructor:	"Ī says ī as in what?"
Student:	"**I**ce cream"
Instructor:	"Ō says ō as in what?"
Student:	"**O**atmeal"
Instructor:	"Ū says ū as in what?"
Student:	"**U**nited States"
Instructor:	"Right! We call these **long vowel sounds** and the mark for the long vowel sounds is a straight line over the letter."

ā for apron

ē for eagle

ī for ice cream

ō for oatmeal

ū for United States ...

- Write the letters, demonstrating: **ā, ē, ī, ō,** and **ū** with straight lines over each.

- Now tell the student there is a song about **Long Vowels** for Step 18. Turn on CD or Cassette #4 for the **Long Vowel Marching Song** (with children singing). Point to the pictures and echo as the leader sings:

LEADER:	STUDENT ECHOES:
ā for apron!	ā for apron!
ē for eagle!	ē for eagle!
ī for ice cream!	ī for ice cream!
ō for oatmeal!	ō for oatmeal!
ū for United States!	ū for United States!
So we do echo!	So we do echo!
	As we march along
	And we sing a song
	Learning our long vowels!

- Have student point to the letters and pictures for the **Long Vowel Song** in **Raceway Book,** p. 115 (top of page) and sing.

ABC Echoes: All Sounds

- Now listen to the **ABC Echoes,** CD or Cassette #4.

	LEADER:	STUDENT:
Pointing to **Aa**:	"ă"	"ă"
	"ā"	"ā"
	"ä"	"ä"
Pointing to **Bb**:	"bh"	"bh"
Pointing to **Cc**:	"c (k)"	"c (k)"
	"c (s)"	"c (s)"
Pointing to **Dd**:	"dh"	"dh"

(Continue in same manner for rest of alphabet.)

ā āpron

fäther ä

ă ăpple

- Next, have student point to each letter in the **ABC Echoes,** p.115 (bottom of page) and give **all sounds** for each letter.

- Practice daily until the student can say all the sounds from A to Z with speed (and rhythm).

- When student can sing the **Long Vowel Song** and say the **ABC Echoes,** (all sounds) initial and date boxes at bottom of p. 115 to indicate successful completion of Step 18.

Now, rejoice! You have taught all the sounds needed in order to read English! Continue daily with singing the songs, playing Letter Cluster Sound-O and Letter Cluster Pick-A-Sound, visiting the Duck Pond, leading the ABC Echoes, and popping the balloons to provide practice until your student can say the individual letter sounds and letter cluster sounds automatically.

Grammar Lesson

RHYMING WORDS

Write each of the following words on an index card: **nest, pest, vest, clock, sock, block, camp, stamp, went, dent, stick, brick, Jill, will**. Ask your student to find the card with the word that answers each riddle.

1. These words rhyme with west. nest, pest, vest
2. These words rhyme with lock. clock, sock, block
3. These words rhyme with lamp. camp, stamp
4. These words rhyme with bent. went, dent
5. These words rhyme with sick. stick, brick
6. These words rhyme with fill. Jill, will

sock

Grammar Chalkboard Lesson

A-B-C ORDER REVIEW

Student will arrange words in alphabetical order by numbering 1, 2, 3.

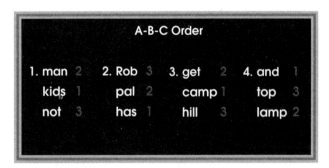

A-B-C Order

1. man	2	2. Rob	3	3. get	2	4. and	1
kids	1	pal	2	camp	1	top	3
not	3	has	1	hill	3	lamp	2

Move Raceway Car to Step **19**

Vocabulary and Reading

Most Frequently Used Words

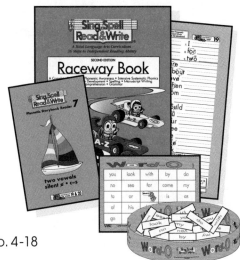

Goals

To read, write, and spell **most frequently used words**
To read most **frequently used words** in context
To practice Grammar Skills

Suggested Pacing

2 days

Materials

1. *Raceway Book*, pp. 116-118
2. Phonetic Storybook Reader 7, *The Sailboat Book*, pp. 4-18
3. **Word-O Game** – Directions/Manual p. 84

PROCEDURE

Instructor:

- Have student open **Raceway Book** to p. 116.
- Tell student this Step has some of the **most frequently used words** in the English language. Some of these words are "Rulebreakers" (they have letters which steal another letter's sound). These may require more time and effort to learn. Use the "Onesy, Twosy, Threesy" technique described on p. 32.
- Have student read, write, and spell all words on p.116.
- Initial and date boxes at the bottom of the page.

Have student:

- Read pp. 4-18 in **Storybook Reader 7**.
- Read each story two or three times for fluency.
- Complete **Raceway Book** pp. 117-118.

Instructor: Introduce **Word-O Game**/Manual p. 84.

Phonics Song(s)/Games

Each day's lesson should begin with one or two previously learned phonics songs and end with a phonics game.

Written Spelling Test

Dictate 10 words per day for a written spelling test. See p. 51 in this Manual for directions.

Phonetic Storybook Reader 7

Comprehension Questions

Snacks for the Cubs • Story 1 • pp. 4-18

Have student read orally the designated pages.
Ask the following questions:

"Come here, Tom," said Mom. "Come here, Jim ! Come here, Linda. Would you come to me ?"

After reading pp. 5-7:
- What is Mom? *(Context Clue)* A bear
- Why are they going to the Snack Hut? *Story Detail)* To buy snacks

After reading pp. 8-11:
- What other snacks do the children want to buy? *(Story Detail)* Nuts, pops, bananas, etc.

After reading pp. 12-15:
- How long did Mom say it would take to get to the Snack Hut? *(Story Detail)* Three seconds

- Why would we say Mama Bear is nice? *(Inference/Drawing Conclusion)* Because she's taking them to the store and buying them snacks.

After reading pp. 16-18:
- How are the cubs feeling at this time? *(predicting)* Happy

*Complete pp. 117-118 in Raceway Book.
See directions below.*

Raceway Book: Comprehension

Fill In The Blank, *pp. 117-118*

Fill in the blanks with the correct word.

pp. 117-118

Word-O Game

TO BE PLAYED FROM STEPS 19-36

Objective
A Bingo-like game which will give the student practice in reading the most frequently used words.

Preparation
- Cut apart Teacher Caller Card found in the package of 5 Word-O Cards.
- Place Callers in the round plastic container labeled **Word-O**.

Directions
1. Distribute the Word-O Cards and see-through game markers.
2. Student will place the blue side of the card face up.
3. Student will put a marker on Gus-the-Bug in the center of the card. This is a free space.
4. Draw a caller from the container and call that word. Use the word in a sentence.
   Example: "has" - "She **has** a book."
5. Student may call "Word-O" when he/she has a straight line vertically, horizontally, or diagonally.
6. Follow these same directions for Side 2, red.

Move Raceway Car to Step **20**

Two Vowel Song

Goals

To learn the **Two Vowels Get Together Song**

To read, write, and spell **two vowel** words

To read **two vowel** words in context

To practice Grammar Skills

Suggested Pacing

3 days

Materials

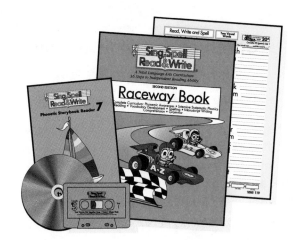

1. *Raceway Book,* pp. 119-122

2. Phonetic Storybook Reader 7, *The Sailboat Book,* pp. 19-39

3. **Two Vowels Get Together Song**, CD or Cassette #5

PROCEDURE

Instructor:

- Tell your student that he/she knows two sounds for each vowel. Now the question is: Which of those two sounds do you use when you are trying to figure out new words? The long vowel sound? Or, the short vowel sound? Here is the answer:

- If the word is a short one with just one vowel in the middle, use the short vowel sound (săt, bĕg, pĭn, hŏp, cŭp).

- If the word has 2 vowels together, as in bo**a**t, the first vowel says its name (ō) and the second vowel (ȧ) is completely quiet (silent).

- Tell the student to go down the list of words on p.119 in **Raceway Book** and cross out the second vowel (boȧt). This will help your student read these words.

- Next, play **Two Vowels Get Together Song**, CD or Cassette #5 and sing down the list of words with student. You may want to sing the remainder of the two vowel words with the music only portion of the CD or cassette.

- Have student read, write and spell all words on pp. 119-121.

- Initial and date boxes at bottom of pages.

Have student:

- Read pp. 19-39 in **Storybook Reader 7**.

- Read each story two or three times for fluency.

- Complete **Raceway Book** pp. 121-122.

Instructor: Teach **Grammar Chalkboard Lesson**/Manual p. 87.

Phonics Song(s)/Games

Each day's lesson should begin with one or two previously learned phonics songs and end with a phonics game. A new song is introduced in this Step.

Written Spelling Tests

Instructor will dictate 10 words per day for a written spelling test. See p. 51 in this Manual for directions.

Phonetic Storybook Reader 7

Comprehension Questions
A Picnic on the Beach
Story 2 • Part 1 • pp. 19-29

Have student read orally the designated pages.
Ask the following questions:

After reading pp. 20-21:

* What kind of insect is in this story?
  (Opinion/Relating Personal Experience)
  An ant

* How many are in this family? Four

* Why can they not go into deep water?
  (Context Clue) The ants cannot swim.

After reading pp. 22-23:

* What did Dad do to protect their health?
  (Inference/Drawing Conclusion) He set up an
  umbrella to protect them from the hot sun.

* Do you think Jack and Sis play well together?
  (Inference/Drawing Conclusion) Yes.

* Read the part that makes you think this.
  "Come sail the boat with me.
  We will have fun."

After reading pp. 24-25:

* What are two toys Sis and Jack have?
  (Story Detail) A sailboat and a pail

* How does it feel to dig in the sand?
  (Personal Experience) Nice and fun

After reading pp. 26-27:

* What did the children do before they ate
  their meal? *(Sequence)* They sat on the mat.

* Why would we say they had a healthy
  meal for their picnic? *(Drawing Conclusion)*
  They had meat and vegetables.

After reading pp. 28-29:

* What will the children sit on to eat their
  meal? *(Story Detail)* The mat

* Would you say these little ants were good
  citizens? *(Cause and Effect)* Yes. They helped
  clean up the beach and they left it nice for
  other people to enjoy.

* Could this story be true? *(Fantasy and
  Realism)* No, because ants cannot act
  like people.

After reading p. 30:

* Where will the family go? *(Context Clue)*
  Up the beach

* What can they do when they go up the
  beach? Name three things. *(Story Detail)*
  1) Feed the gulls
  2) See the swim team
  3) Cheer for the swim team that wins

Comprehension Questions
A Picnic on the Beach
Story 2 • Part 2 • pp. 30-39

Have student read orally the designated pages.
Ask the following questions:

After reading p. 31:

* What is leap frog? *(Picture Clue/ Personal
  Experience)* Leap frog Is a game where you
  leap over someone's back.

* Who will do a *leap frog*? *(Story Detail)*
  Sis and Jack

(Continued on next page)

After reading pp. 32-33:

- Where did the sea weed on the beach come from? *(Personal Experience)* It washed in from the sea.
- Who has walked in hot sand on the beach? Tell us what you did. *(Personal Experience)* Answers will vary.
- Why will Mom not teach them to swim until three o'clock? *(Drawing Conclusion)* They just ate.

After reading pp. 34-35:

- What happened at three o'clock? *(Story Detail)* Mom taught Sis to swim.
- What did Mom tell Sis to do to learn to swim? *(Story Detail)* Kick her feet

After reading pp. 36-37:

- What did Jack learn to do? *(Story Detail)* Float
- Name two things Dad told Jack to do to float. *(Story Detail)* Feet must be up and ears must be in the water

After reading pp. 38-39:

- How did the family cooperate when they left the beach? *(Context Clue)* They helped each other pack.
- Do you believe this family will go to the beach again this summer? Why? *(Predicting)* Yes, because they had fun.

Complete pp. 121 (bottom half) and 122 in Raceway Book. See directions below.

Raceway Book: Grammar/Comprehension

Compound Words, *p. 121 (bottom half)*

Tell the student sometimes two words are put together to make another word. These are called compound words. Have student draw lines to join two words together to make one compound word.

Fill in the Blank, *p. 122*

Fill in the blanks with correct answers.

pp. 121-122

Grammar Chalkboard Lesson

SUBJECT REVIEW

Write the sentences below and have student underline the subject in each.

Subjects
1. Will <u>Jill</u> eat meat?
2. The <u>team</u> will cheer.
3. <u>Pam</u> fed the goats and sheep.
4. <u>I</u> can hike a mile.
5. <u>Mom</u> will slice the meat.

Silent e Song

Goals

To learn the **Silent e Song**

To read, write, and spell **silent e** words

To read **silent e** words in stories

To practice Grammar Skills

To take Book End Assessment

Suggested Pacing

6 days

Materials

1. *Raceway Book*, pp. 123-125
2. Phonetic Storybook Reader 7, *The Sailboat Book*, pp. 40-80
3. Assessment Book: Assessment for Phonetic Storybook Reader 7
4. **Silent e Song**, CD or Cassette #5

PROCEDURE

Instructor:

- For **silent e** words (pp. 123-124), explain that an **e** on the end of a word makes the first vowel in the word "say the letter name" (or long vowel sound). Now, go down the list of **silent e** words with your student and put a long vowel mark over the first vowel and then mark through the **silent e**. Example: (bīt¢).
- Listen to **Silent e Song**, Cassette #5. Follow same procedure used for *Two Vowels Get Together Song* (see Step 20A for directions).
- Practice song daily with your student.
- Have student read, write and spell all **silent e** words in **Raceway Book** pp. 123-124.
- Initial and date boxes at the bottom of pages.

Have student:

- Read pp. 40-80 in **Storybook Reader 7**.
- Read each story two or three times for fluency.
- Complete **Raceway Book** pp. 124-125.

Instructor:

- Teach **Grammar Chalkboard Lesson**/Manual p. 92.
- Administer **Assessment**/Manual p. 93.

Phonics Song(s)/Games

Each day's lesson should begin with one or two previously learned phonics songs and end with a phonics game. A new song is introduced in this Step.

Written Spelling Tests

Instructor will dictate 10 words per day for a written spelling test. See p. 51 in this Manual for directions.

"Would you like to take a bike hike?" said Jake.

"Yes, I would," said Mike. "I will go ask my mom and dad if I may go."

41

Phonetic Storybook Reader 7

Comprehension Questions

The Bike Hike and Dan's Cake
Story 3 • Part 1 • pp. 40-46

Have student read orally the designated pages.
Ask the following questions:

After reading pp. 42-43:

- What is the special event at Mike's house tonight? *(Drawing Conclusion)*
Dan's birthday party

- How do you know how old Dan is? *(Story Detail)* His father said he will be three.

- Who is the oldest, Mike or Dan? How do you know? *(Context Clue)* Mike. He is allowed to go on a bike hike with Jake.

- What time must Mike be home? *(Story Detail)* 6 o'clock

- Why would he have a cake and candles? *(Cause and Effect)* That's how we celebrate birthdays.

- What is Mike thinking about as he leaves for his bike hike? *(Picture Clue)* The party

After reading pp. 44-46:

- Where will Mom get Dan's cake? *(Story Detail)* She will bake it.

- Why do you think that? *(Personal Experience)* He went with Mom into the kitchen to watch.

- What is page 45 mostly about? *(Main Idea)* Mom making a cake

- Why would Dad want the yard work finished by six o'clock? *(Inference/Drawing Conclusion)* So it would be clean for the party.

Comprehension Questions

The Bike Hike and Dan's Cake
Story 3 • Part 2 • pp. 47-53

Have student read orally the designated pages.
Ask the following questions:

After reading p. 47:

- What season of the year is it? *(Drawing Conclusion)* Summer

- What are some things they may see while they are resting? *(Predicting)* Maybe fish, ducks, turtles, and other water creatures

After reading pp. 48-50:

- Look in your book and name in order all the things Jack and Mike saw. *(Sequence)* Duck, bee, snail, goat, robin, and frog

- Which of these animals travel by air? By water? By land? *(Classification)* Air - robin and ducks; water - duck, fish and frog; land - all but the fish.

Part 2
The Bike Hike and Dan's Cake

Jake and Mike had a fine bike hike. They had a rest in the shade. They sat by the pond to rest. Mike stuck his feet in the pond.

47

- What does Mike think will be a good gift for Dan? *(Story Detail)* The green frog

After reading pp. 51-53:

- How did they catch the frog? *(Story Detail)* They chased him to the boat.

- What is another word you could use instead of "yippee"? *(Context Clue/Vocabulary Expansion)* Hurray!

- How did they get the frog to Mike's house? *(Picture Clue)* Mike carried it in his pocket.

- Why do you think he named his frog "Leap"? *(Drawing Conclusion)* He was good at leaping.

- What do you think will happen to Leap next? *(Predicting)* Answers will vary.

Comprehension Questions

Fun on the Trail

Story 4 • pp. 54-65

Have student read orally the designated pages. Ask the following questions:

After reading p. 55:

- Who are the three rabbits in this story? *(Story Detail)* Dave, Pat, and Meg

- Tell me something about Pat. *(Story Detail)* Pat has a big pink nose.

- Tell me about Dave. *(Story Detail)* Dave has a black spot on his left ear.

- Describe Meg. *(Story Detail)* Meg has a tail like a big puff of fuzz.

- Have you ever owned a rabbit? *(Personal Experience)* Answers will vary.

After reading pp. 56-57:

- Look at the picture on page 56. What are Pat, Dave, and Meg doing? *(Context Clue)* Discussing their plans for a hike.

- They are going lots of miles. How long do you think it will take them? *(Predicting)* Probably all day.

- What will they take to help guide them? *(Context Clue)* A trail map.

- What else do you think they will put in their back-pack? *(Predicting)* Some snacks.

After reading pp. 58-59:

- Where does the trail begin? *(Story Detail)* On East Hill Road

- What time must they get back home? *(Story Detail)* 5 o'clock

After reading pp. 60-61:

- What season of the year is it? *(Context Clue)* Summer

- What helped them deal with the hot weather? *(Inference/Drawing Conclusion)* The shade of the trees

- What was the gift Dave was going to take home to Mom? *(Story Detail)* Pine cones

- What does this tell us about Mom and her children? *(Inference/Drawing Conclusion)* They care for each other.

- Could this story be true? Why not? *(Fantasy-Realism)* Rabbits don't bake cakes or drive cars.

After reading pp. 62-63:

- What happened just as they finished Mom's treat? *(Story Detail)* Pat got a bug bite.

- Who came to his rescue? *(Story Detail)* Dave

After reading pp. 64-65:

- How do we know they plan to go again? *(Context Clue)* They said they plan to take Dad the next time.

- Read aloud the part that lets you know Pat, Dave, and Meg enjoy spending time with their Dad. *(Inference/Drawing Conclusion)* "The next time we go on a hike, we will take you, Dad," said Dave.

- How is this story like "A Picnic On The Beach"? *(Comparison)* Both are about animals going on a hike.

- Tell me about this story in a few sentences. *(Summarizing)* Answers will vary.

- What was the setting of this story? *(Analyzing)* Woods or a forest

- Who were the three main characters in this story? *(Main Character)* Pat, Dave, and Meg

- What was Pat's problem? *(Analyzing)* He got a bug bite.

- How was it solved? *(Analyzing)* Dave put a Band-Aid on his nose.

Comprehension Questions

A Visit From Uncle Bruce

Story 5 • pp. 66-80

Have student read orally the designated pages. Ask the following questions:

After reading p. 67:

- What does the word "ice" mean on this page? *(Context Clue)* To add frosting

After reading pp. 68-69:

- Why do you think Uncle Bruce is coming to eat? *(Predicting)*
  He wants to visit his relatives.

- What did Grace mean when she said, "Let me help you get set for Uncle Bruce?" *(Context Clue)* She wants to help Mom with the preparation.

- Read aloud the part that makes us know Mom liked having Grace's help. *(Context Clue)*
  "Mom's face went into a big smile."

After reading pp. 70-73:

- Who do you think Alice is? *(Predicting)* Grace's sister

- What did Grace want to do to make cleaning fun? *(Story Detail)*
  Have a race to dust and wax

- Name the four ways Grace helped in sequence. *(Sequence)*
  1. Diced potatoes
  2. Cleaned the rug
  3. Dusted and waxed
  4. Put the lace tablecloth on the table

After reading pp. 74-75:

- Why did Joe's mother tell him to take the nest back to the tree? *(Personal Experience)*
  So the bird could come back.

- What do you think Mom is thinking about as Joe goes out the door with the nest?
  (Picture Clue/Context Clue)
  What will Joe come home with next?

- Do you think the bird will come back to this nest? *(Predicting)* Probably not

After reading pp. 76-77:

- What errand did Joe do for Mom? *(Story Detail)*
  He went to buy ice cream.

- Do you think Joe likes ice cream and spice cake? Why do you say that?
  (Context Clue) Yes, because he said "Mmm."

After reading pp. 78-80:

- What did Joe mean when he said he had lots of space for ice cream and spice cake?
  (Interpretation) He's hungry.

- Could this story be true?
  (Realism - Fantasy) Yes

- What is the setting for this story?
  (Analyzing) Home

- What kind of person do you think Joe is? (Lead a discussion that will get the student to describe Joe's personality as he/she perceives it: traits such as kind, helpful, mischievous, cooperative, carefree) Answers will vary.

Complete pp. 124 (bottom half) and 125 in Raceway Book.
See directions on next page.

Raceway Book: Grammar/Comprehension

Compound Words, p. 124 (bottom half)
Join two words together to make a compound word and draw pictures for the four compound words shown.

Fill in the Blank, p. 125
Fill in each blank with the correct word.

pp. 124-125

Grammar Chalkboard Lesson

TELLING AND ASKING SENTENCES REVIEW

Have student place a period or question mark at the end of each sentence.

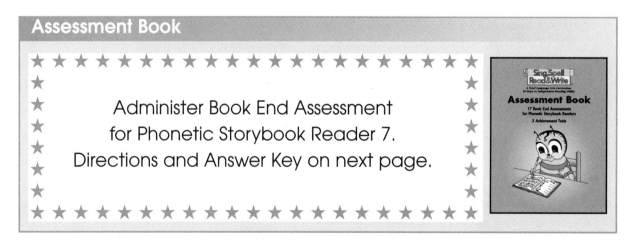

Telling and Asking Sentences
1. Did he sit down ?
2. Mike had a bike hike .
3. Can we feed the gulls ?
4. That was fun .
5. Do we swim here ?

Assessment Book

★ ★

Administer Book End Assessment
for Phonetic Storybook Reader 7.
Directions and Answer Key on next page.

Move Raceway Car to Step **21**

Raceway Step 20

Book End Assessment
Phonetic Storybook Reader 7

Word Recognition: Two Vowels, Silent ∅, c=s Words

Instructor: Direct student to "Put your finger on box #1. Now circle the word in the box that I call... 'beak.' Put your finger on box #2. Now circle the word 'clear,' etc." The words the teacher should call are listed below. Say each word distinctly with emphasis upon initial and final consonants.

1. beak	2. clear	3. leap	4. team	5. stream
6. seal	7. beam	8. feed	9. sheep	10. seen
11. sweet	12. tried	13. queen	14. wheat	15. peak
16. cheer	17. sail	18. maid	19. paint	20. faith

Record scores in the space provided on the front cover of the Student Assessment Record and calculate the Percentage of Mastery Score as indicated.

Word Recognition and Word Comprehension

Name _____

1 beach	2 cream	3 leaf	4 team	5 spear
beak	clear	leap	tear	speak
beast	gear	lean	tea	stream
6 seat	7 beam	feel	8 sheet	9 seed
seal	bead	feed	street	seek
seam	beak	feet	sheep	seen
11 sweep	12 tried	13 screen	14 weep	pie
sweet	tree	green	wheel	peep
sheet	three	queen	wheat	peak
16 cheer	17 snail	18 nail	19 gain	20 faith
creep	nail	mail	paint	fail
coat	sail	maid	pain	hail

Word Recognition _____ Number Correct   Word Comprehension _____ Number Correct

p. 1

Word Comprehension: Two Vowels, Silent ∅, c=s Words

Directions: Tell your student to put his/her finger on box #1 again and listen to what you say:

Instructor: *Underline the word that (is)...*

1. a place to go swimming. beach
2. something your parents might put in their coffee. cream
3. something that is found on a tree. leaf
4. something to drink. tea
5. means to use your voice. speak
6. a place to sit. seat
7. something found in a necklace. bead
8. a part of the body. feet
9. a place where cars travel. street
10. something you put in the ground to grow a plant seed
11. what you do with a broom. sweep
12. a number. three
13. a color. green
14. something found on a car. wheel
15. something that is sweet to eat. pie
16. something to wear. coat
17. something you hit with a hammer. nail
18. something the postman delivers. mail
19. what you feel when you hurt. pain
20. what happens when you do not pass your work. fail

Record scores in the space provided on the front cover of the Student Assessment Record and calculate the Percentage of Mastery Score as indicated.

Raceway Steps 19-20

Sentence Comprehension

"Bubble" Format Directions pp. 69-70

1. B	6. A	11. A	16. C	21. B
2. D	7. D	12. C	17. A	22. A
3. A	8. C	13. B	18. B	23. D
4. C	9. B	14. A	19. D	24. E
5. B	10. D	15. D	20. C	25. C

Story Comprehension

"Bubble" Format Directions pp. 69-70

1. to buy snacks
2. Mom, Jim, Tom and Linda
3. No
4. glad
5. a trip to the Snack Hut
6. nest
7. now
8. So the bird can come back.
9. Yes
10. What can I do?

Vocabulary and Reading

āy̆, y= ī, ge, gi, and gy Words and Related Stories in Storybook Reader 8

Goals
To read, write, and spell **ay̆, y= i, ge, gi, and gy** words
To read numbers and colors,
āy̆, y= ī, and g=j words in context
To practice Grammar Skills

Suggested Pacing
3 days

Materials
1. *Raceway Book*, pp. 126-127

2. Phonetic Storybook Reader 8,
   The Numbers and Colors Book, pp. 3-37

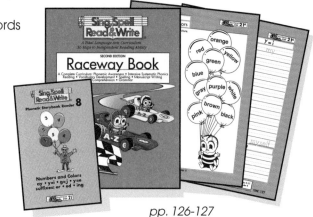

pp. 126-127

PROCEDURE

Instructor:
- Have student open **Raceway Book** to p. 126, and read number and color words. Color the picture.
- In **Raceway Book** p. 127, tell student **y** on the end of a word is a vowel. When two vowels walk together, the first one says its name: dāy, lāy, sāy, y=ī: my, by, try, and gy, gi, ge = soft **g** as in **giant**.
- Have student read, write, and spell all words on p. 127.
- Initial and date boxes at bottom of p. 127.

Have student:
- Read pp. 3-37 in **Storybook Reader 8**.
- Read each story two or three times for fluency.

Instructor:
- Teach **Grammar Chalkboard Lesson**/Manual p. 97.
- Introduce **Sentence Writing with Spelling Words**/Manual p. 97.

Phonics Song(s)/Games

Each day's lesson should begin with one or two previously learned phonics songs and end with a phonics game.

Written Spelling Tests

Dictate 10 words per day for a written spelling test. See p. 51 for directions.

Sing Spell Read & Write

Phonetic Storybook Reader 8

Comprehension Questions

*Red? Green? Blue? Five? Four? Two?
The Winner is Who?*

Story 1 • pp. 3-7

"See the video game," said Tom. "It is a boat race with one, two, three, four, five, six, seven, eight, nine, ten boats!"

4

Have student read orally the designated pages.
Ask the following questions:

After reading pp. 4-7:

- How are these sailboats alike?
  (Classification) All have flags and sails.
- What color was the seventh boat?
  (Story Detail) Brown

- Which boat wins the race?
  (Story Detail) The red boat
- If you were in the winning boat, describe how you would feel. *(Predicting)*
  Thrilled, happy, excited

Comprehension Questions

Ray and the Blue Jay

Story 2 • pp. 8-23

On a nice hot day in May,
Ray went to swim in the bay.

9

Have student read orally the designated pages.
Ask the following questions:

After reading pp. 9-11:

- Who do you think will be the main character in this story? *(Main Character)* Ray
- Where did Ray go to swim? *(Story Detail)*
  The bay
- Which three words on p. 9 rhyme?
  Day; may; bay
- Look on top of the haystack. What other character may be part of this story?
  (Predicting Outcome) A bird

After reading pp. 12-13:

- This story is written to rhyme. Discuss how this is accomplished on each page. The last word on every other line rhymes.
- What kind of bird is this? *(Story Detail)* Blue jay
- What does the blue jay want Ray to do? Why?
  (Story Detail/Predicting) Stay away; she's protecting her eggs.

After reading pp. 14-15:

- Was your prediction right? Why did the blue jay act as he did toward Ray?
  (Drawing Conclusion/Inference)
  Yes; she protected her nest.

After reading pp. 16-17:

- What does Ray promise? *(Story Detail)*
  He'll stay away.
- What is he going to buy? *(Story Detail)*
  A box of clay

After reading pp. 18-21:

- What does he want to do with the clay?
  (Story Detail) Make a model blue jay
- Look back in your book and name the things in sequence that Kay will not be able to do.
  (Sequence) Kay will not say "jay jay"; chase the kids away; lay eggs; speak; or play.
- Has Ray really made this bird of clay or is he thinking about it? How do you know?
  (Picture Clue) He's just thinking about it. There is a bubble around him.

After reading pp. 22-23:

- How are birds alike? How are they different?
  (Classification) Birds have feathers, wings, and fly, but they have different colors, habitats, and behaviors.

Comprehension Questions

The Shy Giant

Story 3 • pp. 24-37

Have student read orally the designated pages.
Ask the following questions:

After reading pp. 25-26:

- When a story begins with "Once upon a time," do you expect it to be true? *(Fantasy/Realism)* No
- Do you think this giant is a young boy or a man? *(Picture Clue)* A young boy
- Why do you think he is so sad? *(Predicting Outcome)* Answers will vary.

After reading pp. 27-30:

- Who wants to help the giant? *(Story Detail)* A little fly
- Why would the fly want to help? *(Cause and Effect)* To be nice
- Why didn't the giant think the fly could help him? *(Story Detail)* Because he's too small.
- Do you agree with the giant? Explain why. *(Analyze)* Yes; answers will vary.
- What did the giant compare his tears to? *(Compare and Contrast)* Rain from the sky
- Why is the giant so sad? *(Story Detail)* He's so shy.
- What does it mean to be *shy*? *(Context Clue)* Shy means to be afraid to speak up and participate.

After reading pp. 30-33:

- The fly had a plan. What was it? *(Story Detail)* To pry up the "sh" from shy and set in "tr".

- Explain what the fly meant when he said, be an "I CAN TRY" giant. *(Drawing Conclusion/Inference)* Answers will vary.
- Tell me exactly what the fly said to do to make the change. *(Summarize)* Pry up the "sh" and set in "tr".

After reading pp. 34-35:

- What did the giant compare it to when he tried it? *(Story Detail)* He said it's like a game.
- How does the giant feel now? *(Drawing Conclusion/Inference)* Very good about himself
- What does "bulge with pride" mean? *(Context Clue)* Filled with happiness

After reading pp. 36-37:

- What did the fly really do to help the giant? *(Drawing Conclusion/Inference)* Made him proud of himself
- Would you ever think a little fly could help a huge giant? *(Fantasy-Realism)* No
- Even though you are little, could you ever do something for a big person? What? *(Personal Experience)* Yes; Answers will vary.
- What problem did the giant have? *(Analyze)* He was shy.
- How was it solved? *(Analyze)* A little fly helped him become an "I can try" giant.

Grammar Chalkboard Lesson

CLASSIFICATION REVIEW

Have student place the words from the word bank under the proper heading.

Person	Classification	Thing
1. Mom		1. boat
2. Dad		2. rug
3. man		3. flag
4. Bill		4. hand
5. Sis		5. peach

Word Bank: boat, Mom, Dad, rug, man, flag, Bill, hand, peach, Sis

Independent Sentence Writing for Homework

To prepare your student for writing sentences independently for "homework" using spelling words, model this skill for a week:

Have student:

- Dictate (as you write) 5 short, simple sentences using spelling words.
- Underline each spelling word used in the sentences.
- Read the sentences.
- Copy the sentences.
- Circle the number of a sentence and illustrate it.

Example:

Writing
1. Patty will eat <u>peach</u> pie.
2. The cat has <u>fleas</u>.
3. The frog is <u>green</u>.
4. I had a <u>dream</u>.
5. We went to the <u>beach</u>.

Note:

- Beginning with Step 22, following the spelling test each day, have your student circle the next 10 words in the Raceway Book and identify these as the new spelling words. These 10 spelling words will be for today's homework (writing sentences), and tomorrow's spelling test.

Vocabulary and Reading

y=ē Words and Related Stories in Storybook Reader 8

p. 128

Goal

To read, write, and spell **y=ē** words

To read **y=ē** words in context

Suggested Pacing

2 days

Materials

1. Raceway Book, p. 128 (top half)
2. Phonetic Storybook Reader 8,
   The Numbers and Colors Book, pp. 38-46

PROCEDURE

Instructor:

* Use **Raceway Book** p. 128 (top half). Tell student that **y** says ē as in **baby**, **Bobby**, **Billy**, etc.
* Have student clap hands when saying the words to hear the two syllables.
* Have student read, write, and spell all words on top half of **Raceway Book** p. 128.
* Initial and date boxes in middle of page.

Have student:

* Read pp. 38-46 in **Storybook Reader 8.**
* Read each story two or three times for fluency.

Phonics Song(s)/Games

Each day's lesson should begin with one or two previously learned phonics songs and end with a phonics game.

Written Spelling Tests

Instructor will dictate 10 words per day for a written spelling test. See Manual p. 51 for directions.

Phonetic Storybook Reader 8

Comprehension Questions

Lucy and the Jellybeans
Story 4 • pp. 38-46

Have student read orally the designated pages. Ask the following questions:

Lucy is nine. She likes to baby-sit. She likes to baby-sit Sally. Sally is pretty and she is happy.
39

After reading p. 39:
* Where do you think Lucy and Sally live? (Predicting) **Answers will vary.**
* Who is the oldest? (Context Clue) **Lucy**

After reading pp. 40-41:
* What does Lucy give Sally? (Story Detail) **Jellybeans**
* Where is Freddy? (Story Detail) **Out to fly his kite**

* What kind of weather do you need to fly a kite? (Personal Experience) **Windy**

After reading pp. 42-43:
* Why did Billy and Gary wait for Freddy? (Inference/Drawing Conclusion) **They knew he would come back because it wasn't windy enough to fly a kite.**

(Continued on next page)

  Copyright © Sue Dickson, Sing Spell Read & Write® is a registered trademark of Pearson Education Inc.

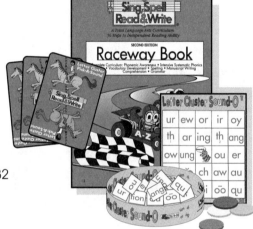

- Why was Freddy upset? *(Drawing Conclusion)* He didn't get to fly his kite.

After reading pp. 44-45:

- Does Freddy understand why his kite won't fly? Read the part that makes you think this. *(Inference/Drawing Conclusion)* Probably not; "It is not funny. My kite will not go up."

- Why would Lucy offer Freddy some jellybeans? *(Cause and Effect)* To distract him from his problem

- What color jellybeans does Freddy like? *(Story Detail)* Red

- Do you think Freddy took five jellybeans? Why? *(Predicting)* No; It says "take two."

After reading p. 46:

- What is the problem on this page? *(Analyze)* Sally is fussy.

- How did Lucy solve this problem? *(Analyze)* Lucy gave her a jellybean and took her home for a nap.

Read, Write and Spell

ed Words

Goals

To read, write, and spell **ed** words
To practice Grammar Skills

Suggested Pacing

2 days

Materials

1. *Raceway Book*, pp. 128 (bottom half), 129, 130, 131, 132

PROCEDURE

Instructor:

- Have student open **Raceway Book** to pp. 128 (bottom half) and 129. Tell him/her **ed** added to a word changes the meaning of the word to mean something that has already happened.
  Example: Today I pack. Yesterday I packed.
- Teach the following one by one as grouped under the headings:
  Sometimes **ed** added to a word says *t* as in pack**ed**.
  Sometimes **ed** added to a word says *d* as in rain**ed**.
  Sometimes **ed** added to a word says *ed* as in want**ed**.
  If a word already ends in **e**, just add **d** for the ending as in **shaved**.
- Have student read, write, and spell all **ed** words in **Raceway Book** pp.128-129.
- Initial and date boxes at bottom of pp. 128-129.
- Have student complete **Raceway Book** pp. 130-132.
- Teach **Grammar Chalkboard Lesson**/Manual p. 100.

Phonics Song(s)/Games

Each day's lesson should begin with one or two previously learned phonics songs and end with a phonics game.

Written Spelling Tests

Instructor will dictate 10 words per day for a written spelling test. See Manual p. 51 for directions.

Raceway Book: Grammar

CLASSIFICATION: Person, Place or Thing, p. 130

Tell student a noun is a **person, place** or **thing**. Draw a chart similar to the one shown below. Write the following words and ask student to help place them in the correct box: **boy, Mom, bat, car, store, girl, Bob, school, park, beach, swing, tree**.

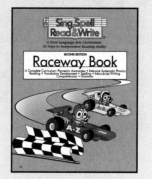

pp. 130-132

Noun Chart		
Person	**Place**	**Thing**
1. boy	1. store	1. bat
2. Mom	2. school	2. car
3. girl	3. park	3. swing
4. Bob	4. beach	4. tree

Next, have your student complete p. 130 in *Raceway Book*.

SOUNDS OF "ed", p. 131

Review with student the three different sounds **ed** can make when added to the end of a word. You may want to refer back to pp. 128-129 in *Raceway Book* to find words to review these sounds.

SUBJECTS AND VERBS, p. 132

Remind student the **subject** of a sentence is the word that tells **who** is doing something, and a **verb** is the word in the sentence that tells **what** the subject is doing. A verb is an action word and is something you can do. Give your student several examples of short simple sentences and ask him/her to identify the subject and verb.

Example: Mary ran home.

Who are we talking about in this sentence? (*Mary-subject*)

What did Mary do? (*ran-verb*)

Grammar Chalkboard Lesson

CLASSIFICATION REVIEW

Write the two headings "Animals" and "Foods" on the board and have student place the words from the word bank under the proper heading.

Animals	Classification	Foods
1. cat		1. jam
2. pig		2. ham
3. pup		3. peach
4. goat		4. banana
5. sheep		5. cake

Word Bank: jam, cat, pig, ham, pup, goat, peach, banana, sheep, cake

Vocabulary and Reading

ed, er, and ing Words and Related Stories in Storybook Reader 8

Goals

To double the final consonant when adding **ed**, **er**, and **ing** to words
To read, write, and spell **ed**, **er**, and **ing** words
To read **ed**, **er**, and **ing** words in context
To take Book End Assessment

Suggested Pacing

4 days

Materials

1. *Raceway Book*, pp. 133-134
2. Phonetic Storybook Reader 8,
   The Numbers and Colors Book, pp. 47-64
3. Assessment Book: Assessment for
   Phonetic Storybook Reader 8

pp. 133-134

PROCEDURE

Instructor:

- Before adding **ed**, **er** and **ing** to short words having one vowel and one consonant, you must double the final consonant.
  Tell student to put a **v** over the one vowel, and a **c** over the one consonant.

  Example:
  $\overset{\text{v c}}{\text{h o p}}$

  Before adding the endings **ed**, **er**, or **ing**, double the final consonant.

  Example: $\overset{\text{v c}}{\text{h o p p e d}}$, $\overset{\text{v c}}{\text{h o p p e r}}$, $\overset{\text{v c}}{\text{h o p p i n g}}$

  - Have student read, write, and spell all words on p. 133.
  - Initial and date boxes at bottom of p. 133.

Have student:

  - Read pp. 47-64 in **Storybook Reader 8**.
  - Read each story two or three times for fluency.
  - Complete **Raceway Book** p. 134.

Instructor:

  - Teach **Creative Writing Lesson**/Manual p. 103.
  - Administer **Assessment**/Manual p. 104.

Phonics Song(s)/Games

Each day's lesson should begin with one or two previously learned phonics songs and end with a phonics game.

Written Spelling Tests

Instructor will dictate 10 words per day for a written spelling test. See p. 51 for directions.

Phonetic Storybook Reader 8

Comprehension Questions

Looking is Fun

Story 5 • pp. 47-64

Have student read orally the designated pages.
Ask the following questions:

It was a **hot** day! Patty and Harry just sat and rested. Patty licked a pop. Harry licked a pop, too! The pops melted fast!
48

After reading pp. 48-49:

• I think it is a very hot day. Why do I think this? *(Context Clue/Picture Clue)* The sun is coming in the window and the popsicle is melting.

• Why will Mom and Dad take the children camping? *(Cause and Effect)* Because they haven't gone on vacation yet this summer.

• What did Patty and Harry have to help them cool off? *(Inference/Drawing Conclusion)* A popsicle

After reading pp. 50-51:

• What was Patty and Harry's reaction to going camping? *(Context Clue)* They were excited.

• What did Dad do to indicate he likes the cake? *(Context Clue)* He smacked his lips and said, "Mmm."

After reading pp. 52-53:

• What will they camp in? *(Picture Clue)* A camper

• Who was the first one to name something? *(Story Detail)* Daddy

After reading pp. 54-57:

• Look back on the pages and name in sequence the six things they saw on these pages. *(Sequence)*
  1. A man painting an ad
  2. A kid playing his flute
  3. A drummer
  4. A baseball game
  5. Three kids jumping rope
  6. A red truck dumping sand

After reading pp. 58-61:

• What did Harry see someone doing that he would like to do when he gets to camp? *(Story Detail)* A kid picking up a rock

• Why do most people jog? *(Drawing Conclusions/Personal Experience)* To keep in shape

After reading pp. 62-64:

• What was the last thing they saw before getting to camp? *(Sequence)* A kid putting a lock on his bike

• How did Patty and Harry show they were glad to get to camp? *(Context Clue)* They clapped and yelled "yippee!"

• What was the setting for most of this story *(Analyzing)* The road

Reference Skills
Open books to p. 2, Table of Contents.
How many stories are in this book? 5
What is the title of the last story? "Looking is Fun"
On what page does **Ray and The Blue Jay** begin? 8
Who is the author of **The Shy Giant**? Sue Dickson

Complete p. 134 in Raceway Book.
See directions on next page.

Raceway Book: Comprehension

Fill in the Blank, *p. 134 (top half)*
Have student complete the sentences.

Alphabetical Order, *p. 134 (bottom half)*
Tell student that putting words in alphabetical order means to arrange them so the first letter of the word follows the order of the alphabet. Use the five words below to practice putting words in A-B-C order.

man 5   big 2   leg 4   at 1   fast 3

Talk about uses for A-B-C order. Example: telephone book, index, etc. Tell student to look at the first letter of the five words on the bottom half of p. 134 and write them in the order of the alphabet next to the numerals 1 to 5.

p. 134

Creative Writing Lesson

This *Creative Writing Lesson* follows the reading of **Looking is Fun**, pp. 46-64 in Phonetic Storybook Reader 8, *The Numbers and Colors Book.*

Ask your student to recreate the scene of the two hikers hiking up a steep hill. Think of what they might say to each other and write it.

Suggestions of things the two hikers might say:
Will we ever get to the top?
I'm too hot.
Let's have a snack.

Assessment Book

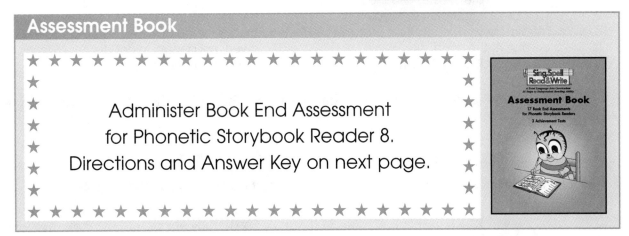

Administer Book End Assessment
for Phonetic Storybook Reader 8.
Directions and Answer Key on next page.

Move
Raceway Car
to Step **22**

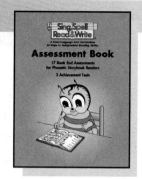

Book End Assessment
Phonetic Storybook Reader 8

Word Recognition: ay, y=i, g=j

Instructor: Direct student to "Put your finger on box #1. Now circle the word in the box that I call... 'pay.' Put your finger on box #2. Now circle the word 'day,' etc." The words the instructor should call are listed below. Say each word distinctly with emphasis upon initial and final consonants.

1. pay	2. day	3. jay	4. clay	5. ray
6. say	7. stay	8. play	9. shy	10. spy
11. try	12. my	13. fry	14. why	15. sky
16. giant	17. hinge	18. page	19. bulge	20. germ

Record scores in the space provided on the front cover of the Student Assessment Record and calculate the Percentage of Mastery Score as indicated.

Word Recognition and Word Comprehension

Name _____

pay	bay	way	clay	say
stay	day	jay	play	ray
play	hay	pay	lay	may

hay	stay	play	shy	pay
bay	ray	clay	sky	spy
say	tray	stay	sly	cry

fly	by	try	sly	sky
fry	my	dry	why	shy
try	why	fry	fly	why

germ	hinge	page	bulge	huge
gem	huge	age	giant	germ
giant	bulge	germ	hinge	page

Word Recognition ____ Number Correct   Word Comprehension ____ Number Correct

p.1

Word Comprehension: ay, y=i, g=j

Directions: Tell your student to put his/her finger on box #1 again and listen to what you say:

Instructor: *Underline the word that (is)...*

1. what you do to have fun. play
2. what you feed to horses. hay
3. what you get for the work that you do. pay
4. means to put something down. lay
5. a word used to ask permission. may
6. a place where water comes into the land. bay
7. something used to carry other things. tray
8. a kind of dirt. clay
9. the area above the earth. sky
10. what you might do if you hurt yourself. cry
11. a way to cook food. fry
12. a word that asks a question. why
13. a word that means not wet. dry
14. what birds can do. fly
15. means the same as bashful. shy
16. something that can make you sick. germ
17. means very large. huge
18. means the number of years old you are. age
19. a very tall person. giant
20. a part of a book. page

Record scores in the space provided on the front cover of the Student Assessment Record and calculate the Percentage of Mastery Score as indicated.

Sentence Comprehension

"Bubble" Format Directions pp. 69-70

1. B	6. C	11. B	16. C	21. A
2. C	7. E	12. D	17. E	22. B
3. A	8. A	13. A	18. B	23. E
4. E	9. B	14. E	19. A	24. C
5. D	10. D	15. C	20. D	25. D

Story Comprehension

"Bubble" Format Directions pp. 69-70

1. nine
2. She is baby-sitting.
3. Sally
4. jellybeans
5. yes
6. sat and rested
7. Pops melt when it is hot.
8. yes
9. summer
10. rain

Vocabulary and Reading

or Words and Related Stories in Storybook Reader 9

Goals

To read, write, and spell words with letter cluster **or**
To practice reading **or** words in context
To practice Grammar Skills

Suggested Pacing

2 days

Materials

1. Phonetic Storybook Reader 9,
   The Orbit Book, pp. 3-13
2. *Raceway Book*, p. 135

p. 135

PROCEDURE

Have student:

- Circle the **or** in each word in **Raceway Book,** p. 135.

- Read, write, and spell all **or** words on p. 135.

Instructor: Initial and date boxes at bottom of page.

Have student:

- Read pp. 3-13 in **Storybook Reader 9**.

- Read each story two or three times for fluency.

Instructor: Teach **Grammar Chalkboard Lesson**/Manual p.106.

Phonics Song(s)/Games

Each day's lesson should begin with one or two previously learned phonics songs and end with a phonics game.

Written Spelling Tests and Homework

Each day dictate the previous day's 10 spelling "homework" words for a written spelling test. Following the test, have your student circle the next 10 words in the Raceway Book. These 10 spelling words will be for today's homework (writing sentences), and tomorrow's test. See p. 97 in this Manual for directions.

Phonetic Storybook Reader 9

Kevin said, "What can we do for fun ?"

"We can make a fort for fun," said Kate.

"OK," said Kevin. "We will need some boxes. We must go to the store."

"Let's ask Mom if we may go," said Kate.

4

Comprehension Questions

A Fort for Kevin and Kate
Story 1 • pp. 3-13

Have student read orally the designated pages.
Ask the following questions:

After reading pp. 4-5:

- Why did Kevin and Kate decide to make a fort?
  (Story Detail) For fun

- What will they use to build their fort?
  (Story Detail) Boxes

- Where do Kevin and Kate expect to get the boxes they need? *(Story Detail)*
  From the grocery store

(Continued on next page)

- What does Mom want the children to get for her? (at the grocery store) *(Story Detail)*
  Pork, corn, and plastic forks

After reading pp. 6-7:

- After Kate paid for Mom's order, what did she ask Mr. Gomez? *(Story Detail)*
  If he has any boxes

- What kind of man does Mr. Gomez seem to be? *(Inference/Drawing Conclusion)* Very nice

After reading pp. 8-9:

- What kind of boxes do Kevin and Kate want? *(Drawing Conclusion)* Big, strong ones

- What kind of box did Kevin almost fall in? *(Picture Clue)* An apple box

After reading pp. 10-11:

- How were they able to take several boxes home at one time? *(Context Clue)*
  By placing the little ones inside the big ones

SUFFIX REVIEW

Student will choose the correct verb to complete the sentence.

- What street do Kevin and Kate live on? *(Drawing Conclusion)* North Street

After reading pp. 12-13:

- What was the first thing they did when they got home? Second? *(Sequence)* They gave Mom the order; they ran to begin the fort.

- Where did they build their fort? *(Picture Clue)* In the yard

- What was Kevin and Kate's problem? *(Analyzing)* Finding the boxes and bringing them home

- If it rains, what will happen to their fort? *(Analyzing)* It will be ruined.

- How did they solve their problem? *(Analyzing)* They put the little boxes inside the big ones and stuck with the job of getting them home.

- Could this story be true? *(Realism/Fantasy)* Yes

Suffixes
1. I will not __rock__ the boat. (rock, rocked)
2. Dad __locked__ the car. (lock, locked)
3. Do not __kick__ the ball. (kick, kicked)
4. Mom __fixed__ the nest. (fix, fixed)
5. I can __jump__. (jump, jumped)

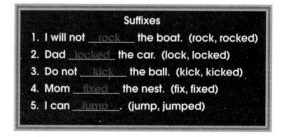

RACEWAY STEP 22ᴮ

Vocabulary and Reading

sh Words and Related Stories in Storybook Reader 9

Goals

To read, write, and spell words with letter cluster **sh**

To practice reading **sh** words in context

To practice Grammar Skills

Suggested Pacing

2 days

Materials

1. Phonetic Storybook Reader 9, *The Orbit Book*, pp. 14-21

2. *Raceway Book*, pp. 136-137

pp . 136-137

PROCEDURE

Have student:
- Circle the **sh** in each word in **Raceway Book**, p. 136. Strike through the silent ¢ on words #2, #13, #18, #22, and #26.
- Read, write, and spell all **sh** words on p. 136.

Instructor: Initial and date boxes at bottom of page.

Have Student:
- Read pp. 14-21 in **Storybook Reader 9**.
- Read each story two or three times for fluency.
- Complete **Raceway Book** p.137.

Phonics Song(s)/Games

Each day's lesson should begin with one or two previously learned phonics songs and end with a phonics game.

Written Spelling Tests and Homework

Each day dictate the previous day's 10 spelling "homework" words for a written spelling test. Following the test, have your student circle the next 10 words in the Raceway Book. These 10 spelling words will be for today's homework (writing sentences), and tomorrow's test. See p. 97 in this Manual for directions.

Phonetic Storybook Reader 9

Comprehension Questions

Sheldon's Bike Crash

Story 2 • pp. 14-21

Have student read orally the designated pages. Ask the following questions:

Sheldon hopped up the street. He held his shin. He left his bike by the side of the street.

15

After reading p. 15:
- Why is Sheldon hopping? *(Predicting Outcome)* He fell off his bike.
- What makes you think this? *(Context Clue/Picture Clue)* He's holding his leg and has a tear in his eye.

After reading pp. 16-17:
- Was your prediction correct? *(Story Detail)* Yes
- What is a shin? *(Vocabulary Expansion)* The front of your lower leg
- Tell me what happened. *(Summarizing)* Sheldon hit a stone and flipped off his bike.
- What is his mom afraid he has done? *(Story Detail)* Crushed his hand
- What caused the accident? *(Story Detail)* A stone in the road

After reading pp. 18-19:
- How does Mom comfort Sheldon? *(Story Detail)* She tells him to sit in the shade, she gets a Band-Aid, and gives him sherbet.

After reading pp. 20-21:
- What did Mom mean when she said Sheldon would "shine"? *(Figurative Language)* He'll feel better.
- How does Sheldon feel at the end of the story? *(Context Clue)* Happy
- What is the problem in this story? *(Analyzing)* Sheldon crashed on his bike.
- How is the problem solved? *(Analyzing)* Mom makes him feel better by taking care of him.

Complete p. 137 in Raceway Book.
See directions on next page.

Raceway Book: Grammar

SUPERLATIVES: Adding er and est, *p. 137*

Superlatives are used for making comparisons. Tell student when adding **er** to these words it means **more**, and **est** means the **most**.

Use the words *big, bigger,* and *biggest* as a practice exercise.

Example: Mom is *big.*
              Dad is *bigger.*
              Grandpa is the *biggest.*

Next, have student write the correct word under each picture on p. 137.

p. 137

ch Words and Related Stories in Storybook Reader 9

Goals
To read, write, and spell words with letter cluster **ch**
To practice reading **ch** words in context
To practice Grammar Skills

Suggested Pacing
3 days

Materials
1. Phonetic Storybook Reader 9, *The Orbit Book*, pp. 22-39
2. *Raceway Book*, pp. 138-139

pp. 138-139

PROCEDURE

Have student:
- Circle the **ch** in each word in **Raceway Book**, p. 138.
- Read, write, and spell all **ch** words on p. 138.

Instructor: Initial and date boxes at bottom of page.

Have student:
- Read pp. 22-39 in **Storybook Reader 9.**
- Read each story two or three times for fluency.
- Complete **Raceway Book** p. 139.

Instructor: Teach **Grammar Chalkboard Lessons**/Manual p. 112.

Phonics Song(s)/Games

Each day's lesson should begin with previously learned phonics song(s) and end with a phonics game.

Written Spelling Tests and Homework

Each day dictate the previous day's 10 spelling "homework" words for a written spelling test. Following the test, have your student circle the next 10 words in the Raceway Book. These 10 spelling words will be for today's homework (writing sentences), and tomorrow's test. See p. 97 in this Manual for directions.

Phonetic Storybook Reader 9

Comprehension Questions
Cherry Hill Ranch
Story 3 • pp. 22-29

Have student read orally the designated pages. Ask the following questions.

Sheldon hopped up the street. He held his shin. He left his bike by the side of the street.

15

After reading p. 23:
- Where did the children go each year? *(Story Detail)* To Cherry Hill Ranch
- How do they get there? *(Picture Clue)* By bus
- How many is a "bunch"? *(Context Clue)* A lot; many

After reading pp. 24-25:
- What would you compare Cherry Hill Ranch to? *(Comparison)* A camp
- Where do they eat lunch? *(Story Detail)* The Lunch Hut
- Read the sentence that tells us they were crowded when they ate. *(Inference/Drawing Conclusion)* "Not one inch of the bench was left to sit on."
- What do the children eat for lunch? *(Story Detail)* Cheese and chicken; cherry punch; peach pie; chocolate cake
- Did they swim *before* or *after* lunch? *(Sequence)* After
- Name in sequence these activities: swim, lunch, rest. *(Sequence)* Lunch; rest; swim
- What does the word "scorch" mean? *(Context Clue)* Burn

After reading pp. 26-27:
- Why do the children swim with a buddy? *(Story Detail)* It is safer
- How do they get a buddy? *(Story Detail)* They pick a buddy themselves.
- Why is the sand not so hot later in the day? *(Personal Experience)* The sun goes down
- What are the children doing in the circle on the beach? *(Predicting Outcome)* Listening to the camp counselor
- Where is the music coming from? *(Picture Clue)* The chapel
- What is a chapel? *(Vocabulary Expansion)* A small church

After reading pp. 28-29:
- How many words on page 29 have the "ch" sound? *(Counting)* 13
- Who is the lady in the picture? *(Context Clue)* A camp counselor or teacher

Comprehension Questions
Cheer the Champ
Story 4 • pp. 30-39

Have student read orally the designated pages. Ask the following questions.

After reading p. 31:

• Do you remember Gus from another book? *(Recall)* Yes

• What is Gus doing in this picture? *(Story Detail)* Dreaming about winning a race

• What will he do with the hot rod he makes? *(Story Detail)* Race it in the Hot Rod Race.

• Does Dad seem interested in this project? How do you know? *(Context Clue)* Yes. He says he'll help Gus.

After reading pp. 32-33:

• Did Gus and Dad make the hot rod in one day? How do you know? *(Context Clue)* No. The story said each day they did more.

• Look back in your book and find in order the two tools Dad needed? *(Sequence)* A chain and a chisel

• Why would Gus need help to build a hot rod? *(Inference/Drawing Conclusion)* It's a big job and he isn't old enough to use big tools.

• Where do you think they are building this hot rod? *(Predicting)* In the garage

After reading pp. 34-35:

• When the hot rod was built, what did Gus need to do to it? *(Story Detail)* Paint it

• Why is Dad painting the bench in the picture? *(Context Clue)* To teach Gus how to paint

• Explain how Dad taught Gus to paint. *(Summarize)* He dips the brush and then presses it on each side so it won't drip.

After reading pp. 36-37:

• Why will Gus only use a little paint? *(Context Clue)* it's just a little hot rod.

• Read aloud the part that lets you know Mom is proud of Gus. *(Inference/Drawing Conclusion)* "Such a fine hot rod! I am glad you chose cherry-red. Maybe you will be champ."

After reading pp. 38-39:

• What kind of treat did Mom prepare for Gus? *(Story Detail)* Punch and a chunk of chocolate

• What did Gus name his hot rod? *(Story Detail)* "Red Flash"

• Why do you think he chose that name? *(Predicting)* Because the red paint was so bright and the hot rod will flash by fast

• What are some words that would describe Mom and Dad? *(Analyzing)* Kind; helpful; loving; caring

• What is the setting for this story? *(Analyzing)* The garage

• Who is the main character? *(Analyzing)* Gus

• What is the problem in this story? *(Analyzing)* Making a hot rod

• How did they solve it? *(Analyzing)* They got busy and built a hot rod.

• Tell me about this story in a few sentences. *(Main Idea/Summarizing)* Answers will vary.

• Would this story be make-believe or real? *(Realism/Fantasy)* Make-believe

• What is another word for make-believe? *(Vocabulary Expansion)* Fantasy; fiction; pretend

Complete p. 139 in Raceway Book.
See directions on next page.

Raceway Book: Phonics

Missing Sounds, *p. 139*
Fill in the missing letters.

p. 139

Grammar Chalkboard Lessons

SUFFIX REVIEW

Choose the correct form of the word for each sentence.

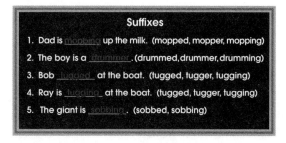

Suffixes

1. Dad is _mopping_ up the milk. (mopped, mopper, mopping)
2. The boy is a _drummer_. (drummed, drummer, drumming)
3. Bob _tugged_ at the boat. (tugged, tugger, tugging)
4. Ray is _tugging_ at the boat. (tugged, tugger, tugging)
5. The giant is _sobbing_. (sobbed, sobbing)

SYLLABICATION REVIEW

On p.137 in the *Raceway Book,* your student used the suffixes **er** and **est**. Sometimes these suffixes add another syllable to the word. Give student more practice in syllabication by dividing the following words into syllables.

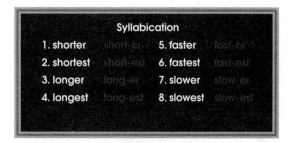

Syllabication

1. shorter	short-er	5. faster	fast-er
2. shortest	short-est	6. fastest	fast-est
3. longer	long-er	7. slower	slow-er
4. longest	long-est	8. slowest	slow-est

Vocabulary and Reading

er, ir, and ur Words and Related Stories in Storybook Reader 9

Goals

To read, write, and spell words with
letter clusters **er**, **ir**, and **ur**

To read stories using **er**, **ir**, and **ur** words in context

To practice Grammar Skills

To take Book End Assessment

Suggested Pacing

4 days

Materials

1. *Raceway Book*, pp. 140-141
2. Phonetic Storybook Reader 9,
   The Orbit Book, pp. 40-64
3. Assessment Book: Assessment for Storybook Reader 9

pp. 140-141

PROCEDURE

Have student:

- Open **Raceway Book** to p. 140 and circle the **er**, **ir**, and **ur** words as indicated in #1.
- Read, write, and spell all **er**, **ir**, and **ur** words.

Instructor: Initial and date boxes at bottom of p.140.

Have student:

- Read pp. 40-64 in **Storybook Reader 9**.
- Read each story two or three times for fluency.
- Complete **Raceway Book** p. 141.

Instructor:

- Teach **Creative Writing Lesson**/Manual p. 115.
- Administer **Assessment**/Manual p. 116.

Phonics Song(s)/Games

Each day's lesson should begin with one or two previously learned phonics songs and end with a phonics game.

Written Spelling Tests and Homework

Each day dictate the previous day's 10 spelling "homework" words for a written spelling test. Following the test, have your student circle the next 10 words in the Raceway Book. These 10 spelling words will be for today's homework (writing sentences), and tomorrow's test. See p. 97 in this Manual for directions.

Phonetic Storybook Reader 9

Comprehension Questions

A Shirt for a Third Grader

Story 5 • pp. 40-49

Have student read orally the designated pages.
Ask the following questions:

After reading pp. 41-43:

- What time of the school year is it?
  (Context Clue) The end of the school year
- What grade will Jenny be in next year?
  (Inference/Drawing Conclusion) Third
- Where does Jenny want to go? *(Story Detail)*
  To the seashore
- Where do Mom and Jenny go to prepare for
  the trip? *(Story Detail)*
  To the shop on Third Street
- What is a clerk? *(Context Clue)*
  A person who helps you in the store

After reading pp. 44-45:

- What does "stern" mean? *(Context Clue)*
  Very serious

After reading pp. 46-47:

- Which outfit did Jenny try on next? *(Sequence)*
  The blue dotted shirt and the red shorts
- Why do you think Mom dislikes flies so much?
  (Predicting/Context Clue)
  They carry germs

After reading pp. 48-49:

- What did Mom purchase for herself?
  (Story Detail) A pretty pink skirt
- What did Jenny choose? *(Story Detail)*
  Green shorts and a yellow skirt
- What could be another title for this story?
  (Main Idea) "Getting Ready for the Beach".

Comprehension Questions

Chocolate Dirt

Story 6 • pp. 50-57

Have student read orally the designated pages.
Ask the following questions:

After reading p. 51:

- What do you believe the title "Chocolate Dirt"
  is referring to? *(Predicting/Context Clue)*
  The mud
- Who do you think will be the main characters
  in this story? *(Context Clue)* Shirley and Bert
- Who do you think Bert is? *(Predicting)*
  He could be her brother, cousin or friend.

After reading pp. 52-54:

- Why does Bert say he can get his shirt dirty?
  (Story Detail) It's old
- Name in order the three steps for making
  "chocolate cake." *(Sequence)*

1) Fill up the pail and stir.
2) Pack it till it is firm.
3) Turn it over and lift up the pail.

- What are Bert and Shirley going to make?
  (Story Detail) Chocolate cake

After reading pp. 55-57:

- What does Bert say the bird is asking?
  (Story Detail) If the cake is real
- What is one thing they will have for lunch?
  (Story Detail) Cake
- What is the setting for this story?
  (Analyzing) The backyard

Chipper was a little black dog. He did not like to stay at home. He had the urge to run away. So one day he did!

59

Comprehension Questions

Chipper Gets Hurt
Story 7 • pp. 58-64

Have student read orally the designated pages. Ask the following questions:

- The title of the story is "Chipper Gets Hurt." Who do you think Chipper is? *(Picture Clue)* A dog

After reading pp. 59-61:

- What did Chipper *not* like to do? *(Story Detail)* Stay at home

- What did he want to do? *(Story Detail)* Run away

- Who did Chipper meet on his way? *(Story Detail)* A big dog

- Name some words to describe Curly *(Inference/Drawing Conclusion)* Daring, brave, curious, bold, mischievous

- What could be the danger of children shooting off rockets? *(Cause and Effect)* Someone may get hurt.

After reading p. 62:

- Were you right? What *did* happen? *(Story Detail)* Chipper fell trying to get away from the rocket.

After reading pp. 63-64:

- Why did Chipper believe Kurt would fix him up? *(Story Detail)* He is his master and loves him.

- How does Chipper feel to be back in Kurt's arms? *(Inference/Drawing Conclusion)* Comforted; relieved

- What part of this story is make-believe? *(Realism/Fantasy)* Dogs talking to each other in English

- What part could be real? *(Realism/Fantasy)* Running away and getting hurt

- What is a lesson to be learned from this story? *(Analyzing)* Stay away from rockets

- Who is the main character? *(Main Character)* Chipper

Reference Skills
Turn to Table of Contents on p. 2.
How many stories are in this book? 7
Which story has two authors?
A Fort For Kevin and Kate
What is the name of the story that begins on p. 40?
A Shirt For a Third Grader
On what page does **A Fort For Kevin and Kate** end? 13

Complete p. 141 in Raceway Book.
See directions below.

Raceway Book: Grammar

Asking Sentences, *p. 141*
Write a question for each telling sentence.

p. 141

Creative Writing Lesson

This *Creative Writing Lesson* follows the reading of **Chocolate Dirt,** pages 50-57 in Phonetic Storybook Reader 9, *The Orbit Book.*

Ask your student to look at the pictures in the story. Suggest that he/she think of something the characters might have said, but didn't. You may wish to give the following example: In the picture on p. 51, Shirley looks as if she's saying, "I'm so happy the rain has stopped. Let's go play outside."

Have student choose one picture and write one or two sentences the characters might have said. Refer to the story and show student how quotation marks are placed around the exact words the person says.

Assessment Book

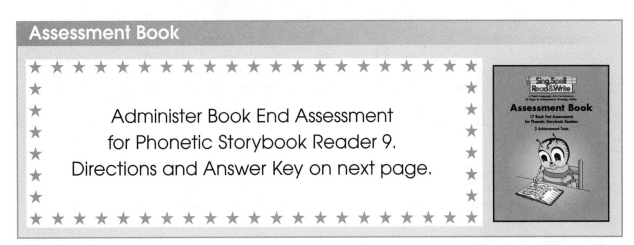

Administer Book End Assessment
for Phonetic Storybook Reader 9.
Directions and Answer Key on next page.

Move Raceway Car to Step **23**

Sing Spell Read & Write.

Raceway Step 22

Book End Assessment
Phonetic Storybook Reader 9

Word Recognition: or, sh, ch

Instructor: Direct student to "Put your finger on box #1. Now circle the word in the box that I call... 'fort.' Put your finger on box #2. Now circle the word 'sort,' etc." The words the instructor should call are listed below. Say each word distinctly with emphasis upon initial and final consonants.

1. fort	2. sort	3. form	4. short	5. for
6. cord	7. thorn	8. order	9. port	10. dash
11. shore	12. crush	13. shin	14. sash	15. sheet
16. hush	17. mush	18. shoot	19. shade	20. she

Record scores in the space provided on the front cover of the Student Assessment Record and calculate the percentage of mastery score as indicated.

p.1

Word Comprehension: or, sh, ch

Directions: Tell your student to put his/her finger on box #1 again and listen to what you say:

Instructor: *Underline the word that (is)...*

1. something you use when eating. fork
2. how your muscles feel when they ache. sore
3. something on a car. horn
4. a place to buy things. store
5. a kind of vegetable. corn
6. a large white bird. stork
7. a direction. north
8. means to burn. scorch
9. another word for a game such as football, baseball or basketball. sport
10. a food that is a mixture of meat and potatoes. hash
11. what a man will do to remove hair from his face. shave
12. another name for money. cash
13. a big boat. ship
14. means to hope for something. wish
15. a pair of pants you might wear in the summer. shorts
16. something you put on your foot. shoe
17. what happens when two cars hit each other. crash
18. what you do when you go out to buy things. shop
19. means to move back and forth quickly. shake
20. a place to put things. shelf

Record scores in the space provided on the front cover of the Student Assessment Record and calculate the percentage of mastery score as indicated.

Sentence Comprehension

"Bubble" Format Directions pp. 69-70

1. B	5. D	9. B	13. B	17. B
2. C	6. C	10. A	14. D	18. A
3. A	7. A	11. D	15. C	19. D
4. D	8. B	12. C	16. A	20. C

Story Comprehension

"Bubble" Format Directions pp. 69-70

1. a hot rod
2. yes
3. no
4. metal
5. It would scorch
6. third
7. So Dad can go with them
8. second grader
9. shorts and shirts
10. happy

Vocabulary and Reading

th, tch Words and Related Stories in Storybook Reader 10

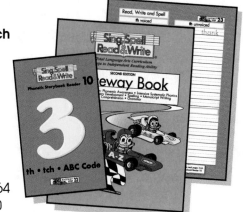

Goals

To read, write and spell words with letter clusters **th** and **tch**

To read stories using **th** and **tch** words in context

To practice Grammar Skills

To take Book End Assessment

Suggested Pacing

5 days

Materials

1. *Raceway Book,* pp. 142-143
2. Phonetic Storybook Reader 10, *The Three Book,* pp. 3-64
3. Assessment Book: Assessment for Storybook Reader 10

PROCEDURE

Have student:

- Open **Raceway Book** to p. 142 and circle the **th** or **tch** in each word.
- Read, write, and spell all words on p. 142.

Instructor: Initial and date boxes at bottom of page.

Have student:

- Read pp. 3-64 in **Storybook Reader 10**.
- Read each story two or three times for fluency.
- Complete **Raceway Book** p. 143.

Instructor:

- Teach **Creative Writing Lesson**/Manual p. 122.
- Teach **Grammar Chalkboard Lessons**/Manual pp. 121-122.
- Administer **Assessment**/Manual p. 123.

Phonics Song(s)/Games

Each day's lesson should begin with one or two previously learned phonics songs and end with a phonics game.

Written Spelling Tests and Homework

Each day dictate the previous day's 10 spelling "homework" words for a written spelling test. Following the test, have your student circle the next 10 words in the Raceway Book. These 10 spelling words will be for today's homework (writing sentences), and tomorrow's test. See p. 97 in this Manual for directions.

Phonetic Storybook Reader 10

Comprehension Questions

Two of These and Three of Those

Story 1 • pp. 3-17

Have student read orally the designated pages. Ask the following questions:

After reading pp. 4-5:

- Why is this day special? *(Inference/Drawing Conclusion)* Today is pay day.
- What do you think pay day is? *(Inference/Drawing Conclusion)* The day they receive their allowance money
- What do Pam and Ann do to earn their money? *(Context Clue)* Help make beds and do dishes

After reading pp. 6-7:

- What are Pam and Ann going to buy? *(Story Detail)* Candy
- In what kind of store would you buy candy? *(Classification)* Candy store; grocery store

After reading pp. 8-11:

- How do we know Pam and Ann had been to this store before? *(Inference/Drawing Conclusion)* The owner knew them by name.
- What did Ann want two of? *(Story Detail)* Gum

After reading pp. 12-13:

- How many pieces of candy has Ann chosen? *(Context Clue)* Eight

Pam and Ann can help Mom. They will make their beds. Then they will help with the dishes.
4

- What are the two kinds of candy Pam has chosen? *(Story Detail)* Taffy and chocolate cherries

After reading pp. 14-15:

- In what way were Pam and Ann kind to their parents? *(Context Clue)* They bought some mints for them.

After reading pp. 16-17:

- How did Pam and Ann show their good manners? *(Context Clue)* They said "thank you."
- On page 16, in the last line the word "you" is written in bold print. Why? Read it with the correct expression. *(Oral Expression)* To tell the reader to say it louder for expression
- Who are the main characters? *(Analyzing)* Pam and Ann
- Could this be a true story? *(Reality/Fantasy)* Yes

Comprehension Questions

Bobby Smith Likes Thick Icing

Story 2 • pp. 18-25

Have student read orally the designated pages. Ask the following questions:

After reading p. 19:

- What is the problem here? *(Context Clue)* Bobby fell from the tree.

After reading pp. 20-21:

- What does Bobby have to do as a result of his fall? *(Story Detail)* Stay in bed and rest
- What did Bobby's mom do to help him feel better? *(Inference/Drawing Conclusion)* Bake cupcakes

Bobby Smith slipped and fell from the tree. What a thump!
Thump!
19

- What is another word for pal? *(Vocabulary Expansion)* Friend

After reading pp. 22-23:

- What does Bobby want to have on his cupcakes? *(Story Detail)* Thick icing
- What are the three kinds of icing Mom puts on the cupcakes? *(Story Detail)* Chocolate, vanilla, and mint

(Continued on next page)

After reading pp. 24-25:

- Why did Bobby want his mother to have a cupcake? *(Story Detail)* So she'll feel better too.
- What could be another title for this story? (Main Idea) "Bobby Fell from a Tree"
- Who is the main character, Bobby or Mom?

(Elicit that Bobby is on almost every page.) *(Analyzing)* Bobby

- Tell, in sequence, the main events in this story. *(Sequence/Summarizing/Main Idea)* Bobby fell, went to bed, and had cupcakes.

Comprehension Questions
The Baseball Match
Story 3 • pp. 26-43

Have student read orally the designated pages. Ask the following questions:

After reading p. 27:

- How were the children divided into teams? *(Story Detail)* One girl team; one boy team

After reading pp. 28-29:

- What was a problem the boys team had? *(Story Detail)* Their catcher was on crutches.
- Why was Bobby chosen to be catcher? *(Context Clue)* He can catch very well.

After reading pp. 30-33:

- What is an inning? *(Context Clue)* When each team has had a time at bat. (There are 9 innings per game.)
- How many runs were scored in the first four innings? *(Story Detail)* No runs were scored.

After reading pp. 34-37:

- Name in order where Gretchen's ball went? *(Sequence)* Over the pitcher, past the shortstop, and into the back fence
- What is the difference between a run and a home run? *(Personal Experience)* A run is when a batter doesn't make it around all 3 bases and on to home plate. A home run is when the batter runs by all three bases and back home without being tagged out.

After reading pp. 38-41:

- What do you think the boys are doing in the huddle on p. 38? *(Predicting)* They're deciding how they are going to play in order to win.

 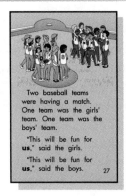

Two baseball teams were having a match. One team was the girls' team. One team was the boys' team.

"This will be fun for **us**," said the girls.

"This will be fun for **us**," said the boys. 27

- Read aloud the line that tells what Bobby's team members yelled. *(Oral Expression)* "You are up, Bobby. Let 'em have it!"
- What did Bobby do? *(Story Detail)* He hit the very first pitch and ran to first base.
- What three things happened next? *(Sequence/Story Detail)*
  1) Jimmy and Mike struck out,
  2) Butch got a hit, and
  3) Bobby ran to home plate.

After reading pp. 42-43:

- The next batter struck out and what happened next? *(Sequence)* It began to rain.
- Was Bobby pleased that it started to rain? How do you know? *(Inference/Drawing Conclusion)* No; He said "Oh, no!"
- What makes him a little pleased? *(Context Clue)* The score is tied.
- Do you believe the two teams are showing good sportsmanship? *(Context Clue)* Yes
- What does the hand clasp at the end of the story mean? *(Inference/Drawing Conclusion)* They are good sports and enjoyed being good team players.
- What is the setting of this story? *(Analyzing)* A baseball field

Comprehension Questions
Mitch and His Bean Bag
Story 4 • pp. 44-57

Mitch has a little cat. Her name is Puff. Puff is one year old.

45

Have student read orally the designated pages. Ask the following questions:

After reading pp. 45-47:

• What is another name for a young cat? *(Vocabulary Expansion)* Kitten

• How old is Puff? *(Story Detail)* One year

• What does Mitch like to use when he plays with Puff? *(Picture Clue)* A red bean bag

• Where did Mitch get the bean bag? *(Story Detail)* He made it.

• Read aloud the sentence that tells us Mitch and Puff play together well. *(Context Clue)* "They make a good team."

After reading pp. 48-49:

• Where did Mitch's bean bag land? *(Picture Clue)* On the peak of the roof

• What did Puff see that she thought was the bean bag? *(Story Detail)* A red leaf

• Why would Puff leap for the bean bag? *(Predicting)* She thought she had a red bean bag too.

• What is another word for leap? *(Vocabulary Expansion)* Jump

After reading pp. 50-51:

• What are the words that describe the dog? *(Vocabulary Expansion)* Big; mean

• Why was Puff able to jump on the shed so quickly? *(Personal Experience)* She was afraid.

• Where is the peak of the shed? *(Vocabulary Expansion)* The very tip-top of the roof

• What does it mean when it said, "Puff was on the shed in a streak?" *(Context Clue)* She went up as fast as she could.

After reading pp. 52-55:

• Read aloud with expression what Mitch yelled at the dog. *(Oral Expression)* "Go away, dog! Go away! Do you hear?"

• What did Puff discover on the shed? *(Story Detail)* The bean bag

• How did Puff get the bean bag back to Mitch? *(Story Detail)* She pushed it, and it slid down.

After reading pp. 56-57:

• How did Mitch show he was proud of Puff and what was the reward for Puff? *(Story Detail)* He said, "You are the best cat," and he will give her a dish of meat.

• Why did Mitch think Puff could win any race? *(Story Detail)* She is very fast.

• What is the setting for this story? *(Analyzing)* The back yard

• Tell me the first and last thing that happened in this story. *(Sequence)*
  1) Mitch and Puff are playing together.
  2) Mitch gave Puff a big hug.

Comprehension Questions
The ABC Code
Story 5 • pp. 58-64

Have student read orally the designated pages, and then ask him/her the following questions:

By the time you read this, your Raceway car may be speeding on the Language Arts Raceway to Step 23! Why are you doing this? So you will be a good reader!

59

After reading pp. 59-64

- What is good about being able to read all by yourself? *(Analyzing)* You don't have to depend on anyone else to read for you.

- How can books be helpful to you? *(Analyzing)* You can learn about any subject you want.

- Where can you go to find many books to read? *(Picture Clue)* The library

- Where does the writer say the whole world is? *(Story Detail)* Right at your finger tips

- What does she mean by that? *(Figurative Language)* You can read about anything in a book which means it's right at your finger tips.

- What kind of books do you like best? *(Personal Experience)* Answers will vary.

Reference Skills

Turn to Table of Contexts p. 2.

1) How many stories are in this book? 5

2) What is the title of the fourth story?
Mitch and His Bean Bag

3) On what page does *Mitch and his Bean Bag* end? 57

4) Who is the author of the first story? Hetty Hubbard

Complete p. 143 in Raceway Book.
See directions below.

Raceway Book

Missing Sounds, *p. 143*
Fill in the missing letters and color the pictures.

p. 143

Grammar Chalkboard Lessons

SUFFIX REVIEW

Write the words shown below and help the student understand that sometimes **er** at the end of a word stands for someone who does something. Have the student write the words and draw a picture to go with each word.

Suffixes
1. **work** + **er** = worker
2. **paint** + **er** = painter
3. **teach** + **er** = teacher
4. **help** + **er** = helper
5. **sing** + **er** = singer

SUPERLATIVE REVIEW

Write the sentences shown below. Have student choose the correct word to complete each sentence.

Superlatives

1. Tom is the shortest boy in the class. (shorter, shortest)
2. This cord is shorter than Dad. (shorter, shortest)
3. My rope is the longest. (longer, longest)
4. My bike is longer than your bike. (longer, longest)

Creative Writing Lesson

This *Creative Writing Lesson* follows the reading of the story, **The Baseball Match**, pp. 26-43 in Phonetic Storybook Reader 10, *The Three Book*.

WRITING A NOTE:

- Tell student to imagine that each baseball team found a note the next day that was written to them from the other team. Ask him/her to think about what the girls' team wrote to the boys' team and what the boys' team wrote to the girls' team.

For example, the girls may have written:
"We're too good for you! We'll show you next week."

- Ask a boy to write a note to the girls' team and vice versa. Have student follow the pattern below.

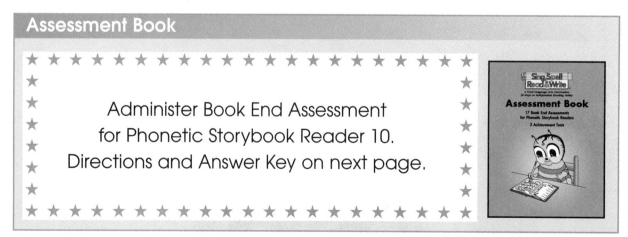

Dear Boys' Team,
_____
_____
_____
_____
                    Love,
                    Girls' Team

Assessment Book

★ ★

Administer Book End Assessment
for Phonetic Storybook Reader 10.
Directions and Answer Key on next page.

Sing Spell Read & Write
A Total Language Arts Curriculum
36 Steps to Independent Reading Ability
Assessment Book
17 Book End Assessments
for Phonetic Storybook Readers
3 Achievement Tests

Move
Raceway Car
to Step **24**

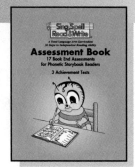

Raceway Step 23

Book End Assessment
Phonetic Storybook Reader 10

Word Recognition: th, tch

Instructor: Direct student to "Put your finger on box #1. Now circle the word in the box that I call... 'the.' Put your finger on box #2. Now circle the word 'there,' etc." The words the instructor should call are listed below. Say each word distinctly with emphasis upon initial and final consonants.

1. the	2. there	3. cloth	4. this	5. that
6. Smith	7. catch	8. thank	9. these	10. pitch
11. ditch	12. stretch	13. moth	14. three	15. both
16. itch	17. crutch	18. those	19. they	20. with

Record scores in the space provided on the front cover of the Student Assessment Record and calculate the percentage of mastery score as indicated.

Word Comprehension: th, tch

p.1

Directions: Tell your student to put his/her finger on box #1 again and listen to what you say:

Instructor: *Underline the word that (is)...*

1. means those people. them
2. a number. three
3. a kind of soup. broth
4. what you do with your brain. think
5. what you do when someone gives you something. thank
6. what you do when you sew. stitch
7. what Mother may put over a hole in your jeans. patch
8. another word for fat. thick
9. means you want two. both
10. a kind of drawing. sketch
11. what makes you want to scratch. itch
12. something that will help you walk, if you hurt your leg. crutch
13. another word for together. with
14. means in that place. there
15. what clothes are made of. cloth
16. a word that means to throw. pitch
17. what you will try to do with a ball thrown at you catch
18. means to pull. stretch
19. means at that time. then
20. means the opposite of thick. thin

Record scores in the space provided on the front cover of the Student Assessment Record and calculate the percentage of mastery score as indicated.

Sentence Comprehension

"Bubble" Format Directions pp. 69-70

1. A	5. A	9. C	13. A	17. B
2. D	6. D	10. A	14. B	18. C
3. C	7. C	11. D	15. D	19. D
4. B	8. B	12. B	16. C	20. A

Story Comprehension

"Bubble" Format Directions pp. 69-70

1. Candy Shop
2. gum
3. a trip to the Candy Shop
4. taffy and chocolate cherries
5. had fun buying candy
6. Step 23
7. so you will be a good reader
8. read
9. you can read about anyplace in the world
10. reading

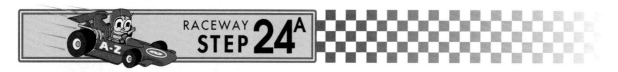

Vocabulary and Reading

ow and ou Words and Related Stories in Storybook Reader 11

Goals

To read, write, and spell words with letter clusters **ow** and **ou**

To practice reading **ow** and **ou** words in context

Suggested Pacing

2 days

Materials

1. *Raceway Book*, p. 144
2. Phonetic Storybook Reader 11,
   The Owl Book, pp. 3-27

p . 144

PROCEDURE

Have student:

- Open **Raceway Book** to p. 144 and circle the **ow** and **ou** in each word as indicated in #1.
- Read, write, and spell words on p. 144.

Instructor: Initial and date boxes at bottom of p. 144.

Phonics Song(s)/Games

Each day's lesson should begin with one or two previously learned phonics songs and end with a phonics game.

Written Spelling Tests and Homework

Each day dictate the previous day's 10 spelling "homework" words for a written spelling test. Following the test, have your student circle the next 10 words in the Raceway Book. These 10 spelling words will be for today's homework (writing sentences), and tomorrow's test. See p. 97 in this Manual for directions.

Sing-Spell Read&Write.

Phonetic Storybook Reader 11

Comprehension Questions

Bozo the Clown Comes to Town
Story 1 • pp. 3-19

Have student read orally the designated pages.
Ask the following questions:

Andy jumped from his bed and ran to take a shower. Then he dried with his towel and ran to get dressed.

Today was Andy's big day. The circus had come to town at last!

4

After reading pp. 4-7:

- Why is Andy excited today? *(Context Clue)* He is going to the circus.
- Who will meet them at the big tent? *(Story Detail)* Uncle Howard
- How long do they have to get there? *(Analyzing)* One hour

After reading pp. 6-7:

- What were the two jobs to be done before they could leave for the circus? *(Story Detail)* Open the gate for Brown Cow and feed Lassie

After reading pp. 8-9:

- How did Andy feel when he saw the big tent? *(Inference/Drawing Conclusion)* Surprised at its size
- Where did Andy and Uncle Howard go next? *(Story Detail)* To see Bozo the Clown get dressed

After reading pp. 10-11:

- What was the third thing Bozo put on? The first? The second? *(Sequence)*
  3) A big red spot on each cheek
  1) Thick white cream
  2) Fat red lips

After reading pp. 12-13:

- What is the last thing Bozo put on? *(Story Detail/Sequence)* His big red nose
- What did Andy not want to miss? *(Story Detail)* The first act
- How do you think Andy will feel when Bozo waves to him? *(Predicting)* Proud; excited

After reading pp. 14-19:

- Name some different kinds of clowns *(Context Clue)* Fat, skinny, red, brown, and upside down
- On p.18, what was the clown really doing when he said he could howl? *(Interpretation)* Laughing
- Which clown do you think is the funniest? Why? *(Personal Experience)* Answers will vary.
- What part of this story could be true? *(Reality/Fantasy)* All of it
- Why was Uncle Howard especially important to Mom and Andy today? *(Analyzing)* Because he was Bozo's friend
- Why was Uncle Howard able to take Andy behind the stage to see Bozo put on his makeup? *(Inference/Drawing Conclusion)* Because they were friends

Comprehension Questions

A Brownie Scout at Joan's House
Story 2 • pp. 20-27

Joan ran into the house. "Mommy!" she shouted. "Look at this paper. My teacher gave it to me. It says that I may be a Brownie Scout!"

21

Have student read orally the designated pages. Ask the following questions:

After reading p. 21:

- Why is Joan excited? *(Context Clue)* Because she is invited to become a Brownie Scout.

After reading pp. 22-23:

- How many girls will be Scouts? *(Story Detail)* Lots; many

- Does it seem that Mom would like Joan to be a Scout? Why do you think so? *(Inference/Drawing Conclusion)* Yes. She said, "It sounds like fun."

- Who will be the leader? *(Story Detail)* Miss Proud

- What are the two things Mom needs to do before they go see Miss Proud? *(Story Detail)*
  1) Finish the pie crust
  2) Wipe the flour from her hands

After reading pp. 24-25:

- When Mom and Joan got to Miss Proud's house, how did she greet them? *(Story Detail)* She said, "Come in."

- What does this tell you about Miss Proud? *(Inference/Drawing Conclusion)* That she is friendly

- What did Miss Proud tell them they would do in Scouting? *(Story Detail)* Go camping and sleep in tents

- What is the main idea of p. 25? *(Main Idea)* The different activities they will be doing

- What is Joan going to need if she joins Scouts? *(Story Detail)* A sleeping bag

After reading pp. 26-27:

- Whose sleeping bag could Joan use? *(Story Detail)* Her dad's

- How old do you think it is? *(Analyzing)* Very old because it was Dad's when he was a Scout

- Describe Joan's personality. *(Inference/Drawing Conclusion)* Happy; outgoing

- Why does Mom need to go home now? *(Story Detail)* She has a pie in the oven.

- What is the happy word Joan shouted? *(Context Clue)* Yippee!

- What else did Joan do to show her excitement? *(Story Detail)* Bounce up and down on the sofa

- Write these sentences and have the student number them in sequence. *(Sequence)*
  Joan yelled, "Yipee!" 3
  Joan brought home a paper telling about Scouts. 1
  Miss Proud told Mom and Joan about Scouts. 2

- What is this story about? *(Analyzing)* Joan wants to become a Brownie Scout.

Vocabulary and Reading

ōw and ew Words and Related Stories in Storybook Reader 11

Goals

To read, write, and spell words with letter clusters **ōw** and **ew**

To practice reading **ōw** and **ew** words in context

To practice Grammar Skills

Suggested Pacing

3 days

Materials

1. *Raceway Book*, p. 145
2. Phonetic Storybook Reader 11, *The Owl Book*, pp. 28-43

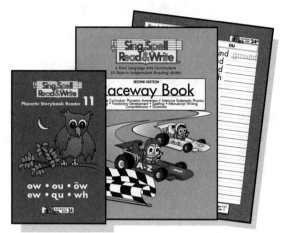

p. 145

PROCEDURE

Have student:

- Open **Raceway Book** to p. 145 and circle the **ōw** and **ew** in each word as indicated in #1.
- Read, write, and spell words on p. 145.

Instructor: Initial and date boxes at bottom of p. 145.

Have student:

- Read pp. 28-43 in **Storybook Reader 11**.
- Read each story two or three times for fluency.

Instructor: Teach **Grammar Lesson**/Manual p.129.

Phonics Song(s)/Games

Each day's lesson should begin with one or two previously learned phonics songs and end with a phonics game.

Written Spelling Tests and Homework

Each day dictate the previous day's 10 spelling "homework" words for a written spelling test. Following the test, have your student circle the next 10 words in the Raceway Book. These 10 spelling words will be for today's homework (writing sentences), and tomorrow's test. See p. 97 in this Manual for directions.

Phonetic Storybook Reader 11

Comprehension Questions

The Snowman

Story 3 • pp. 28-34

Have student read orally the designated pages. Ask the following questions:

It was the first snow of the winter. Ted, Karen and Liz ran out to make a big snowman.

29

After reading p. 29:

• What season of the year is it?
(Story Detail) Winter

• Why are the children bundled up in heavy clothing? *(Inference/Drawing Conclusion)* It is cold outside.

• What do they plan to make?
(Story Detail) A snowman

After reading pp. 30-31:

• What does Dad say the north wind will bring?
(Story Detail) Snow and a snowman

• What did Liz add to the snowman? Ted? Karen? *(Story Detail)*
1) A bow
2) A carrot nose
3) Two black coals

After reading pp. 32-34:

• Who else became interested in working on the snowman? *(Context Clue)* Mom and Dad

• What did Mom and Dad add?
(Story Detail) A hat; a pipe

• What did the children use for buttons?
(Story Detail) Stones

• What did Mom mean when she said Dad would never grow up? *(Context Clue)* He was still playful.

• What else did Mom suggest they do besides build a snowman?
(Story Detail) Go in for hot chocolate

• Read aloud the part that shows Dad is proud of the snowman. *(Context Clue)* "Now there's a snowman to crow about!" said Dad.

• What was the last thing to happen in this story? *(Sequence)* They looked out the window at their snowman.

• Why would hot chocolate be a good treat? *(Personal Experience)* It will warm them.

• What does it mean in the last sentence, "If it keeps on snowing, we may see him **grow!**" *(Interpretation)* The falling snow will stick to the snowman and make him larger.

Sing Spell Read & Write.

Comprehension Questions
The New Crew
Story 4 • pp. 35-43

Bobby and Steve lived near a pond.

"Let's make a raft to sail on the pond," said Steve.

"Yes," said Bobby. "We can get some logs at my house."

36

"I will get a hammer and nails and screws," said Steve.

"Wait," said Bobby. "I must go home to eat now. I will meet you after lunch."

"OK," said Steve.

37

Have student read orally the designated pages. Ask the following questions:

After reading pp. 36-37:

• What are Bobby and Steve planning to make? *(Story Detail)* A raft

• Do you think Bobby and Steve live in the same neighborhood? *(Context Clue)* Yes

• What will each one bring from their homes to use for making the raft? *(Story Detail)* Bobby- logs; Steve- hammer, nails, and screws

After reading pp. 38-39:

• What does the word *crew* mean on p. 38? *(Context Clue)* The sailors

• Why did Mom pack cookies and gum? (Story Detail) For a snack

After reading pp. 40-41:

• What did Bobby invite Willy to do? (Story Detail) To come with them

• How did Willy let Bobby know he wanted to be with him? (Inference/Drawing Conclusion) He meowed and rubbed Bobby's leg.

• What does it mean, "Hammers and nails flew"? (Interpretation) They were very busy.

• Do you think the raft was finished in one day? *(Inference/Drawing Conclusion)* Yes

After reading pp. 42-43:

• Why did Willy jump on the raft? *(Story Detail)* To get the bird

• At the same time Willy jumped on the raft, what happened? *(Story Detail)* The wind blew and the raft went out into the pond.

• Who is the new crew? *(Picture Clue)* The bird and Willy, the cat

• How do Bobby and Steve feel about this? *(Context Clue)* They think it's funny.

• What is the setting for most of the story? *(Analyzing)* The yard and pond

• Tell me about the story in a few sentences. *(Summarizing)* Answers will vary.

Grammar Lesson

NOUNS AND VERB REVIEW

Write each word below on an index card and give cards to your student. Ask student to tell if the word on the card is a noun or a verb and then use the word in a sentence orally.

Words to put on index cards:

1. **shoe**	noun	6. **sheep**	noun
2. **jump**	verb	7. **hit**	verb
3. **boy**	noun	8. **play**	verb
4. **farm**	noun	9. **girl**	noun
5. **sing**	verb	10. **store**	noun

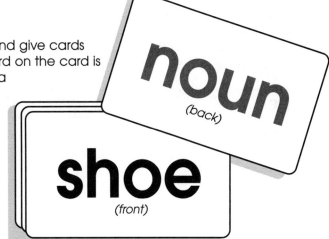

noun *(back)*

shoe *(front)*

Vocabulary and Reading

wh and qu Words and Related Stories in Storybook Reader 11

Goals

To read, write, and spell words with letter clusters **wh** and **qu**

To practice reading **wh** and **qu** words in context

To practice Grammar Skills

To take Book End Assessment

Suggested Pacing

5 days

Materials

1. *Raceway Book,* pp. 146-150
2. Phonetic Storybook Reader 11, *The Owl Book,* pp. 44-64
3. Assessment Book: Assessment for Storybook Reader 11

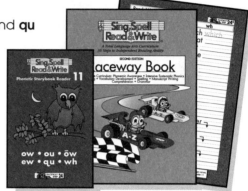

pp. 146-150

PROCEDURE

Have student:

- Open **Raceway Book** to p. 146 and circle **wh** or **qu** in each word as indicated in #1.
- Read, write, and spell words on p. 146.

Instructor: Initial and date boxes at bottom of p. 146.

Have student:

- Read pp. 44-64 in **Storybook Reader 11**.
- Read each story two or three times for fluency.
- Complete **Raceway Book** pp. 147-150.

Instructor:

- Teach **Creative Writing Lesson**/Manual p. 133.
- Administer **Assessment**/Manual p. 134.

Phonics Song(s)/Games

Each day's lesson should begin with one or two previously learned phonics songs and end with a phonics game.

Written Spelling Tests and Homework

Each day dictate the previous day's 10 spelling "homework" words for a written spelling test. Following the test, have your student circle the next 10 words in the Raceway Book. These 10 spelling words will be for today's homework (writing sentences), and tomorrow's test. See p. 97 in this Manual for directions.

Sing Spell Read & Write®

Phonetic Storybook Reader 11

Comprehension Questions
Quite a Surprise
Story 5 • pp. 44-49

Jean was so quiet! Mom asked, "What are you doing, Jean? What are those little scraps of cloth?"
45

Have student read orally the designated pages. Ask the following questions:

After reading p. 45:
• What do you think Jean is doing with these little scraps of cloth? *(Predicting)*
She is going to make something.

After reading pp. 46-47:
• What is Jean planning to do?
(Story Detail) Make a surprise for her mom
• Why did Mom say she hoped it wasn't a dress?
(Inference/Drawing Conclusion) Because of all the small scraps and colors
• We know now it's a surprise for Mom but we don't know what the occasion is for the surprise. When do you plan surprises for people?
(Cause and Effect) Birthdays; anniversaries, etc.

After reading pp. 48-49:
• What was the occasion for the surprise?
(Story Detail) Mom's birthday
• When that special day came, how did Jean's mother act? *(Context Clue)* Very surprised
• What was Jean's answer to Mom that made her feel so good? *(Story Detail)*
"You are my queen, Mom."
• What did Mom mean, "I will always see your love in each little stitch of that quilt."
(Interpretation) Every time she looks at the quilt, she will think of Jean's love and hard work.
• Tell me in one sentence the main idea of this story. *(Main Idea)* Jean makes a quilt for her mom.

Comprehension Questions
The New White Car
Story 6 • pp. 50-63

The Millers have a new white car. They are going on a trip in it. Mom is going to look at the map to see which roads to take.
51

Have student read orally the designated pages. Ask the following questions:

After reading p. 51:
• Why is Mom looking at a road map?
(Context Clue) To see which roads to take

After reading p. 53:
• Do you believe Dad will drive the entire trip? Why? *(Context Clue)* No. It says he will just drive for awhile.

After reading pp. 54-57:
• What do the road signs tell you?
(Story Detail/Picture Clue)
Which way to go; when to turn, etc.

• How do you know Dad likes his new car?
(Inference/Drawing Conclusion)
He said, "I just love this new steering wheel."
• Are they driving in the city or country? How do you know? *(Context Clue)*
The country; there are wheat fields.
• What is wheat used for?
(Personal Experience)
Bread, cakes, doughnuts, pies, etc.

(Continued on next page)

After reading pp. 58-61:

- Why do you think Dad thought about hamburger rolls for something made from wheat? *(Inference/Drawing Conclusion)* Maybe he's hungry and he sees the hamburger sign ahead.
- What does "whiz" mean? *(Vocabulary Expansion)* Fast
- What is the name of the restaurant? *(Picture Clue)* Whiz Inn
- What else could you buy there besides hamburgers and soda? *(Classification)* French fries
- What about pizza? *(Classification)* Probably not
- How do we know the wind is blowing? *(Picture Clue)* The flag is whipping in the wind.

After reading pp. 62-63:

- Who will drive next? Why? *(Story Detail)* Mom; it's her turn.
- Could this story be true? *(Reality/Fantasy)* Yes

- What part of this story do you like best? *(Opinion)* Answers will vary.

Reference Skills

Turn to Table of Contents on p. 2.

1) How many stories are in this book? 7
2) Which story could be about a birthday? Quite a Surprise
3) Which page does **The Snowman** begin on? 28 End on? 34
4) Which stories have two authors? Where's That Popsicle Man? The New Crew

Complete pp. 147-150 in Raceway Book. See directions below.

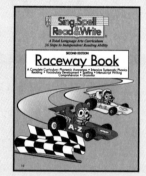

Raceway Book: Grammar

QUESTION WORDS, p. 147

Write the correct question word.

QUESTION WORDS, p. 148

Write the correct question word.

Remind student when beginning a sentence with the words *Is, Do, Which, Where, When, Why, How* or *What*, the sentence is going to ask a question. Practice using these words in sentences orally.

QUESTIONS, p. 149

Read each sentence. Put a (?) or (.) at the end of each sentence. Write "yes" if the sentence asks a question. Write "no" if the sentence does not ask a question.

MISSING SOUNDS, p. 150

Fill in the missing letters and color the pictures.

pp. 147-150

Creative Writing Lesson

This *Creative Writing Lesson* follows the reading of **The New White Car**, pp. 50-63 in Phonetic Storybook Reader 11, *The Owl Book*.

Dialogue

Talk about the story and how the children saw wheat growing in the field. They discussed with their parents the different foods that come from wheat. Ask your student to name some different kinds of foods and things which can be made from them.
Example:

Food	What you can make from it
Corn	Cereal
Potatoes	French Fries
Flour	Cupcakes
Chocolate	Candy

Have your student choose a food from the list and write it on a piece of paper. Draw a picture of something that can be made from that food and write a descriptive sentence about it.

My chocolate cupcake has icing with a strawberry on it.

Assessment Book

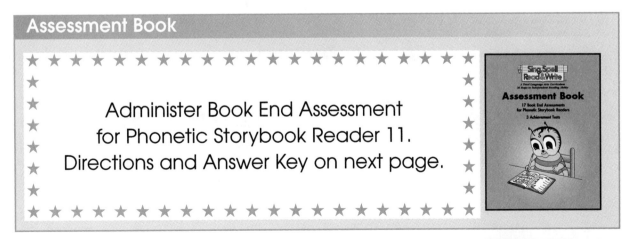

Administer Book End Assessment
for Phonetic Storybook Reader 11.
Directions and Answer Key on next page.

Move Raceway Car to Step **25**

Sing Spell Read & Write®

Raceway Step 24

Book End Assessment
Phonetic Storybook Reader 11

Word Recognition: ow, ou

Instructor: Direct student to "Put your finger on box #1. Now circle the word in the box that I call... 'round.' Put your finger on box #2. Now circle the word 'growl,' etc." The words the instructor should call are listed below. Say each word distinctly with emphasis upon initial and final consonants.

1. round	2. growl	3. sour	4. down	5. loud
6. drown	7. about	8. ground	9. shower	10. howl
11. now	12. proud	13. out	14. flower	15. frown
16. couch	17. how	18. clown	19. snout	20. brown

Record scores in the space provided on the front cover of the Student Assessment Record and calculate the Percentage of Mastery Score as indicated.

Word Recognition and Word Comprehension

Name _____

1 found / round / sound	2 towel / town / growl	3 sour / out / snout	4 gown / clown / down	5 loud / cloud / sprout
6 crown / drown / frown	7 mouth / scout / about	8 couch / pound / ground	9 shower / flower / flour	10 ow! / howl / bow
11 how / now / cow	12 shout / proud / brown	13 owl / out / bow	14 towel / shower / flower	15 frown / round / scout
16 couch / about / loud	17 mouth / how / sour	18 sound / cloud / shout	19 snout / sprout / clown	20 flour / brown / ground

Word Recognition ____ Number Correct   Word Comprehension ____ Number Correct

p.1

Word Comprehension: ow, ou

Directions: Tell your student to put his/her finger on box #1 again and listen to what you say:

Instructor: *Underline the word that (is)...*

1. the opposite of lost. found
2. a place to live. town
3. the opposite of "in" out
4. a person who might make you laugh clown
5. something that you can see in the sky. cloud
6. an unhappy look. frown
7. a part of the body found on the face. mouth
8. a place to sit down. couch
9. a pretty plant. flower
10. what you say when you hurt yourself. ow !
11. an animal that gives milk. cow
12. a dark color. brown
13. a kind of bird. owl
14. what you use to dry your hands. towel
15. the shape of a circle. round
16. means "not quiet." loud
17. the taste that is opposite of sweet. sour
18. something you hear. sound
19. a loud yelling sound. shout
20. something that you put in a cake. flour

Record scores in the space provided on the front cover of the Student Assessment Record and calculate the Percentage of Mastery Score as indicated.

Sentence Comprehension

"Bubble" Format Directions pp. 69-70

1. B	6. A	11. A	16. D	21. D
2. D	7. B	12. C	17. E	22. B
3. A	8. C	13. B	18. B	23. A
4. C	9. B	14. C	19. A	24. D
5. D	10. D	15. A	20. C	25. C

Story Comprehension

"Bubble" Format Directions pp. 69-70

1. Uncle Howard
2. thick white cream
3. Bozo's big red nose
4. a red spot on each cheek
5. yes
6. quilt
7. her mother's birthday
8. She wanted to surprise Mom.
9. She gave Jean a hug and thanked her.
10. She stitched it.

Vocabulary and Reading

ar Words and Related Stories in Storybook Reader 12

Goals

To read, write, and spell words with letter cluster **ar**

To practice reading **ar** words in context

Suggested Pacing

2 days

Materials

1. *Raceway Book*, p. 151

2. Phonetic Storybook Reader 12, *The Car Book*, pp. 3-27

p. 151

PROCEDURE

Have student:

- Open **Raceway Book** to p. 151 and circle the **ar** in each word.
- Read, write, and spell all words on p. 151.

Instructor: Initial and date at bottom of p. 151.

Have student:

- Read pp. 3-27 in **Storybook Reader 12**.
- Read each story two or three times for fluency.

Phonics Song(s)/Games

Each day's lesson should begin with one or two previously learned phonics songs and end with a phonics game.

Written Spelling Tests and Homework

Each day dictate the previous day's 10 spelling "homework" words for a written spelling test. Following the test, have your student circle the next 10 words in the Raceway Book. These 10 spelling words will be for today's homework (writing sentences), and tomorrow's test. See p. 97 in this Manual for directions.

Comprehension Questions
Harmony Hill Farm
Story 1 • pp. 3-27

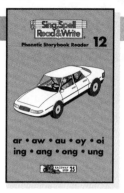 

Have student read orally the designated pages.
Ask the following questions:

After reading pp. 4-5:
- Where do Mark and Carl live?
  (Story Detail) Harmony Hill Farm
- How old are Mark and Carl?
  (Story Detail) Seven and five

After reading pp. 6-7:
- Who is Sparky?
  (Story Detail) Their dog
- What do you think Dad is doing at the barn?
  (Predicting)
  Feeding the animals or milking the cows

After reading pp. 8-9:
- Do you think the barn is near the home?
  (Analyzing) Yes
- What is Dad doing? *(Story Detail)*
  Lifting hay into a cart
- What do you think the hay will be used for?
  (Personal Experience) To feed the animals
- Who did Mark say "good morning" to?
  (Story Detail) The lark
- What is a lark? *(Context Clue)* A bird

After reading pp. 10-11:
- How can Mark help Dad? *(Context Clue)*
  By feeding Old Martha, the cow
- How did Old Martha show she did not want
  Sparky around? *(Context Clue)*
  She went "moo!"

After reading pp. 12-13:
- Why did Mark say Sparky was smart?
  (Context Clue)
  He came when he was called.
- Who else is smart? Why? *(Context Clue)*
  Mom, because she can play the harp.

After reading pp. 14-15:
- Where would you most likely see a harp?
  (Personal Experience) In an orchestra

- Why did Carl and Mark go to the park?
  (Story Detail) To catch bugs
- What time do Mark and Carl need to be
  home? *(Story Detail)* By dark
- Is that an exact time? Explain why not.
  (Analyzing) No; it gets dark at different times.
- Why would Mom suggest Carl and Mark take
  Sparky with them? *(Predicting)*
  Sparky probably likes the park.

After reading pp. 16-17:
- What would be the latest Mark and Carl
  would come home? Why? *(Context Clue)*
  Six o'clock; they want to see "Stars and
  Planets" on TV.
- What did Mom remind Mark and Carl to take
  with them? *(Story Detail)* Their jars

After reading pp. 18-19:
- How many bugs did Carl catch? Mark?
  (Story Detail) Six; seven
- How many did they catch all together?
  (Analyzing) Thirteen
- What does Miss Marcy Sharp have in her
  basket? *(Story Detail)* Red yarn
- How would you describe Sparky's behavior?
  (Analyzing) Playful

After reading pp. 20-21:
- Describe what Sparky is doing. *(Context Clue)*
  He is running off with the yarn.
- Read the part that lets us know Miss Marcy
  Sharp was not happy with Sparky.
  (Oral Expression/Context Clue) "No! Come
  back with my yarn! You are a bad dog!"

After reading pp. 22-23:
- Where did Sparky go next? *(Story Detail)*
  He ran to some kids playing in the sandbox.

(Continued on next page)

- How much yarn did Mark have to roll up? *(Story Detail)* He guessed 500 yards.

- About what time was it when they got home? *(Context Clue)* About six o'clock

After reading pp. 24-25:

- What did Carl do with the yarn? *(Story Detail)* He gave it back to Miss Marcy Sharp.

After reading pp. 26-27:

- What is the setting of this story? *(Analyzing)* A farm and a park

RACEWAY STEP **25**^B

Vocabulary and Reading

aw, au Words and Related Stories in Storybook Reader 12

Goals

To read, write, and spell words with letter clusters **aw** and **au**

To practice reading **aw** and **au** words in context

Suggested Pacing

3 days

Materials

1. *Raceway Book*, pp. 152-153
2. Phonetic Storybook Reader 12, *The Car Book*, pp. 28-46

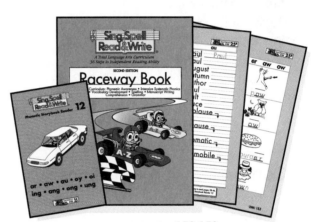

pp. 152-153

PROCEDURE

Have student:

- Open **Raceway Book** to p. 152 and circle the **aw** and **au** in each word.
- Read, write, and spell all words on p. 152.

Instructor: Initial and date boxes at bottom of p. 152.

Have student:

- Read pp. 28-46 in **Storybook Reader 12**.
- Read each story two or three times for fluency.
- Complete **Raceway Book** p. 153.

Instructor: Teach **Creative Writing Lesson** / Manual p. 139.

Phonics Song(s)/Games

Each day's lesson should begin with one or two previously learned phonics songs and end with a phonics game.

Written Spelling Tests and Homework

Each day dictate the previous day's 10 spelling "homework" words for a written spelling test. Following the test, have your student circle the next 10 words in the Raceway Book. These 10 spelling words will be for today's homework (writing sentences), and tomorrow's test. See p. 97 in this Manual for directions.

Phonetic Storybook Reader 12

Comprehension Questions

A Fawn at Dawn

Story 2 • pp. 28-37

Have student read orally the designated pages.
Ask the following questions:

After reading pp. 29-37:

Let student read each page aloud through the complete poem.

- **What was the same on each page?**
  Point out that the last word on lines 2 and 4 rhyme.

- Find rhyming words on each page.
- Let students say in their own words what each page is about.

Student and instructor may read poem together in unison.

Comprehension Questions

Saul and Paul

Story 3 • pp. 38-46

Have student read orally the designated pages.
Ask the following questions:

After reading p. 39:

- **How old are Saul and Paul?** *(Story Detail)*
  Seven years old

- **How do we know they like each other?**
  (Context Clue) It says, "They hardly ever find fault in each other."

After reading pp. 40-41:

- **What season of the year is it?**
  (Story Detail) Autumn

- **What is another word for autumn?**
  (Vocabulary Expansion) Fall

- **What happens to the leaves on the trees in autumn?** *(Inference/Drawing Conclusion)*
  They turn colors and fall off the trees.

- **What did Saul and Paul use to haul leaves?**
  (Picture Clue) A red pedal car and wagon

After reading pp. 42-43:

- **Did the twins play in the leaves *before* or *after* working hard?** *(Sequence)* After

- **How did Dad show he was proud of Paul and Saul?** *(Story Detail)* He gave them applause.

- **What does applause mean?**
  (Vocabulary Expansion) Clapping your hands

After reading pp. 44-46:

- **Why did Mom and Dad give them a treat?**
  (Story Detail) For doing a good job

- **What was the treat?** *(Story Detail)* Ice cream

- **Tell me how the leaf truck works.**
  (Inference/Drawing Conclusion)
  Like a huge vacuum

(Continued on next page)

- Why would Dad say they would ask Santa Claus for a leaf truck? *(Predicting)*
  So they wouldn't have to work so hard

- Do you think a family would ever own a truck like that? Why? *(Context Clue)*
  No; it's too expensive.

- In this story there are lots of leaves on the ground. Why? *(Cause and Effect)* It's fall.

- What could be another title for this story? *(Main Idea)* Answers will vary.

Complete p. 153 in Raceway Book. See directions below.

Raceway Book: Phonetic Analysis

Missing Sounds, *p. 153*
Fill in the missing letters and color the pictures.

p. 153

Creative Writing Lesson

This *Creative Writing Lesson* follows the reading of **Saul and Paul**, pp. 28-46 in Phonetic Storybook Reader 12, *The Car Book*.

- Have student think about where Saul and Paul played, worked, and things they did. Discuss the season when this story took place. Talk about some words that would describe autumn. Put the responses in a web as modeled below.
  Example:

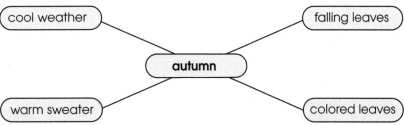

- Have student draw an autumn scene and write one or two sentences describing the picture.

Pretty colored leaves are falling to the ground in autumn.

RACEWAY STEP 25^C

Vocabulary and Reading

ing, ang, ong, and ung Words and Related Stories in Storybook Reader 12

Goals

To read, write, and spell words with letter clusters
ing, ang, ong, ung, oi, and **ou.**

To practice reading **ing, ang, ong, ung, oi,** and **ou**
words in context

To practice Grammar Skills

To take Book End Assessment

Suggested Pacing

3 days

Materials

1. *Raceway Book,* pp. 154-155

2. Phonetic Storybook Reader 12, *The Car Book,* pp. 47-64

3. Assessment Book for Phonetic Storybook Reader 12

pp. 154-155

PROCEDURE

Have student:

- Open **Raceway Book** to p. 154.
- Circle **ing, ang, ong, ung, oy** or **oi** in all the words.
- Read, write, and spell all words on p. 154.

Instructor: Initial and date boxes at bottom of p. 154.

Have student:

- Read pp. 47-64 in **Storybook Reader 12**.
- Read each story two or three times for fluency.
- Complete **Raceway Book** p. 155.

Instructor:

- Teach **Grammar Lessons**/Manual pp. 142-143.
- Introduce **Writing Stories for Spelling Homework**/Manual p. 143.
- Administer **Assessment**/Manual p. 144.

Phonics Song(s)/Games

Each day's lesson should begin with one or two previously learned phonics songs and end
with a phonics game.

Written Spelling Tests and Homework

Each day dictate the previous day's 10 spelling "homework" words for a written spelling test.
Following the test, have your student circle the next 10 words in the Raceway Book. These 10
spelling words will be for today's homework (writing sentences or a story), and tomorrow's test.
See pp. 97 and 143 in this Manual for directions.

140

Phonetic Storybook Reader 12

Comprehension Questions

A Play in the Basement, Bong!

Story 4 • pp. 47-60

Have student read orally the designated pages. Ask the following questions:

After reading pp. 48-49:

- Who gave a play and where was it?
  (Story Detail) Some kids; Eddy's basement
- Why would strong lungs be helpful to Joan?
  (Inference/Drawing Conclusion)
  Because she's a singer.

After reading pp. 50-51:

- What was the gong going to be used for?
  (Context Clue) Whenever King Edward would make a wish, the gong would ring.
- What was King Edward's first wish?
  (Story Detail) For a pretty bird to sing to him
- How do you think they will produce the things the king wishes for? *(Predicting)*
  Other kids will bring them in.

After reading pp. 52-53:

- Where did the bird come from? *(Picture Clue)*
  From under the table

After reading pp. 54-55:

- What are the three wishes that have been made? *(Story Detail)*
  1) A bird to sing
  2) An animal to ride
  3) A handsome prince to marry the princess

After reading pp. 56-67:

- How was the princess to get her handsome prince? *(Context Clue)* By kissing a frog

After reading pp. 58-59:

- Describe to me what happened. *(Story Detail)*
  The bird flew up, the throne toppled, the horse ran away, the ladder fell, and the gong went flying.

After reading p. 60:

- Which parts of this story could be true? Not true? *(Reality/Fantasy)* All of it could be true.
- Do you think this play was a success or failure? Why? *(Cause and Effect)* Success; everybody had a good time.
- Name the two groups of characters in this play. *(Classification)*
  People: King Eddie, Joan, and Danny
  Animals: a dog, a bird, a frog

Comprehension Questions

Enjoy! Enjoy!

Story 5 • pp. 61-64

Have student read orally the designated pages. Ask the following questions:

After reading pp. 62-64:

- This story is written as a poem. What makes it a poem? Rhythm and rhyming words
- On p. 62, what does "toil" mean? *(Vocabulary Expansion)* Work
- On page 62, what are the two rhyming pairs of words? On page 63? On page 64?
  Page 62: toil-boil; cream-dream
  Page 63: spoil-foil; join-coin
  Page 64: toy-enjoy; boy-joy

(Continued on next page)

- What made the picnic special? *(Context Clue)*
  Treats; Roy showed his wind-up toy.

Student and instructor may read poem in unison.

Reference Skills

Turn to Table of Contents on p. 2.

1) How many stories are in this book? 5

2) Which story does not have Sue Dickson as the author? A Fawn at Dawn

3) Which story may be about two boys? Saul and Paul

4) What page does **Harmony Hill Farm** begin on? End on? 3; 27

   Complete p. 155 in Raceway Book.
   See directions below.

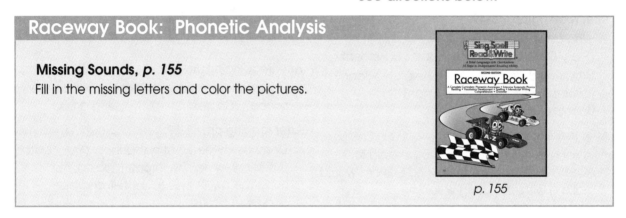

Raceway Book: Phonetic Analysis

Missing Sounds, p. 155

Fill in the missing letters and color the pictures.

p. 155

Grammar Chalkboard Lesson

ASKING SENTENCES REVIEW

Have student choose the correct question word from the Word Bank to complete the sentences.

Example: _Can_ you help me?

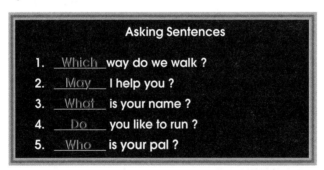

Asking Sentences

1. _Which_ way do we walk ?
2. _May_ I help you ?
3. _What_ is your name ?
4. _Do_ you like to run ?
5. _Who_ is your pal ?

Word Bank: Who, Do, What, Which, May

Grammar Lesson

TELLING AND ASKING SENTENCES REVIEW

Give your student two 3x5 cards. Write a period on one and a question mark on the other. Read aloud an asking or a telling sentence. Have student raise the card with the appropriate ending for each sentence.

Example: What did you eat for lunch?

   (Student holds up card with "?")

   I ate a sandwich and some fruit.

   (Student holds up card with ".")

Continue in same manner with examples of your own.

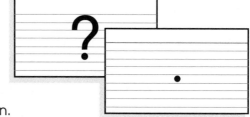

Writing Stories for Spelling Homework

Fold two sheets of paper and staple in the fold. This will make an eight page booklet. Have student write a title on the front cover. Write spelling words on the inside cover. Next, have student write a storybook using spelling words and illustrate each page.

Assessment Book

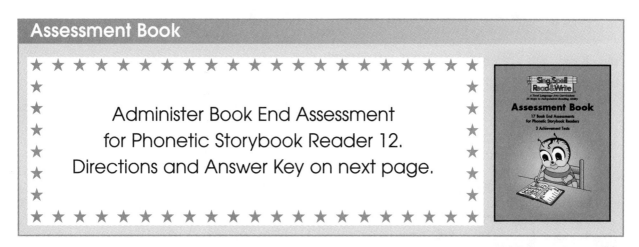

★ ★

Administer Book End Assessment
for Phonetic Storybook Reader 12.
Directions and Answer Key on next page.

Move Raceway Car to Step **26**

Directions and Answer Key

Book End Assessment
Phonetic Storybook Reader 12

Word Recognition: ar

Instructor: Direct student to "Put your finger on box #1. Now circle the word in the box that I call... 'harm.' Put your finger on box #2. Now circle the word 'tar,' etc." The words the instructor should call are listed below. Say each word distinctly with emphasis upon initial and final consonants.

1. harm	2. tar	3. dart	4. shark	5. spark
6. march	7. far	8. garden	9. sharp	10. yarn
11. cart	12. hard	13. park	14. charm	15. bar
16. mark	17. smart	18. Carl	19. yard	20. dark

Record scores in the space provided on the front cover of the Student Assessment Record and calculate the Percentage of Mastery Score as indicated.

p.1

Word Comprehension: ar

Directions: Tell your student to put his/her finger on box #1 again and listen to what you say:

Instructor: *Underline the word that (is)...*

1. a musical instrument. harp
2. something in which you ride. car
3. means to be intelligent. smart
4. something worn around the neck. scarf
5. something seen in the sky at night. star
6. a name for one of the planets. Mars
7. a glass container. jar
8. a kind of celebration. party
9. the sound made by a dog. bark
10. a place usually behind the house. yard
11. a place where a farmer keeps his animals. barn
12. means the same as begin. start
13. a place where flowers are grown. garden
14. a part of the body. arm
15. a class where you can learn how to draw. art
16. means the same as big. large
17. something you use if you are making a sweater. yarn
18. something you may get for your birthday. card
19. where you would shoot an arrow. target
20. a place where you might go to play. park

Record scores in the space provided on the front cover of the Student Assessment Record and calculate the Percentage of Mastery Score as indicated.

Raceway Step 25B

Book End Assessment
Phonetic Storybook Reader 12

Word Recognition: aw, au

Instructor: Direct student to "Put your finger on box #1. Now circle the word in the box that I call... 'awful.' Put your finger on box #2. Now circle the word 'fawn,' etc." The words the instructor should call are listed below. Say each word distinctly with emphasis upon initial and final consonants.

p. 2

1. awful	2. fawn	3. saw	4. because	5. sauce
6. bawl	7. raw	8. claw	9. automatic	10. haul
11. straw	12. lawn	13. dawn	14. autumn	15. crawl
16. applause	17. automobile	18. jaw	19. fault	20. flaw

Record scores in the space provided on the front cover of the Student Assessment Record and calculate the Percentage of Mastery Score as indicated.

Word Comprehension: aw, au

Directions: Tell your student to put his/her finger on box #1 again and listen to what you say:

Instructor: *Underline the word that (is)...*

1. a season of the year. autumn
2. the grassy area around the house. lawn
3. an animal's foot. paw
4. means to clap your hands. applause
5. something used to sip soda. straw
6. to move on your hands and knees. crawl
7. the rules that people must follow. law
8. something you can do with crayons. draw
9. a person who writes a book. author
10. means to blame. fault
11. a food that is put on top of other food. sauce
12. a carpenter's tool. saw
13. a baby deer. fawn
14. one of the months of the year. August
15. means to cry very loudly. bawl
16. a covering over the outside of a window or doorway. awning
17. means something that is very bad. awful
18. a large bird. hawk
19. a boy's name. Paul
20. means not cooked. raw

Record scores in the space provided on the front cover of the Student Assessment Record and calculate the Percentage of Mastery Score as indicated.

Directions and Answer Key

Book End Assessment
Phonetic Storybook Reader 12

Word Recognition: ing, ang, ong, oy, oi

Instructor: Direct student to "Put your finger on box #1. Now circle the word in the box that I call... 'clang.' Put your finger on box #2. Now circle the word 'song,' etc." The words the instructor should call are listed below. Say each word distinctly with emphasis upon initial and final consonants.

1. clang	2. song	3. king	4. sang	5. boy
6. enjoy	7. boil	8. joint	9. oil	10. strong
11. along	12. spoil	13. hang	14. annoy	15. rang
16. coin	17. Roy	18. royal	19. foil	20. thing

Record scores in the space provided on the front cover of the Student Assessment Record and calculate the Percentage of Mastery Score as indicated.

p.3

Word Comprehension: ing, ang, ong, oy, oi

Directions: Tell your student to put his/her finger on box #1 again and listen to what you say:

Instructor: *Underline the word that (is)...*

1. what the telephone did. rang
2. the opposite of weak. strong
3. something you wear on your finger. ring
4. a loud noise. bang
5. a play thing. toy
6. means to bother. annoy
7. a shiny metal paper. foil
8. to use your finger to show where something is. point
9. another name for dirt. soil
10. something you might put your clothes on. hanger
11. means to take it with you. bring
12. a name for metal money. coin
13. a part of a bird's body. wing
14. a way to cook food. broil
15. what you did to a song. sang
16. means to bring together. join
17. a child. boy
18. means to like very much. enjoy
19. a place where two things come together. joint
20. the man who rules a country. king

Record scores in the space provided on the front cover of the Student Assessment Record and calculate the Percentage of Mastery Score as indicated.

Sentence Comprehension

"Bubble" Format Directions pp. 69-70

1. D	6. B	11. C	16. B
2. C	7. D	12. A	17. D
3. E	8. A	13. B	18. E
4. A	9. E	14. E	19. A
5. B	10. C	15. D	20. C

Story Comprehension

"Bubble" Format Directions pp. 69-70

1. like
2. seven in August
3. autumn
4. to haul leaves
5. to fall in the leaves
6. at a picnic
7. Scouts and Brownies
8. worked
9. happy
10. candy

Vocabulary and Reading

o͝o Words and Related Stories in Storybook Reader 13

pp. 156-158

Goals

To read, write, and spell words with letter cluster o͞o

To practice reading o͞o words in context

Suggested Pacing

2 days

Materials

1. *Raceway Book*, pp. 156-158
2. Phonetic Storybook Reader 13, *The Boot Book*, pp. 3-31

PROCEDURE

Have student:

- Circle o͞o in all the words as indicated in #1 in **Raceway Book**, p.156.
- Read, write, and spell o͞o words on p. 156.

Instructor: Initial and date boxes at bottom of p. 156.
Have student:

- Read pp. 3-31 in **Storybook Reader 13**.
- Read each story two or three times for fluency.
- Complete **Raceway Book** pp.157-158.

Phonics Song(s)/Games

Each day's lesson should begin with one or two previously learned phonics songs and end with a phonics game.

Written Spelling Tests and Homework

Each day dictate the previous day's 10 spelling "homework" words for a written spelling test. Following the test, have your student circle the next 10 words in the Raceway Book. These 10 spelling words will be for today's homework (writing sentences or a story), and tomorrow's test. See pp. 97 and 143 in this Manual for directions.

Phonetic Storybook Reader 13

"Here we are at the zoo," said Janet.

"We can buy our tickets at this booth," said Fred. "This will be fun for us. The animals have lots of room to play in this zoo."

4

"See the seals swimming in that pool," said Janet. "They do tricks, too. See that one up on the stool. He has a big yellow balloon. Look at that one on the rock with a boot !"

"They **are** funny," said Fred.

5

Comprehension Questions

A Trip to the Zoo

Story 1 • pp. 3-13

Have student read orally the designated pages. Ask the following questions:

After reading pp. 4-5:

• Do you have to buy tickets to visit all zoos or are some free? *(Personal Experience)* Some may be free but most have to charge to help pay for the upkeep of the animals.

• Why do people go to zoos? *(Inference/Drawing Conclusion)* To see the animals and have fun

After reading pp. 6-7:

• What are the two kinds of animals in the pool? *(Context Clue)* Seals and polar bears

After reading pp. 8-9:

• Why does Janet think the tiger is sad? *(Story Detail)* The tiger wants food.

• What kind of food do you think the zookeeper has for the monkey? *(Predicting)* Answers will vary.

After reading pp. 10-13:

• What part of the zoo do they go to next? *(Story Detail)* The Children's Zoo

• How is this part of the zoo different from the part we first read about? *(Analyzing/Reality/Fantasy)* It has make believe animals.

• Why will Fred and Janet probably want to go back to the zoo someday? *(Context Clue)* They had a good time.

• What is the main idea of this story? *(Main Idea)* Going to the zoo

Suggestion:

• Check with your public library for a Mother Goose Nursery Rhyme book and share some favorite rhymes with your student.

Comprehension Questions

The Loose Tooth

Story 2 • pp. 14-31

Have student read orally the designated pages. Ask the following questions:

After reading p. 15:

• Who is going to be the main character in this story? *(Context Clue)* Tom Booth

• What do you know about him? *(Story Detail)* He is six years old and in first grade.

After reading pp. 16-17:

• Why was it necessary for Tom to get up on time? *(Context Clue)* He had to go to school.

• What did Tom do that shows he was in a good mood? *(Analyzing)* He jumped up.

Tom Booth is six years old. He is in the first grade at school.

15

After reading pp. 18-19:

• What did Tom have for breakfast? *(Story Detail)* An egg and some toast

• Why did Tom want his mom to eat with him? *(Inference/Drawing Conclusion)* So he wouldn't eat breakfast alone.

• What was the chore Tom had to do before he went to school? *(Story Detail)* He had to feed his pet goose.

(Continued on next page)

After reading pp. 20-21:

- As Tom was tying his shoe lace, what was the goose thinking? *(Story Detail)* "Tom is smart. He can tie his own shoes, That looks hard."
- What did Tom have to do to get to the bus on time? *(Story Detail)* He had to rush and run.

After reading pp. 22-23:

- Why is the bus honking its horn? *(Context Clue)* Because a puppy ran in front of the school bus.
- Why did Tom enjoy his day at school? *(Context Clue)* He played "Pop the Balloons."
- What made playing "Pop the Balloons" so much fun? *(Inference/Drawing Conclusion)* The boys and girls in his class clapped.

After reading pp. 24-25:

- What may happen if you bite into an apple with a loose tooth? *(Predicting)* It may come out.

After reading pp. 26-27:

- What did happen to Tom's loose tooth? *(Story Detail)* It came out in the apple.
- Do you think it hurt him to lose his tooth? *(Context Clue)* Probably not
- What would you do if your tooth came out at school? *(Personal Experience)* Answers will vary.

After reading pp. 28-29:

- What is the root of a tooth? *(Personal Experience)* The part that anchors the tooth to the gum

- Read aloud what Rick said to Tom. What does this tell us about Rick? *(Context Clue)* "Why don't you glue it back in with tooth-paste?" Rick likes to tease.
- Where do you think Tom kept his tooth the rest of the day? *(Predicting)* Probably in his pocket
- Do you think you will lose a tooth each time you bite into an apple? Why did Tom's tooth come out when he bit into the apple? *(Inference/Drawing Conclusion)* No; it was already loose.

After reading pp. 30-31:

- Why did Tom put his tooth under his pillow? *(Inference/Drawing Conclusion)* So the Tooth Fairy would come
- How does Tom feel this morning? *(Story Detail)* Tom is in a good mood.
- Why is he so happy? *(Context Clue)* Because the Tooth Fairy left him fifty cents
- What do you think Tom will share at Show and Tell? *(Predicting)* The money from the Tooth Fairy
- Who is the main character in this story? *(Analyzing)* Tom

Complete pp. 157-158 in Raceway Book. See directions below.

Raceway Book: Phonetic Analysis/Grammar

MISSING SOUNDS, *p. 157*
Fill in the missing letters and color the pictures.

PLURALS, *p. 158*
Tell student when a word ends in **sh, ch, s, x,** or **z,** add **es** to make it mean "more than one".

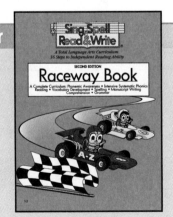

pp. 157-158

Vocabulary and Reading

o͝o Words and Related Stories in Storybook Reader 13

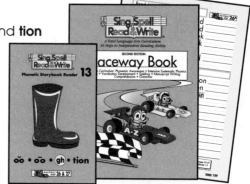

pp. 159-162

Goals

To read, write, and spell words with letter clusters **o͝o** and **tion**

To practice reading **o͝o** and **tion** words in context

To practice Grammar Skills

Suggested Pacing

3 days

Materials

1. *Raceway Book,* pp. 159-162
2. Phonetic Storybook Reader 13,
   The Boot Book, pp. 32-47

PROCEDURE

Have student:

- Circle **o͝o** and **tion** in all the words as indicated in #1 in **Raceway Book** p.159.
- Read, write, and spell all words on p. 159.

Instructor: Initial and date boxes at bottom of p. 159.

Have student:

- Read pp. 32-47 in **Storybook Reader 13**.
- Read each story two or three times for fluency.
- Complete **Raceway Book** pp. 160-162.

Instructor: Teach **Grammar Chalkboard Lesson**/Manual p. 152.

Phonics Song(s)/Games

Each day's lesson should begin with one or two previously learned phonics songs and end with a phonics game.

Written Spelling Tests and Homework

Each day dictate the previous day's 10 spelling "homework" words for a written spelling test. Following the test, have your student circle the next 10 words in the Raceway Book. These 10 spelling words will be for today's homework (writing sentences or a story), and tomorrow's test. See pp. 97 and 143 in this Manual for directions.

Note: After Step 26, if some of the spelling seems too difficult for your student, drop the spelling, (or just choose some of the easier words on each list), but continue all the way through the reading and writing. Whatever it takes, get to Step 36! It's worth the effort to know that your student has independent reading ability.

Phonetic Storybook Reader 13

Comprehension Questions

A Book, Hook-A-Fish, or Paint

Story 3 • pp. 32-38

Have student read orally the designated pages. Ask the following questions:

After reading p. 33:
- What is the teacher's name? *(Story Detail)* Miss Brooks
- Why are the kids clapping? *(Context Clue)* They like Choosing Time.

After reading pp. 34-35:
- Who wanted to look at books? *(Story Detail)* Bill, Patty, Kim, and Donna
- What is the title of Bill's book? *(Picture Clue)* "Robin Hood"

After reading pp. 36-37:
- Who was playing "Hook-a-Fish?" *(Story Detail)* Steve and Ann
- What do Jenny, Sally and Brad choose? *(Story Detail)* The big wooden blocks
- Why does Brad want them to look at him? *(Context Clue)* Because he's on one foot

- Why would we say Brad has good balance? *(Inference/Drawing Conclusion)* Because he's on one foot
- What will Brad do next? *(Sequence)* He will hop to the rug.

After reading p. 38:
- What other activities did some children choose? *(Story Detail)* Painting
- Who chose to paint? *(Story Detail)* Paul, Judy, and Janet
- What kind of personality do you think Miss Brooks has? *(Context Clue/Picture Clue)* Kind, patient, not bothered by noise and activity, loves children
- Name the three activities the children chose for "Choosing Time." *(Story Detail)* Blocks, painting, and books
- What could be another title for this story? *(Main Idea)* "Fun in School"

Comprehension Questions

Our Nation

Story 4 • pp. 39-47

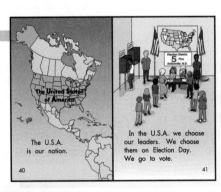

Have student read orally the designated pages. Ask the following questions:

After reading pp. 40-41:
- In the U.S.A., when do we choose our leaders? *(Story Detail)* On Election Day
- How do we choose our leaders? *(Story Detail)* We vote for them.
- Can you vote to choose our leaders? Who can vote? *(Personal Experience)* No; citizens who are 18 years old and up.

After reading pp. 42-43:
- What do men or women do who want to be leaders of our country? *(Context Clue)* They speak on TV/ give information/ tell us what they will do/ ask us to vote for them/ they tell us to take action to stop pollution

(Continued on next page)

- What is pollution? *(Picture Clue/Personal Experience)* Dirty air and/or water/trash

After reading pp. 44-45:

- Read what the man on television is saying. Tell me what it means. *(Interpretation)* People should obey the laws so we can keep our freedoms.

- Are all people always good? *(Personal/Experience)* No

- What is the "list of laws" called? *(Story Detail)* The Constitution

- What happens to people who do not follow the laws? *(Personal Experience)* They get in trouble and have to go to court.

- What do we have in our nation to help us do what is right? *(Inference/Drawing Conclusion)* Answers will vary.

After reading pp. 46-47:

- Why do we celebrate the Fourth of July? *(Story Detail)* It is the birthday of our nation.

- What are ways we celebrate the birthday of our nation? *(Inference/Drawing Conclusion)* We have parades and fireworks to show our appreciation for our nation.

- If you have a question about the U.S.A., what books could you look in? *(Story Detail)* A history book or sometimes a big dictionary

- Do you know how your family celebrates the Fourth of July? *(Personal Experience)* Answers will vary.

- Does this story give us some true information? How? *(Analyzing)* Yes; it tells us something about our nation.

- What did you learn from this story? *(Personal Experience)* Answers will vary.

Complete pp. 160-162 in Raceway Book. See directions below.

Raceway Book: Phonetic Analysis/Grammar

MISSING SOUNDS, pp. 160-161

Fill in the missing letters and color the pictures.

JUST FOR FUN, p. 162

Tell student we are sometimes lazy with our speech and slur words together. Words "have to" come out sounding like "hafta." This page is for fun and to stress correct pronunciation of phrases.

pp. 160-162

Grammar Chalkboard Lesson

CLASSIFICATION REVIEW

Write three headings, "Toys, Foods, and Buildings". Ask student to classify the following words under the correct heading: **hamburger, school, house, potatoes, bike, ball, skateboard, apple, store, church, banana, hotel, skates, beans, and doll**. Write the words under the appropriate heading.

Toys	Foods	Buildings
1. bike	1. hamburger	1. school
2. ball	2. potatoes	2. house
3. skateboard	3. apple	3. store
4. skates	4. banana	4. church
5. doll	5. beans	5. hotel

Move Raceway Car to Step **27**

Gh Clown Song

Gh Clown Song, gh Words, and Related Stories in Storybook Reader 13

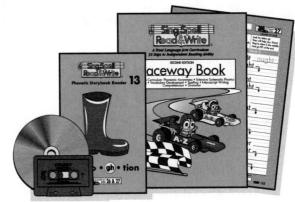

pp. 163-165

Goals
To learn the Gh Clown Song
To read, write, and spell words with **gh**
To practice reading **gh** words in context
To practice Grammar Skills
To take Book End Assessment, and
  Achievement Test 2

Suggested Pacing
5 days

Materials
1. *Raceway Book*, pp. 163-165
2. Phonetic Storybook Reader 13,
   The Boot Book, pp. 48-64
3. **Gh Clown Song**, CD or Cassette #6
4. Assessment Book: Assessment for Phonetic Storybook Reader 13/
               Achievement Test #2

PROCEDURE

Instructor:

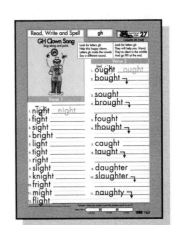

p. 163

- Have student open **Raceway Book** to p. 163 and draw a circle around letters **gh** in each word as shown.

- Explain to your student that **gh** is silent and doesn't say ANYTHING (in this list). **Gh** always causes the vowel(s) to say a different sound from what they usually say.

- Have student draw a slash mark through **gh**, as in #1, Verse 1.

- Have student draw the long vowel mark over each **i**, #1-12, Verse 1.

- Have student read down through the "**ight**" words. When you get to "**knight**", tell student to cover the **k** at the beginning and say the word. Talk about the meanings of **night** and **knight**. Tell him/her the knight in armor who helps the **k**ing always has a **k** for **king** at the beginning of the word.

- Play the **Gh Clown Song** for your student. Then, play it again and have student sing along through the chorus and Verse 1 (noting that **gh** is silent in each word and the vowel does say a different sound).

Chorus

Look for letters gh
Help this happy clown
Letters gh make the vowels
Say a different sound.

Look for letters gh
They will help you, friend,
They're silent in the middle
And go fff! at the end.

Verse 1

n-i-g-h-t says *night*   l-i-g-h-t says *light*
f-i-g-h-t says *fight*   t-i-g-h-t says *tight*
s-i-g-h-t says *sight*   r-i-g-h-t says *right*
b-r-i-g-h-t *bright*   s-l-i-g-h-t *slight*

(Sing Chorus)

Also teach *knight, fright, might, flight*
Instructor:
• Have student read, write, and spell all words for Verse #1.

p. 163

Verse 2

o-u-g-h-t says *ought*   f-o-u-g-h-t *fought*
b-o-u-g-h-t *bought*   t-h-o-u-g-h-t *thought*
s-o-u-g-h-t *sought*   c-a-u-g-h-t *caught*
b-r-o-u-g-h-t *brought*   t-a-u-g-h-t *taught*

(Sing Chorus)

Also teach *daughter, slaughter, naughty.*

Instructor:
• Tell student that **ou=au.** (**ou** sounds like **au** in these **gh** words.)
• Have student read, write, and spell all words for Verse #2.
• Initial and date boxes at bottom of p.163.

• Have student mark all **eigh=ā** words as shown in#1 Raceway Book, p. 164 and read the words.
• Next, have student read, write, and spell words #1-11.

Verse 3

l-a-u-g-h says *laugh*   Teacher: AGAIN!
c-o-u-g-h says *cough*   Chanting: E-N-O-U-G-H
r-o-u-g-h says *rough*   ENOUGH!
t-o-u-g-h says *tough*

(Sing Chorus)

Instructor:
• Tell student that **gh** on the end of words (in Verse 3) is not silent but goes **fff!** on the end. Read words #1-6, Verse 3 in **Raceway Book**.
• Have student read, write, and spell all words for Verse 3.
• In the last group of 6 words, tell student **gh** does not say **fff!** on the end but still changes the vowel sound.
• Have student read, write, and spell words.
• Initial and date boxes at bottom of p. 164.
• Continue to sing the **Gh Clown Song**.

p. 164

(Continued on next page)

Have student:
- Read pp. 48-64 in **Storybook Reader 13**.
- Read each story two or three times for fluency.
- Complete **Raceway Book** p. 165.

Instructor:
- Teach **Grammar Chalkboard Lessons**/Manual p. 157.
- Teach **Creative Writing Lesson**/Manual p.158.
- Administer **Assessment**/Manual p. 159.
- Administer **Achievement Test 2**/Manual p. 163.

Phonetic Storybook Reader 13

Comprehension Questions

The Neighborhood Costume Party
Story 5 • pp. 48-56

Have student read orally the designated pages.
Ask the following questions:

After reading p. 49:
- Who will be the main characters? *(Story Detail)* **Mark and Maria**
- What kind of party is it? *(Story Detail)* **A costume party**
- What kind of costume is Mark wearing? *(Story Detail)* **A knight**
- How will Mark help Maria? *(Story Detail)* **He'll collect the party food from the neighbors.**

After reading pp. 50-51:
- What is Maria doing to prepare for the party? *(Story Detail)* **Decorating a cake**
- What will Mark put the food in? *(Story Detail)* **A bag**
- Why could we say Mark is a responsible person? *(Inference/Drawing Conclusion)* **He is in charge of going out to get the party food from the neighbors.**

After reading pp. 52-53:
- How was Jenny dressed? *(Story Detail)* **As a pilgrim**
- What do you know about Pilgrims? *(Using Prior Knowledge)* **They had the first Thanksgiving.**
- Do you think most of the families in this neighborhood know each other? Why do you think this? *(Inference/Drawing Conclusion)* **Yes. Answers will vary.**

- What did Mr. Jones have for the party food? *(Story Detail)* **Doughnuts**

After reading pp. 54-55:
- Do you think Mr. Jones likes Mark and Jenny? Why do you say this? *(Inference/Drawing Conclusion)* **Yes. Because he compliments them.**
- After Mark and Jenny left Mr. Jones' house, what exciting thing happened? *(Story Detail/ Sequence)* **They saw two cats in a fight.**
- How do we know Jenny was a little frightened? *(Inference/Drawing Conclusion)* **She said she was glad Mark was with her when the two cats started to fight.**
- What did Dr. Mink have for the party food? *(Story Detail)* **Popcorn and apples**

After reading p. 56:
- How much is a ton? *(Expanding Vocabulary)* **Think of a pound of butter - Now think of 2,000 pounds of butter. That's a ton. The weight of a garbage truck is approximately a ton.**
- Did their bags really weigh a ton? What did they mean? *(Analyzing)* **No, they just meant their bags were heavy.**

(Continued on next page)

Comprehension Questions
The Tough Knight
Story 6 • pp. 57-64

One day King Tweek's daughter, Ann, was riding in a sleigh through her neighborhood. All at once...
58

...a naughty dragon jumped out at her! He was eighty feet long! He could cough a big bright fire!
59

Have student read orally the designated pages. Ask the following questions:

After reading pp. 58-59:

• Who is Ann? *(Inference/Drawing Conclusion)* A princess

• What was she riding in? *(Story Detail)* A sleigh

• What kind of weather do you need to use a sleigh? *(Inference/Drawing Conclusion)* Snow

• Describe what happened. *(Summarizing)* She was riding in her sleigh when a dragon jumped out of the woods.

• Try to compare the length of the dragon to something the students can identify with. The school building; cafeteria; etc.

After reading pp. 60-61:

• Why did the horses return to the palace? *(Context Clue)* They were afraid.

• What does "neighed" mean? *(Context Clue)* The sound that horses make

• Why would King Tweet call for a tough knight? *(Inference/Drawing Conclusion)* He needed someone who could fight.

• How long did the battle last? *(Story Detail)* Eight days

• What did the tough knight use to fight with? *(Picture Clue)* His hands and a shield

After reading pp. 62-63:

• What did the knight do that made the dragon give up? *(Story Detail)* He caught the dragon by the tail and the dragon fell on a big rock.

• What promise did the dragon make? *(Story Detail)* He promised not to frighten the princess again.

After reading p. 64:

• What is the lesson the dragon learned? Is it a lesson we all need to learn? *(Story Detail)* He learned that it is best not to fight or frighten anyone. Yes

• Where did the dragon go to live? *(Story Detail)* To the hills

• Why would we say this story ends like a fairy tale? *(Analyzing)* The knight and the princess got married and lived happily ever after.

• How do we know Princess Ann was happy with the tough knight? *(Inference/Drawing Conclusion)* She married him.

• Which characters in the story could be real? Fanciful? *(Reality/Fantasy)* The princess, king, and knight; the dragon

• What is the main idea of this story? *(Main Idea)* A knight captures a dragon for the king.

• What was the problem in this story? *(Analyzing)* A dragon was frightening a princess.

• How was it solved? *(Analyzing)* The knight caught the dragon.

Reference Skills

Turn to Table of Contents p. 2.

1) How many stories are in this book? 6

2) Which story has two authors? Our Nation

3) What page does **The Tough Knight** begin on? page 57

4) Can we tell what page it ends on? No Why? It's the last story in the book.

5) Which story may be about our country? Our Nation

Complete p. 165 in Raceway Book.
See directions on next page.

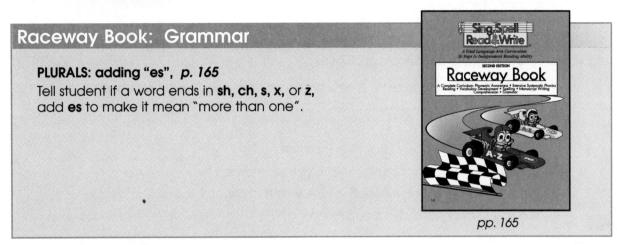

Raceway Book: Grammar

PLURALS: adding "es", *p. 165*
Tell student if a word ends in **sh, ch, s, x,** or **ż,**
add **es** to make it mean "more than one".

pp. 165

Grammar Chalkboard Lessons

CLASSIFICATION REVIEW

Write the headings **Fo͞od** and **Bo͝ok**. Student will place words from the word bank under the correct heading. Words that have o͞o will go under the heading **Food** and words with o͝o will go under the heading **Book**.

Fo͞od	Classification	Bo͝ok
1. loop		1. wool
2. cool		2. wood
3. root		3. hook
4. tooth		4. good
5. loose		5. foot
6. goose		6. stood

Word Bank: loop, cool, wool, wood, hook, root, good, tooth, loose, foot, stood, goose

NOUN AND VERB REVIEW

Write the sentences shown below. Student will underline the verb and circle the noun in each sentence.

Example: The (boy) ran away.

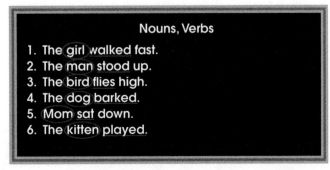

Nouns, Verbs
1. The girl walked fast.
2. The man stood up.
3. The bird flies high.
4. The dog barked.
5. Mom sat down.
6. The kitten played.

Creative Writing Lesson

This *Creative Writing Lesson* follows the reading of the story **The Tough Knight**, Phonetic Storybook Reader 13, *The Boot Book*, pp. 57-64.

- Tell student he/she is going to write a new ending for the story **The Tough Knight**. Have student think about what might have happened if the knight had not defeated the dragon. Help student organize thoughts by asking these questions:

  - Would the dragon have harmed the princess?
  - Would the princess and Knight have gotten married?
  - Would the princess have fallen in love with the prince?
  - Would Princess Ann have been frightened?

- Have student write a different ending for the story based on the discussion, then illustrate the new ending.

Assessment Book

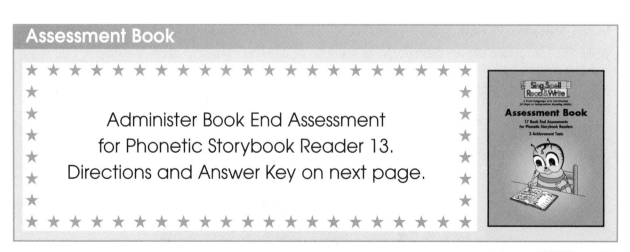

Administer Book End Assessment
for Phonetic Storybook Reader 13.
Directions and Answer Key on next page.

Move
Raceway Car
to Step **28**

Raceway Step 26A

Book End Assessment
Phonetic Storybook Reader 13

Word Recognition: o͞o

Instructor: Direct student to "Put your finger on box #1. Now circle the word in the box that I call... 'root.' Put your finger on box #2. Now circle the word 'pool,' etc." The words the instructor should call are listed below. Say each word distinctly with emphasis upon initial and final consonants.

1. root	2. pool	3. loop	4. mood	5. bloom
6. smooth	7. soon	8. tool	9. hoop	10. loose
11. fool	12. noon	13. cool	14. balloon	15. stoop
16. stool	17. food	18. tooth	19. broom	20. shoot

Record scores in the space provided on the front cover of the Student Assessment Record and calculate the Percentage of Mastery Score as indicated.

p.1

Word Comprehension: o͞o

Directions: Tell your student to put his/her finger on box #1 again and listen to what you say:

Instructor: *Underline the word that (is)...*

1. the sound a toy trumpet makes. toot
2. something a carpenter uses. tool
3. the time we go to lunch. noon
4. a place to go and see animals. zoo
5. what you use to sweep the floors. broom
6. something found in your mouth. tooth
7. something you use when eating. spoon
8. a place to sit. stool
9. a part of a house. room
10. something to eat. food
11. a place to go swimming. pool
12. something you may see in the night sky. moon
13. something to wear on your foot. boot
14. a large bird. goose
15. the top of a house. roof
16. means to trick someone. fool
17. the part of the tree that grows in the ground. root
18. another name for a flower. bloom
19. means to have very little money. poor
20. a child's toy. balloon

Record scores in the space provided on the front cover of the Student Assessment Record and calculate the Percentage of Mastery Score as indicated.

Raceway Step 26B

Book End Assessment
Phonetic Storybook Reader 13

Word Recognition: ŏŏ, tion

Instructor: Direct student to "Put your finger on box #1. Now circle the word in the box that I call... 'brook.' Put your finger on box #2. Now circle the word 'hood,' etc." The words the instructor should call are listed below. Say each word distinctly with emphasis upon initial and final consonants.

1. brook	2. hood	3. took	4. crook	5. stood
6. book	7. foot	8. shook	9. wood	10. good
11. addition	12. action	13. foundation	14. invention	15. nation
16. station	17. information	18. attention	19. election	20. vacation

Record scores in the space provided on the front cover of the Student Assessment Record and calculate the Percentage of Mastery Score as indicated.

p. 2

Word Comprehension: ŏŏ, tion

Directions: Tell your student to put his/her finger on box #1 again and listen to what you say:

Instructor: *Underline the word that (is)...*

1. what you use to catch a fish. hook
2. the opposite of bad. good
3. something you get from trees. wood
4. the hair of sheep. wool
5. to have moved back and forth quickly. shook
6. what you might do to food. cook
7. what you do with your eyes. look
8. a small stream. brook
9. something to wear over your head. hood
10. something to read. book
11. something you might do in the summer. vacation
12. a place where you go to get on the train or bus. station
13. means to watch carefully. attention
14. things that make the air, water and land dirty. pollution
15. a time to go and vote. election
16. a big party. celebration
17. a book that tells you what words mean. dictionary
18. the bottom part of a building. foundation
19. means two numbers added together. addition
20. something that someone makes. invention

Record scores in the space provided on the front cover of the Student Assessment Record and calculate the Percentage of Mastery Score as indicated.

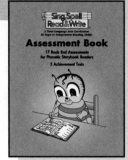

Book End Assessment
Phonetic Storybook Reader 13

Word Recognition: gh

Instructor: Direct student to "Put your finger on box #1. Now circle the word in the box that I call... 'slaughter.' Put your finger on box #2. Now circle the word 'fright,' etc." The words the instructor should call are listed below. Say each word distinctly with emphasis upon initial and final consonants.

1. slaughter	2. fright	3. might	4. thought	5. fight
6. naughty	7. flight	8. bright	9. ought	10. knight
11. taught	12. fight	13. slight	14. caught	15. brought
16. daughter	17. tight	18. right	19. sight	20. bright

Record scores in the space provided on the front cover of the Student Assessment Record and calculate the Percentage of Mastery Score as indicated.

p. 3

Word Comprehension: gh

Directions: Tell your student to put his/her finger on box #1 again and listen to what you say:

Instructor: *Underline the word that (is)...*

1. what you hear after someone tells a joke. laughter
2. a man that wore armor. knight
3. what you turn on when it is dark. light
4. what you did when you paid money for something. bought
5. the opposite of left. right
6. what a teacher did. taught
7. what the two boxers did. fought
8. the opposite of day. night
9. a girl is this to her parents. daughter
10. the opposite of loose. tight
11. something you think. thought
12. what you did with a ball thrown at you. caught
13. an airplane trip. flight
14. what our eyes provide us. sight
15. another word for power. might
16. means to be shiny. bright
17. means to act badly. naughty
18. an argument using fists. fight
19. means perhaps you should. ought
20. means to have looked for something. sought

Record scores in the space provided on the front cover of the Student Assessment Record and calculate the Percentage of Mastery Score as indicated.

Raceway Step 27

Book End Assessment
Phonetic Storybook Reader 13

Word Recognition: gh

Instructor: Direct student to "Put your finger on box #1. Now circle the word in the box that I call... 'dough.' Put your finger on box #2. Now circle the word 'trough,' etc." The words the instructor should call are listed below. Say each word distinctly with emphasis upon initial and final consonants.

1. dough	2. trough	3. through	4. eighty	5. enough
6. freight	7. eightieth	8. tough	9. rough	10. sigh
11. eight	12. neighbor	13. sleigh	14. neigh	15. weigh
16. eighteen	17. though	18. weight	19. laugh	20. cough

Record scores in the space provided on the front cover of the Student Assessment Record and calculate the Percentage of Mastery Score as indicated.

p. 4

Word Recognition: gh

Directions: Tell your student to put his/her finger on box #1 again and listen to what you say:

Instructor: *Underline the word that (is)...*

1. the number that is after seven. eight
2. a vehicle that can move over the snow. sleigh
3. a person that lives next door to you. neighbor
4. what you might do if you have a cold. cough
5. the measure of how heavy something is. weight
6. the sound that a horse makes. neigh
7. the number that comes after 17. eighteen
8. a sound of happiness. laugh
9. a feeding place for animals. trough
10. uncooked bread. dough
11. means to be strong. tough
12. the place where you live. neighborhood
13. the cargo carried by a train, plane, truck or boat. freight
14. a sound made when you are sad or tired. sigh
15. a number. eighty
16. means to have what you need. enough
17. means going in one side and out the opposite side. through
18. the opposite of low. high
19. a number. eightieth
20. means not smooth. rough

Record scores in the space provided on the front cover of the Student Assessment Record and calculate the Percentage of Mastery Score as indicated.

Sentence Comprehension

"Bubble" Format Directions pp. 69-70

1. B	6. D	11. C	16. D	21. E
2. C	7. B	12. D	17. A	22. C
3. A	8. E	13. A	18. E	23. A
4. E	9. A	14. E	19. B	24. B
5. D	10. C	15. B	20. C	25. D

Story Comprehension

"Bubble" Format Directions pp. 69-70

1. U.S.A.
2. on Election Day
3. Yes
4. leaders
5. an important day
6. The Constitution
7. the leaders who started our nation
8. freedom
9. U.S.A.
10. the Constitution

DIRECTIONS FOR ACHIEVEMENT TEST 2

Achievement Test 2 may be used:

- As a post assessment to measure growth
- To determine mastery of skills

TO BEGIN

- Remove Achievement Test #2 from back of student's Assessment Book.

ADMINISTERING

SECTION A: Letter Cluster Sounds

- Direct student to write the letter cluster for each picture in the spaces provided.
- Stop when you see the **STOP** .

SECTION B: Word Recognition

- Look at the pictures in each box and circle the word that names the picture.
- Read all four words before choosing your answer.
- Stop when you complete #8 and see the **STOP** .

SECTION C: Word Comprehension

- Read the underlined word at the top of each box and then read the four words below it.
- Circle the word that means almost the same as the underlined word.
- Use this example:

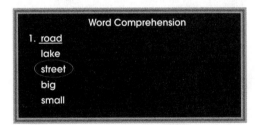

Word Comprehension

1. road
   lake
   street
   big
   small

- Stop when you complete #4 and see the **STOP** .

SECTION D: Compound Words

- Draw lines to match words and make a compound word.
- Remember that compound words are two words put together to make one word.
- Use this example:

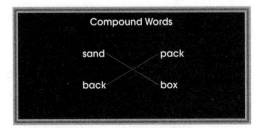

Compound Words

sand   pack

back   box

- Stop when you complete #4 and see the **STOP** .

SECTION E: Alphabetical Order

- Arrange the two groups of words in A-B-C order by using 1, 2, 3.
- Use this example:

Alphabetical Order

1. bib 2
   pop 3
   apple 1

- Stop when you are finished and see the (STOP).

SECTION F: Sentence Comprehension

- Look at the four pictures in each box.
- Read the sentence in the box and put an X on the picture that goes with the sentence.
- Stop when you complete #6 and see the (STOP).

SECTION G: Rhyming Words

- Read the three words in each box.
- Circle the two words in each box that rhyme.
- Use this example:

Rhyming Words

1. (book)
   sun
   (look)

- Stop when you complete #8 and see the (STOP).

SECTION H: Punctuation

- Read the two sentences and put a period or question mark at the end of each sentence.
- Stop when you complete #2 and see the (STOP).

SCORING ACHIEVEMENT TEST 2

- There are 50 items on Achievement Test 2.
- Score each Section, total the number of items correct, and multiply by 2. This will give the student's Percentage of Mastery Score.
- 40 items correct x 2 = 80%. (40 x 2 = 80%)
- **If student scores 80% or above, it is suggested that he/she is ready for Raceway Step 28.**

164

ACHIEVEMENT TEST 2

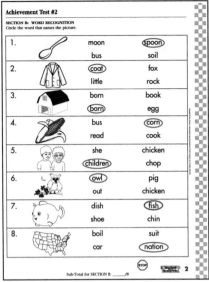

Achievement Test #2

SECTION A: Letter Cluster Sounds
Have student write the letter cluster for each box. Allow 5 seconds per item. Draw a line through each miscue.

o w l		o r bit
sn o w man		c h andelier
p h one		c h ild
c a r		bo o k
m oo n		a r m
s h ell		na t io n
ya w n		ha n g er
t u r tle		r o y alty

1   Sub-Total for SECTION A: _____/16   STOP

Achievement Test #2

SECTION B: WORD RECOGNITION
Circle the word that names the picture.

1.	moon	(spoon)
	bus	soil
2.	(coat)	fox
	little	rock
3.	born	book
	(barn)	egg
4.	bus	(corn)
	read	cook
5.	she	chicken
	(children)	chop
6.	(owl)	pig
	out	chicken
7.	dish	(fish)
	shoe	chin
8.	boil	suit
	car	(nation)

Sub-Total for SECTION B: _____/8   STOP   2

Achievement Test #2

SECTION C: Word Comprehension
Read the underlined word at the top of each box. Read the four words below it. Circle the word that means almost the same as the underlined word.

1. **shout**	2. **large**	3. **hop**	4. **boat**
(yell)	slow	sleep	car
wave	pet	(jump)	bike
ask	fast	listen	(ship)
laugh	(big)	climb	clock

STOP

Total for SECTION C: _____/4

SECTION D: Compound Words
Draw lines to match words and make compound words. Remember that compound words are two words put together to make one word.

1. sun — cake
2. cup — boat
3. sail — bow
4. rain — shine

STOP

Total for SECTION D: _____/6

SECTION E: Alphabetical Order
Arrange the two groups of words in A-B-C order by using 1, 2, 3.

goat	3	hay	1
dear	1	want	3
face	2	rest	2

STOP

Total for SECTION E: _____/4

Total for SECTION F: _____/2

3

Achievement Test #2

SECTION F: Sentence Comprehension
Look at the four pictures in each box. Read the sentence in the box and put an x on the picture that goes with the sentence.

1. Mark the flowers.
2. Here are two apples.
3. This is a girl.
4. The dog is under the table.
5. What will make you hot?
6. Mark the sign that says you cannot go in.

STOP   4

Total for SECTION D: _____/6

Achievement Test #2

SECTION G: Rhyming Words
Read the three words in each box. Circle the two words in each box that rhyme.

1. look	2. (log)	3. (corn)	4. (hook)
(moon)	big	(horn)	like
(soon)	(frog)	gain	(crook)
5.(less)	6.(long)	7. boy	8.(come)
(mess)	(song)	(soil)	love
this	sing	(boil)	(some)

STOP

Total for SECTION G: _____/8

SECTION H: Punctuation
Read the sentences and put a period or question mark at the end of each sentence.

1. The girl can curl her hair .
2. Is the little bird hurt ?

STOP

Total for SECTION H: _____/2

5

Sing, Spell Read & Write

Vocabulary and Reading

all, ar=or, dge, and ue Words and Related Stories in Storybook Reader 14

Goals

To read, write, and spell words with **all**, **ar=or**, **dge**, and **ue**

To practice reading **all**, **ar=or**, **dge**, and **ue**
words in context

To practice Grammar skills

Suggested Pacing

2 days

Materials

1. *Raceway Book*, pp. 166-167
2. Phonetic Storybook Reader 14, *The Ball Book*, pp. 3-29

pp. 166-167

PROCEDURE

Have student:

- Circle the **all, ar=or, dge, and ue** in all the words as indicated in #1.
- Open **Raceway Book to** p.166 and read, write, and spell all words on p. 166.

Instructor: Initial and date boxes at bottom of p. 166.

Have student:

- Read pp. 3-29 in **Storybook Reader 14.**
- Read each story two or three times for fluency.
- Complete **Raceway Book** p. 167.

Instructor: Teach **Grammar Chalkboard Lesson**/Manual p. 169.

Phonics Song(s)/Games

Each day's lesson should begin with one or two previously learned phonics songs and end with a phonics game.

Written Spelling Tests and Homework

Each day dictate the previous day's 10 spelling "homework" words for a written spelling test. Following the test, have your student circle the next 10 words in the Raceway Book. These 10 spelling words will be for today's homework (writing sentences or a story), and tomorrow's test. See pp. 97 and 143 in this Manual for directions.

Phonetic Storybook Reader 14

Comprehension Questions

The Baseball Team

Story 1 • pp. 3-7

Have student read orally the designated pages.
Ask the following questions:

After reading pp. 4-5:

- What are all these children hoping for? *(Story Detail)* To be picked for the basketball team
- Do you think someone who is not tall, but plays basketball very well would have a chance to be chosen? *(Predicting)* Yes
- Who is very confident they will be chosen? *(Story Detail)* The tall kids

After reading pp. 6-7:

- How did Coach Dobbs let the children know if they made the team? *(Context Clue)* He called them into his office one by one.
- Why was Nick chosen for the team? *(Context Clue)* Because he's fast.
- What did Nick say that tells us he will work hard? *(Inference/Drawing Conclusion)* "We will all do our best for the team."

Comprehension Questions

No War

Story 2 • pp. 8-14

Have student read orally the designated pages.
Ask the following questions:

After reading pp. 9-14:

- Tell me what happened on p. 9. *(Summarizing)* A sailor washed ashore after his boat wrecked in a storm.
- Who are the natives? *(Context Clue)* The people who live on the island
- What are the natives afraid of? *(Context Clue)* The huge man with a loud snore
- What do they want to do to prevent war? *(Context Clue)* Prepare for war and tie up the stranger
- Tell me what happened on pp. 12-13. *(Summarizing)* They poked him on his wart and he woke up with an awful snort.

- Why are the giant and the native shaking hands on page 1 *(Inference/Drawing Conclusion)* They decided to treat each other right and be friends.
- Go back and find the rhyming words on each page. (Point out this is what gives it rhyme and rhythm.) *(Decoding/Rhyming)*

  page 10: down - town; roar - war
  page 11: tight - tonight; be - me
  page 12: wart - snort
  page 13: sky - high
  page 14: right - fight; you - do
  more - war

Instructor and student will read poem in unison.

Comprehension Questions

Mrs. Hodge's Surprise

Story 3 • pp. 15-23

The boys missed Mrs. Hodges! She had gone to Park Ridge. She had been away for weeks now. She always let Ray and David play dodge-ball in her yard. She was a very nice neighbor.
16

"Let's fix up her yard," said Ray and David.

Ray and David ran to get the lawn mower. Ray lifted the latch of the tool shed. There was the mower wedged way in the back.
17

Have student read orally the designated pages. Ask the following questions:

After reading pp. 16-17:

- Where had Mrs. Hodges gone? *(Story Detail)* To Park Ridge
- Why did Ray and David think Mrs. Hodges is a good neighbor? *(Inference/Drawing Conclusion)* She let them play dodge ball in her yard.
- What did they decide to do for her? *(Story Detail)* Fix up her yard
- Do you think they will be able to fix up the yard by themselves? *(Predicting)* Probably

After reading pp. 18-19:

- Write the following sentences and have student number them in sequence. *(Sequence)*

  2 Ray lifted the tools out of the way.

  1 Ray ran home to get the lawn mower.

  4 He nudged the mower away from the window.

  3 The handle was caught under the ledge.

After reading pp. 20-21:

- What two things did Ray and David do in Mrs. Hodges' yard? *(Story Detail)* They cut the lawn and trimmed the hedge.
- How do you think Mrs. Hodges will feel when she sees her yard? *(Predicting)* Wonderful

After reading pp. 22-23:

- What was the surprise? *(Story Detail)* A box of fudge
- What is a pledge? *(Vocabulary Expansion/Context Clue)* A promise
- What did Ray and David pledge to do? *(Story Detail)* To take care of Mrs. Hodges' lawn every week
- Could this story be true? *(Reality/Fantasy)* Yes
- What is the main idea of this story? *(Main Idea)*

  Mrs. Hodges went away for weeks.

  The lawn mower was caught under the window ledge.

  ✓ Mrs. Hodges and Ray and David are good neighbors.

Comprehension Questions

Sue Makes Valentines

Story 4 • pp. 24-29

Sing Spell Read&Write

Phonetic Storybook Reader 14

all • ar=or • dge • ue • ie
x=cks • eā • ēa • ear=er
f to ves

RACEWAY STEP 28

Sue helped her mother open the fireplace flue. They made a nice warm fire.

"February 14 will be here soon," said Sue. "I must make my valentines today."

Have student read orally the designated pages. Ask the following questions:

After reading p. 25:

- Which holiday is coming soon? *(Story Detail)* Valentine's Day

- What does Sue say she must do today? *(Story Detail)* Make her valentines

(Continued on next page)

- What is a fireplace flue? Why does it need to be open? *(Personal Experience)* A door-like thing in the chimney that needs to be open to let the smoke go up and out.

After reading pp. 26-27:

- What are four things that Sue used to make her valentines? *(Context Clue)* Scissors, glue, paper, and lace

- Read what she wrote on each one? *(Story Detail)* "It is true, I love you."

After reading pp. 28-29:

- Instead of writing her name, what did Sue use? *(Story Detail)* A number code

- Explain this code to me. *(Interpretation)* 19=S (the 19th letter of the alphabet, etc.)

    21=U   5=E

- How did she get her valentine to her friends? *(Story Detail)* She mailed them.

- Who is the main character in this story? *(Analyzing)* Sue

- What was the problem in this story? *(Analyzing)* Sue needed to make her valentines and mail them that day.

- How did she solve it? *(Analyzing)* She got to work and completed the job.

Complete p. 167 in Raceway Book. See directions below.

Raceway Book: Comprehension

FILL IN THE BLANK, p. 167
Read each sentence and choose a word from the word bank to complete it.

p. 167

Grammar Chalkboard Lesson

A-B-C ORDER REVIEW

Write the following groups of words. Student will arrange them in A-B-C order by numbering 1-4.

Example: Gus   2
              Max   4
              hum   3
              can   1

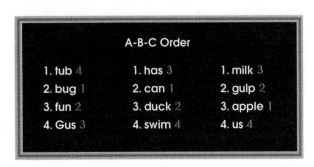

A-B-C Order

1. tub 4	1. has 3	1. milk 3
2. bug 1	2. can 1	2. gulp 2
3. fun 2	3. duck 2	3. apple 1
4. Gus 3	4. swim 4	4. us 4

Vocabulary and Reading

x = cks, i¢ = ē, and ¢a = ā Words and Related Stories in Storybook Reader 14

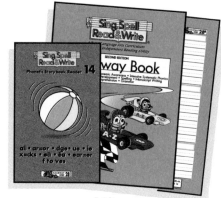

p.168

Goals

To read, write, and spell words with

x = cks, ie = ē, ¢a = ā

To read stories with **x = cks, ie = ē, and ¢a = ā** words in context

To practice Grammar Skills

Suggested Pacing

2 days

Materials

1. *Raceway Book*, p. 168
2. Phonetic Storybook Reader 13, *The Ball Book*, pp. 30-44

PROCEDURE

Have student:

- Open **Raceway Book** to p.168 and mark all the words as indicated in #1.
- Read, write, and spell all words on p. 168.

Instructor: Initial and date boxes at bottom of p. 168.

Have student:

- Read pp. 30-44 in **Storybook Reader 14**.
- Read each story two or three times for fluency.

Instructor:

- Teach **Grammar Chalkboard Lessons**/Manual p. 172.
- Teach **Creative Writing Lesson**/Manual p. 173.

Phonics Song(s)/Games

Each day's lesson should begin with one or two previously learned phonics songs and end with a phonics game.

Written Spelling Tests and Homework

Each day dictate the previous day's 10 spelling "homework" words for a written spelling test. Following the test, have your student circle the next 10 words in the Raceway Book. These 10 spelling words will be for today's homework (writing sentences or a story), and tomorrow's test. See pp. 97 and 143 in this Manual for directions.

Sing Spell Read&Write

Phonetic Storybook Reader 14

Comprehension Questions
Uncle Max
Story 5 • pp. 30-36

Tony loved to help his Uncle Max. Uncle Max could fix anything. He could do so many things.
31

Have student read orally the designated pages. Ask the following questions:

After reading p. 31:
- Describe Uncle Max. *(Summarizing)* He can fix anything.

After reading pp. 32-33:
- Name the three things Tony helped Uncle Max do. *(Story Detail)*
  1) Make a toolbox
  2) Sharpen an ax
  3) Clean and wax his car

After reading pp. 34-35:
- What did Uncle Max ask Tony to do next? *(Story Detail)* Mix the paint
- Why do you think Tony was glad to do something by himself? *(Predicting)* To show Uncle Max how grown-up he is

- What did Uncle Max compare Tony to? *(Comparing)* An ox and a fox
- Why would he use an ox and a fox to make this comparison? *(Inference/Drawing Conclusion)* Because an ox is strong and a fox is smart.

After reading p. 36:
- What did Tony sit down to do? *(Story Detail)* Relax
- What is another word for relax? *(Vocabulary Expansion)* Rest
- What is the setting of this story? *(Analyzing)* Probably the garage or basement

Comprehension Questions
The Jewel Thief
Story 6 • pp. 37-40

Jill was reading The Greenfield News to her mom. Jill said, "The Chief of Police believes a thief stole a briefcase full of jewels from the Greenfield Pier."

Jill went on reading...
38

The Greenfield N

Jewel Thief at Pier

A priest and his niece, who were on the pier yesterday, saw a big car leave the pier at a fierce speed.

"It went through a yield sign," said the priest. "It made so much dust, I had to shield my face for a brief time. I did not get the license plate number."

39

Have student read orally the designated pages. Ask the following questions:

After reading pp. 38-40:
- What is the name of the newspaper? *(Story Detail)* The Greenfield News
- Tell me in a few words what has happened? *(Summarizing)* A thief stole a briefcase full of jewels.
- Where did the theft occur? *(Story Detail)* At the Greenfield Pier

- Where would a pier be located? *(Personal Experience)* By a river or other body of water
- What do you think Jill's mother thinks of their police chief? *(Inference/Drawing Conclusion)* She likes him and believes he will do his job.
- What is the main idea of this story? *(Main Idea)* A thief has stolen a briefcase full of jewels in a town called Greenfield.

At break of day
Sat Little Dan
Cooking his steak
42 In a frying pan.

Out of the woods came a
great big bear !
43

Comprehension Questions

A Bear's Steak

Story 7 • pp. 41-44

Have student read orally the designated pages.
Ask the following questions:

After reading pp. 42-44:

- Tell me what happened. *(Summarizing)* Dan
  is cooking a steak at a cookout when a big
  brown bear came out of the woods. Dan
  climbed a tree to safety.

- Did Dan have the breakfast he had planned
  to have? *(Inference/Drawing Conclusion)* No

- Find the rhyming words on page 42. (Pages
  43 and 44 go together.) *(Decoding/Rhyming
  Words)* 42) Dan - pan; 43 & 44) bear - pear

*Student and Instructor will read together
in unison.*

Grammar Chalkboard Lessons

SUPERLATIVE REVIEW: er and est

Ask student to name words to which **er** and **est** could be added. Write them.
Example:

Superlatives

cold, colder, coldest
warm, warmer, warmest
tall, taller, tallest
short, shorter, shortest
big, bigger, biggest
cool, cooler, coolest

SYLLABICATION

Review with student the different ways of dividing words into parts or syllables.

Syllabication

1. hunted hunt-ed
2. hilltop hill-top
3. silly sil-ly
4. longest long-est
5. sunset sun-set

1. quickest quick-est
2. marry mar-ry
3. dustpan dust-pan
4. little lit-tle
5. shorter short-er

Sing Spell Read & Write

RACEWAY STEP 28^B

Creative Writing Lesson

This *Creative Writing Lesson* follows the reading of the story **A Bear's Steak**, pp. 41-44, in *Phonetic Storybook Reader 14, The Ball Book*.

- Have student think about other animals (besides the bear) that could have come out of the woods. Tell student to close his/her eyes and visualize this animal.

  - What does it look like?

  - Is it scary?

  - Would Dan have climbed a tree to get away?

- Ask your student to write three or four sentences to describe the animal and illustrate it.

RACEWAY STEP 28^C

Vocabulary and Reading

ea̸ = ĕ, ea̸ r=er, f to "ves" Words and Related Stories in Storybook Reader 14

Goals
To read, write, and spell words with letter cluster **ea̸ = ĕ, ea̸r=er, f to "ves"**
To practice reading **ea̸ = ĕ, ea̸r=er, f to "ves"** words in stories
To practice Grammar Skills
To take Book End Assessment

Suggested Pacing
3 days

Materials
1. *Raceway Book*, pp. 169-170
2. Phonetic Storybook Reader 14, *The Ball Book*, pp. 45-64
3. Assessment Book: Book End Assessment for Phonetic Storybook Reader 14

PROCEDURE

Have student:

- Open **Raceway Book** to p.169 and mark each word as indicated in #1.
- Read, write, and spell each word on p. 169.

Instructor: Initial and date boxes at bottom of p. 169.

Have student:

- Read pp. 45-64 in **Storybook Reader 14**.
- Read each story two or three times for fluency.
- Complete **Raceway Book** p. 170.

Instructor:

- Teach **Grammar Chalkboard**/Manual p. 176.
- Administer **Assessment**/Manual p. 177.

Phonics Song(s)/Games

Each day's lesson should begin with one or two previously learned phonics songs and end with a phonics game.

Written Spelling Tests and Homework

Each day dictate the previous day's 10 spelling "homework" words for a written spelling test. Following the test, have your student circle the next 10 words in the Raceway Book. These 10 spelling words will be for today's homework (writing sentences or a story), and tomorrow's test. See pp. 97 and 143 in this Manual for directions.

Phonetic Storybook Reader 14

Comprehension Questions

A Breath of Spring

Story 8 • pp. 45-53

"The weather is perfect," said Heather. "Not a cloud in heaven. Spring must be here at last!"
"Let's get ready to go out in our boat," said Gus.
46

"Fine," said Mother. "Put on your sweaters or your leather jackets. It is still cool."
Mother tied a scarf on her head.
47

Have student read orally the designated pages. Ask the following questions:

After reading pp. 46-47:

- What season of the year is it? *(Context Clue)* Spring
- What season comes before spring? after spring? *(Sequence)* Winter/Summer
- Why do Gus and Heather think the weather is perfect? *(Story Detail)* There are no clouds in the sky.
- What are they going to do to enjoy the spring day? *(Story Detail)* Take a boat ride
- Why do they need a sweater or jacket? *(Cause and Effect)* It is still cool.

After reading pp. 48-49:

- When Gus saw men catching fish, what did it help him remember? *(Inference/Drawing Conclusion)* That eating fish is good for your health

- What will she serve with the fish? *(Story Detail)* Fresh bread and butter
- What could they catch besides fish? *(Predicting)* Crabs, old tires, tin cans, etc.

After reading pp. 50-51:

- If a feather landed on your head, could you feel it? Why not? *(Analyzing)* Maybe not. A feather is very light.

After reading pp. 52-53:

- What is Gus' problem? *(Analyzing)* A button caught on a nail
- How did he solve it? *(Analyzing)* He put it in his pocket.
- Who helped him solve it? *(Story Detail)* Mom
- What is Mom's opinion about their outing? *(Inference/Drawing Conclusion)* She said it was good for their health.

Comprehension Questions

The Search for the Pearls

Story 9 • pp. 54-64

Have student read orally the designated pages.
Ask the following questions:

After reading p. 55:

- What season of the year do you think it is?
  (Context Clue/Picture Clue) Fall
- What does Grandfather ask Earl?
  (Story Detail) If he had ever heard the story
  "The Search for the Pearls."

After reading pp. 56-57:

- What do you think Grandmother meant
  when she said they had earned some bread?
  (Context Clue) They worked very hard
  at raking.
- How many loaves had Grandmother baked?
  (Story Detail) Three

After reading p. 58:

- Do you think Grandfather was happy with
  Grandmother? Read what makes you think
  this. *(Inference/Drawing Conclusion)* Yes! He
  said, "Of all the wives on earth, you are the
  best wife."

After reading pp. 59-64:

- When did Grandfather begin his story?
  (Story Detail) After they finished eating
- Who were the characters in Grandfather's
  story? *(Story Detail)* Sam, Ben, and their wives
- What were Sam, Ben and their wives doing?
  (Context Clue) Looking for the lost pearls
- What do you think they did with the pearls?
  (Predicting) They brought them up
  to the boat.

- What mistakes did Sam, Ben and the wives
  make? *(Context Clue)* Nobody stayed on the
  boat to guard the pearls.
- Why did the thieves ship sink? *(Context Clue)*
  A fierce storm came.
- What is the lesson to be learned from this
  story? *(Analyzing)* Answers will vary.
- Why do you think the pearls have never been
  found? *(Predicting)* Answers will vary.

Reference Skills

Turn to Table of Contents p. 2.

1) How many stories are in this book? 9
2) Which story has three authors?
   The Search for the Pearls
3) Four stories have only one author. Who is she?
   Hetty Hubbard
4) Which story is about a season of the year?
   A Breath of Spring
5) On what page does that story begin? End
   on? 45, 53

Complete p. 170 in Raceway Book.
See directions on next page.

Raceway Book: Comprehension

SINGULAR AND PLURAL, *p. 170*

Draw a line from the words to the matching pictures.

p. 170

Grammar Chalkboard Lesson

QUESTION REVIEW

Student will choose the correct question word to complete the sentence.

Example: _Do_ you know my name?

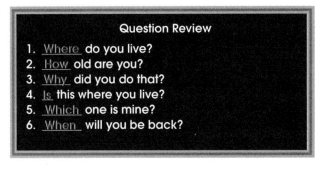

Question Review

1. _Where_ do you live?
2. _How_ old are you?
3. _Why_ did you do that?
4. _Is_ this where you live?
5. _Which_ one is mine?
6. _When_ will you be back?

Word Bank: Which, Where, Why, How, Is, Do, When

Assessment Book

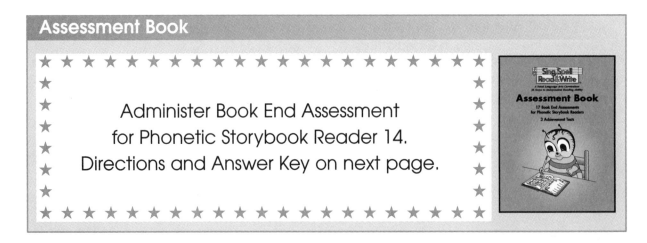

Administer Book End Assessment
for Phonetic Storybook Reader 14.
Directions and Answer Key on next page.

Move
Raceway Car
to Step **29**

Book End Assessment
Phonetic Storybook Reader 14

Word Recognition: all, ar=or, dge, ue

Instructor: Direct student to "Put your finger on box #1. Now circle the word in the box that I call... 'hall.' Put your finger on box #2. Now circle the word 'reward,' etc." The words the instructor should call are listed below. Say each word distinctly with emphasis upon initial and final consonants.

1. hall	2. reward	3. wedge	4. flue	5. small
6. wart	7. cue	8. ledge	9. call	10. budge
11. warn	12. due	13. toward	14. dodge	15. fudge
16. true	17. tall	18. all	19. hedge	20. glue

Record scores in the space provided on the front cover of the Student Assessment Record and calculate the Percentage of Mastery Score as indicated.

Word Recognition and Word Comprehension*

Name _____

1	2	3	4	5
ball	(reward)	fudge	true	Tuesday
(hall)	swarm	dodge	(flue)	midget
tall	toward	(wedge)	blue	(small)

6	7	8	9	10
warm	all	pledge	(call)	tall
(wart)	(cue)	(ledge)	clue	(budge)
wall	edge	judge	glue	Sue

11	12	13	14	15
fall	(due)	Tuesday	midget	(fudge)
(warn)	cue	reward	(dodge)	flue
wedge	war	(toward)	hedge	fall

16	17	18	19	20
swarm	blue	call	warm	edge
warn	ledge	(all)	wedge	pledge
(true)	(tall)	ball	(hedge)	(glue)

Word Recognition _____ Number Correct   Word Comprehension _____ Number Correct

p.1

Word Comprehension: all, ar=or, dge, ue

Directions: Tell your student to put his/her finger on box #1 again and listen to what you say:

Instructor: *Underline the word that (is)...*

1. the opposite of short. tall
2. means to go in the direction of something. toward
3. a sweet chocolate candy. fudge
4. the opposite of false. true
5. one of the days of the week. Tuesday
6. a place to hang a picture. wall
7. means everything or everyone. all
8. the person that works in a court. judge
9. something that will stick things together. glue
10. a girl's name. Sue
11. means to let something drop. fall

12. a big fight between countries. war
13. a gift given for doing something good. reward
14. a row of bushes. hedge
15. opens and closes in the fireplace chimney. flue
16. a big group of bees. swarm
17. a color. blue
18. a toy. ball
19. means to feel some heat, but you aren't really hot. warm
20. means to make a promise. pledge

Record scores in the space provided on the front cover of the Student Assessment Record and calculate the Percentage of Mastery Score as indicated.

Book End Assessment
Phonetic Storybook Reader 14

Word Recognition: x=cks, iē, eā

Instructor: Direct student to "Put your finger on box #1. Now circle the word in the box that I call... 'wax.' Put your finger on box #2. Now circle the word 'believe,' etc." The words the instructor should call are listed below. Say each word distinctly with emphasis upon initial and final consonants.

1. wax	2. believe	3. great	4. excuse	5. relief
6. break	7. Max	8. shield	9. fix	10. tear
11. chief	12. fierce	13. relax	14. pear	15. brief
16. thief	17. pier	18. steak	19. niece	20. bear

Record scores in the space provided on the front cover of the Student Assessment Record and calculate the Percentage of Mastery Score as indicated.

Word Recognition and Word Comprehension

1 box	2 fierce	3 bear	4 relax	5 piece
wax	believe	wear	excuse	relief
tax	priest	great	six	grief

6 pear	7 ax	8 pier	9 mix	10 thief
streak	Max	brief	fox	field
break	ox	shield	fix	tear

11 chief	12 excuse	13 relax	14 piece	15 brief
yield	believe	relief	niece	box
niece	fierce	great	fox	break

16 tear	17 six	18 steak	19 grief	20 yield
tax	mix	field	niece	bear
thief	pier	priest	wear	Max

Word Recognition ____ Number Correct   Word Comprehension ____ Number Correct

p. 2

Word Comprehension: x=cks, iē, eā

Directions: Tell your student to put his/her finger on box #1 again and listen to what you say:

Instructor: *Underline the word that (is)...*

1. the amount of money paid to the government. tax
2. means to be cruel. fierce
3. a large animal. bear
4. means to rest. relax
5. means a part of something larger. piece
6. a kind of fruit. pear
7. a tool. ax
8. a place to tie up ships. pier
9. to stir things together. mix
10. someone who steals things. thief
11. the girl child of your brother or sister. niece
12. a reason given for doing something. excuse
13. another word for fantastic. great
14. an animal that looks something like a dog. fox
15. a thing that can hold other things. box
16. means the same as rip. tear
17. a number. six
18. an open area of land. field
19. something you do with clothes. wear
20. a person's name. Max

Record scores in the space provided on the front cover of the Student Assessment Record and calculate the Percentage of Mastery Score as indicated.

Sing Spell Read & Write

Directions and Answer Key

Book End Assessment
Phonetic Storybook Reader 14

Word Recognition: ea=ea, ear=er, f to "ves"

Instructor: Direct student to "Put your finger on box #1. Now circle the word in the box that I call... 'feather.' Put your finger on box #2. Now circle the word 'earn,' etc." The words the instructor should call are listed below. Say each word distinctly with emphasis upon initial and final consonants.

1. feather	2. earn	3. leaf	4. head	5. knives
6. breath	7. loaves	8. instead	9. search	10. steady
11. heaven	12. thief	13. leather	14. heavy	15. wealth
16. deaf	17. ready	18. leaves	19. learn	20. earth

Record scores in the space provided on the front cover of the Student Assessment Record and calculate the Percentage of Mastery Score as indicated.

p. 3

Word Comprehension: ea=ea, ear=er, f to "ves"

Directions: Tell your student to put his/her finger on box #1 again and listen to what you say:

Instructor: *Underline the word that (is)...*

1. the climate; such as heat or cold, rain or snow. weather
2. another name for the ground or dirt. earth
3. the shape of bread. loaf
4. unable to hear. deaf
5. things found on trees and plants. leaves
6. means the body is in good condition. health
7. something used to cut other things. knife
8. something to eat. bread
9. used in jewelry. pearl
10. a word that describes something that weighs a lot. heavy
11. something to wear in cool weather. sweater
12. something to use when sewing. thread
13. what you are expected to do in school. learn
14. what you did with your ears. heard
15. a word for married ladies. wives
16. something found on a bird. feather
17. what you did to a book. read
18. a material made from cowhide. leather
19. the air that goes in and out of your mouth. breath
20. another word for sky. heaven

Record scores in the space provided on the front cover of the Student Assessment Record and calculate the Percentage of Mastery Score as indicated.

Sentence Comprehension

"Bubble" Format Directions pp. 69-70

1. E	6. E	11. D	16. B	21. A
2. C	7. D	12. C	17. C	22. C
3. A	8. B	13. A	18. D	23. B
4. B	9. A	14. B	19. E	24. E
5. D	10. C	15. E	20. A	25. D

Story Comprehension

"Bubble" Format Directions pp. 69-70

1. No	7. Yes
2. in the hall	8. happy because Tony did a good job
3. paint	9. quickly
4. Coach Dobbs	10. ox, fox
5. Nick	
6. Tony and Uncle Max	

Vocabulary and Reading

long i, long o, u=o͝o, air, and ui=o͞o Words and Related Stories in Storybook Reader 15

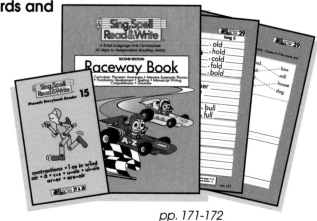

pp. 171-172

Goals

To read, write, and spell **long i**, **long o**, **u=o͝o**, **air**, and **ui=o͞o** words

To read **long i**, **long o**, **u=o͝o**, **air**, and **ui=o͞o** words in context

To practice Grammar Skills

Suggested Pacing

2 days

Materials

1. *Raceway Book*, pp. 171-172

2. Phonetic Storybook Reader 15, *The Wind-Up Book*, pp. 3-13

PROCEDURE

Have student:

- Open **Raceway Book** to p. 171 and read, write, and spell each word.

Instructor: Initial and date boxes at bottom of page.

Have student:

- Read pp. 3-13 in **Storybook Reader 15**.
- Read each story two or three times for fluency.
- Complete **Raceway Book** p. 172.

Instructor:

- Initial and date boxes at bottom of p. 172.
- Teach **Grammar Chalkboard Lessons**/Manual p. 182.

Phonics Song(s)/Games

Each day's lesson should begin with one or two previously learned phonics songs and end with a phonics game.

Written Spelling Tests and Homework

Each day dictate the previous day's 10 spelling "homework" words for a written spelling test. Following the test, have your student circle the next 10 words in the Raceway Book. These 10 spelling words will be for today's homework (writing sentences or a story), and tomorrow's test. See pp. 97 and 143 in this Manual for directions.

Phonetic Storybook Reader 15

Comprehension Questions
Help the Blind
Story 1 • pp. 3-8

Have student read orally the designated pages. Ask the following questions:

After reading p. 4:

- Why do blind people have dogs at their side? *(Context Clue)* They're seeing eye dogs that help lead the blind.

After reading p. 5:

- What time of day does it always feel like when you are blind? *(Context Clue)* Night

After reading p. 6:

- When you are walking near a blind person, where should you walk? *(Context Clue)* Beside him/her

- Why is it better to walk beside him/her? *(Analyzing)* So you can speak to and guide him/her

After reading p. 7:

- Tell me what this verse means. *(Interpretation)* He'll make you appreciate your eyes.

After reading p. 8:

- What are some things you can learn from the blind? *(Analyzing)* How to get along if you don't have sight

Comprehension Questions
A Fair Day, A Bad Day
Story 2 • pp. 9-13

Have student read orally the designated pages. Ask the following questions:

After reading pp. 10-11:

- What season of the year do you think it is? *(Picture Clue/Drawing Conclusion)* Summer

- What does "fair" mean in this story? *(Context Clue)* Sunny and nice

- What is Tim going to do? *(Story Detail)* Read a book

- Why did the squirrel run away when it saw Tim coming? *(Analyzing)* Squirrels are usually afraid of people.

- What had the squirrel been eating? *(Context Clue/Predicting)* Nuts

- What is the name of the book Tim is reading? *(Story Detail)* Butch, the Silly Bull

- Who is the character in Tim's book? *(Story Detail)* Butch

- How is Butch like a person? *(Context Clue)* He eats at a table.

- What do Butch and Tim like to do that is the same? *(Context Clue)* Put cream on their pudding

After reading pp. 12-13:

- What does nuisance mean? *(Context Clue)* A bothersome event

- What was a nuisance to Tim? *(Story Detail)* The wind was blowing his hair and the pages of the book.

- What did he decide to do instead? *(Story Detail)* Go in and get some juice

- What happened next? *(Story Detail)* He tripped and spilled the juice.

(Continued on next page)

- Write the following sentences and have student number them in sequence. *(Sequence)*
  2 Tim cleaned the shells off the chair.
  1 Tim's Mom called him back to close the door.
  4 Tim spilled his juice.
  3 Tim read a book about Butch.

- What is the last problem in this story? *(Analyzing)* **Tripping on the stair**
- Does Tim solve it in this story? *(Analyzing)* **No**
- How do you think he will solve it? *(Predicting)* **By changing his clothes**

*Complete p. 172 in Raceway Book.
See directions below.*

Raceway Book: Grammar

Missing Sounds, *p. 172*
Have student make compound words, write them, and draw pictures.

Raceway Book

p. 172

Grammar Chalkboard Lessons

PERIOD AND QUESTION MARK REVIEW
Write the sentences shown below. Student will place the appropriate mark at the end of each sentence.

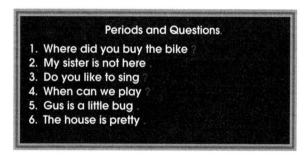

Periods and Questions
1. Where did you buy the bike ?
2. My sister is not here .
3. Do you like to sing ?
4. When can we play ?
5. Gus is a little bug .
6. The house is pretty .

PLURALS: Changing *f* to *ves*
Write the sentences shown below below. Student will choose the correct form of the word to complete the sentence.

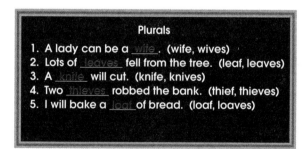

Plurals
1. A lady can be a _wife_. (wife, wives)
2. Lots of _leaves_ fell from the tree. (leaf, leaves)
3. A _knife_ will cut. (knife, knives)
4. Two _thieves_ robbed the bank. (thief, thieves)
5. I will bake a _loaf_ of bread. (loaf, loaves)

Move Raceway Car to Step **30**

Vocabulary and Reading

or=er Words and Related Stories in Storybook Reader 15

Goals

To read, write, and spell words with **or=er (after w and at the end of words)**

To read **or=er** words in context

To practice Grammar Skills

Suggested Pacing

2 days

Materials

1. *Raceway Book*, pp. 173-174
2. Phonetic Storybook Reader 15, *The Wind-Up Book*, pp. 14-29

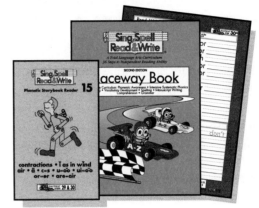

pp. 173-174

PROCEDURE

Have student:

- Open **Raceway Book** to p. 173 (top half) and tell him/her **or** sounds like **er after w** and at the **end of a word.**
- Read, write, and spell all words on p. 173 (top half).
- Read pp. 14-29 in **Storybook Reader 15**.
- Read each story two or three times for fluency.
- Complete **Raceway Book** pp. 173-174.

Instructor:

- Teach **Grammar Lesson**/Manual p. 186.
- Teach **Creative Writing Lesson**/Manual p. 186.

Phonics Song(s)/Games

Each day's lesson should begin with one or two previously learned phonics songs and end with a phonics game.

Written Spelling Tests and Homework

Each day dictate the previous day's 10 spelling "homework" words for a written spelling test. Following the test, have your student circle the next 10 words in the Raceway Book. These 10 spelling words will be for today's homework (writing sentences or a story), and tomorrow's test. See pp. 97 and 143 in this Manual for directions.

Phonetic Storybook Reader 15

Comprehension Questions

Mayor, Janitor, Doctor? What Will You Be?

Story 3 • pp. 14-24

Have student read orally the designated pages.
Ask the following questions:

After reading p. 15:

● What is a mayor? *(Personal Experience)*
The leader of a town or city

● What does an author do? Janitor?
(Picture Clue/Personal Experience) Authors
write books, and janitors take care of buildings.

After reading pp. 16-17:

● When you choose what you will do for a job,
what is important to remember? *(Context Clue)*
To pick something you like to do

● When you have a job what should you always
do? *(Context Clue)* Do it well

● What is more important than being important?
(Story Detail) Being nice

After reading pp. 18-19:

● What are two other jobs you may have?
(Story Detail) Conductor/fixing motorboats

After reading pp. 20-21:

● What two words rhyme on pp. 20-21?
(Decoding/Rhyming Word) Laws and jaws

● This story has rhyme and rhythm. What do we
call this? A poem

● What city is Eric in? *(Context Clue)* Washington

After reading pp. 22-23:

● Does James like the pie? *(Inference)* Yes

After reading p. 24:

● What does a doctor do? *(Context Clue)*
Take care of sick people

● Why is it important to choose a career you will
enjoy? *(Inference)* To be happy

Comprehension Questions

Don't We Have Any Ice Cream?

Story 4 • pp. 25-29

Have student read orally the designated pages.
Ask the following questions:

After reading pp. 26-27:

● What is Jeff looking for? *(Story Detail)* Ice cream
● Where did he look? *(Story Detail)* In the freezer
● Did he find any ice cream? *(Story Detail)* No
● What is the difference between the freezer
and the refrigerator? *(Personal Experience)*
The temperature in the freezer is lower than in
the refrigerator.
● What else besides ice cream would you keep
in the freezer? *(Personal Experience)*
Meats; frozen vegetables

● What did Mom suggest Jeff have instead?
(Context Clue) Popsicles
● Were there any popsicles? *(Story Detail))* No

After reading pp. 28-29:

● Is Jeff willing to forget about a snack? How do
you know? *(Inference/Drawing Conclusion)*
No, because he said he'd love some Jello.
● What did Mom tell Jeff she would do?
(Story Detail) Go to the store
● Why doesn't Jeff go with Mom? *(Context Clue)*
He has a baseball game.

(Continued on next page)

- What did Jeff find to eat?
  (Context Clue) Jello
- Was the Jello in the freezer or the refrigerator?
  (Personal Experience) Refrigerator
- How do you know Jeff enjoyed the Jello?
  (Inference/Drawing Conclusion)
  He said "Mmm".
- What did Jeff say to show his appreciation to Mom? *(Story Detail)* He said, "Thanks!"
- What was Jeff's problem? *(Analyzing)*
  He wanted ice cream.
- List in sequence the three foods he looked for.
  (Sequence) Ice cream, Popsicles, Jello

- Go back to p. 26 and list all the contractions you can find throughout the story. Review them. *(Decoding/Contraction)*

don't	aren't	they're
I'm	you'd	we'll
can't	I'll	we're
there's	it's	haven't
you're		

Complete pp. 173 (bottom half) and 174 in Raceway Book. See directions below.

Raceway Book: Grammar

CONTRACTIONS, p. 173 (bottom half) p. 174 in Raceway Book.

- Write **don't** and **do not**. Tell student **don't** is a contraction that stands for the two words **do** and **not**. Explain that the apostrophe takes the place of a missing letter **o**.

- Write **they're** and **they are**. Tell student **they're** is a contraction for **they are**. Explain that the apostrophe takes the place of a missing letter **a**.

- Write the sentences shown below.

- Have student read the following sentences and ask him/her to identify the contraction. Underline the contractions and have student name the two words the contraction stands for.

pp. 173-174

> 1. We <u>don't</u> like ice cream. do not
> 2. They <u>aren't</u> in school. are not
> 3. Tom <u>can't</u> come to play. can not
> 4. <u>We're</u> going to the store. we are
> 5. <u>They're</u> not very happy. they are
> 6. We <u>haven't</u> had our cookies. have not

- Next, have student complete pp. 173 (bottom half) and 174 in the **Raceway Book**.

Grammar Lesson

CONTRACTIONS

- Teach student to write a contraction by leaving out a letter and inserting an apostrophe in its place.
- Next, show student how to write a contraction with **are** and **not**.
- The following is a list of words to use while practicing contractions.

Words to use for **"not"** contractions:

are n~~o~~t - aren't	has n~~o~~t - hasn't
is n~~o~~t - isn't	do n~~o~~t - don't
did n~~o~~t - didn't	should n~~o~~t - shouldn't
could n~~o~~t - couldn't	were n~~o~~t - weren't
have n~~o~~t - haven't	would n~~o~~t - wouldn't

Words to use for **"are"** contractions:

we ~~a~~re - we're

you ~~a~~re - you're

they ~~a~~re - they're

Creative Writing Lesson

- Tell student: In the story, **Don't We Have Any Ice Cream?** Jeff wanted ice cream and popsicles, but there were none in the refrigerator. Pretend Jeff wrote a note to his mom asking her to buy some special things at the grocery store. Model this note on paper.

Dear Mom,

Please buy some ice cream and popsicles at the store. I like chocolate ice cream.

You're a nice mom!

Love,
Jeff

- Have student write a note to a family member asking him/her to do something. Remind your family member about the note Jeff wrote.

Vocabulary and Reading

ā̸re = air, ä = ŏ, and c=s before e, i, or Words and Related Stories in Storybook Reader 15

Goals

To read, write, and spell words with **ā̸re=air, ä=ŏ,** and **c=s**

To read the words with **ā̸re=air, ä=ŏ,** and **c=s** in context

To practice Grammar Skills

To take Book End Assessment

Suggested Pacing

3 days

Materials

1. *Raceway Book,* pp. 175-176
2. Phonetic Storybook Reader 115, *The Wind-Up Book,* pp. 30-47
3. Assessment Book: Assessment for Phonetic Storybook Reader 15

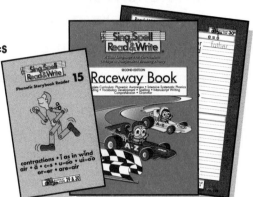

pp. 175-176

PROCEDURE

Have student:

- In **Raceway Book** p. 175, mark the sound in each word as indicated in #1.
- Read, write, and spell each word on p. 175.

Instructor: Initial and date boxes at bottom of p. 175.

Have student:

- Read pp. 30-47 in **Storybook Reader 15**.
- Read each story two or three times for fluency.
- Complete **Raceway Book** p. 176.
- Complete **Assessment**/Manual p. 190.

Phonics Song(s)/Games

Each day's lesson should begin with one or two previously learned phonics songs and end with a phonics game.

Written Spelling Tests and Homework

Each day dictate the previous day's 10 spelling "homework" words for a written spelling test. Following the test, have your student circle the next 10 words in the Raceway Book. These 10 spelling words will be for today's homework (writing sentences), and tomorrow's test. See pp. 97 and 143 in this Manual for directions.

Phonetic Storybook Reader 15

Comprehension Questions

A Flat Tire and A Good Spare

Story 5 • pp. 30-36

Have student read orally the designated pages.
Ask the following questions:

After reading p. 31:
- When did this family have a flat tire?
  (Story Detail) After the toll booth
- What sound did it make? *(Story Detail)*
  Bump, bump, bump, bump

After reading pp. 32-33:
- Where did Mom say they would need to go to change the tire? *(Story Detail)*
  To the side of the road
- Why did Dad light a flare? *(Story Detail)*
  For other cars to see them
- Where was the spare tire?
  (Story Detail) In the trunk

After reading pp. 34-36:
- Why did the tire go flat? *(Story Detail)*
  It was bare and worn.

- What else could make a tire go flat?
  (Personal Experience) nail
- What does *rare* mean in this story?
  (Context Clue) It doesn't happen often.
- Why would people stare at them as they drove by? *(Predicting)* People are curious.
- Who stopped to help this family?
  (Story Detail) A state trooper
- What else may a state trooper do?
  (Predicting/Personal Experience)
  Stop speeders and give tickets
- What was the problem in this story? *(Analyzing)*
  The family had a flat tire.
- How was it solved? *(Analyzing)*
  They stopped and put on the spare tire.

Comprehension Questions

Buzzy Wasp Finds Something

Story 6 • pp. 37-43

Have student read orally the designated pages.
Ask the following questions:

After reading pp. 38-39:
- What did Buzzy like to do all day? *(Story Detail)*
  He watched his father as he worked.
- Where does Buzzy live?
  (Story Detail) By a swamp

After reading pp. 40-41:
- Instead of Father letting Buzzy help him, what did he tell Buzzy to do? *(Story Detail)*
  Play with the other little wasps
- Why do you think Father wouldn't let Buzzy help?
  (Inference/Drawing Conclusion)
  He wasn't old enough.

- What do you think Father is doing with the mud and leaves? *(Predicting)* Building a nest
- Where did Buzzy go to play?
  (Story Detail) In the mud
- What do you think he has spotted?
  (Predicting) Answers may vary.
- What does Buzzy think has happened?
  (Context Clue) The moon fell into the swamp.

After reading pp. 42-43:
- Describe this object to me. *(Summarizing)*
  It's as round as the moon, and muddy and dirty.

(Continued on next page)

- What did Buzzy and Father do? *(Story Detail)*
  They washed it.

- Do you think Father is interested in Buzzy's find? Why do you think this? *(Analyzing)*
  Yes, because he helped him.

- What did they find? *(Story Detail)*
  A 100 watt light bulb

- How do you think Father and Buzzy felt? *(Context Clue)* Surprised

- Could this story be true? Why not? *(Reality/Fantasy)* No, because wasps do not talk.

Comprehension Questions

The Prince of France
Story 7 • pp. 44-47

Have student read orally the designated pages.
Ask the following questions:

After reading pp. 45-47:

- What had been going on in France for a long time? *(Context Clue)* A war

- Why did the prince announce a celebration? *(Context Clue)* The war was over.

- Who could we compare the Prince of France to in our country? *(Expanding Knowledge)*
  An important leader

- Describe the celebration? *(Summarizing)*
  People danced, sang, and drank cider.

- What is the setting for this story?
  (Analyzing) France; city streets; parks

Reference Skills

Turn to the Table of Contents p. 2

1) How many stories are in this book? 7

2) Which story has two authors?
   Mayor? Janitor? Doctor? Which will you be?

3) What page does **The Prince of France** begin on? 44

4) Read the title of the story that has food in it.
   Don't We Have Any Ice Cream?

Complete p. 176 in Raceway Book.
See directions below.

Raceway Book: Grammar

SUPERLATIVES, p. 176

Tell student to add **er** or **est** to a describing word to make comparisons.

Example: It is *cold* today.
            Yesterday was *colder*.
            Tomorrow will be the *coldest*.

Next, have student write the correct word under each picture on p. 176.

p. 176

Assessment Book

★ ★
★   ★
★   Administer Book End Assessment   ★
★   for Phonetic Storybook Reader 15.   ★
★   Directions and Answer Key on next page.   ★
★   ★
★ ★

Move
Raceway Car
to Step **31**

Raceway Step 29

Book End Assessment
Phonetic Storybook Reader 15

Word Recognition: ī as in find, u as in o͞o, air, ui=o͞o

Instructor: Direct student to "Put your finger on box #1. Now circle the word in the box that I call... 'grind.' Put your finger on box #2. Now circle the word 'fair,' etc." The words the instructor should call are listed below. Say each word distinctly with emphasis upon initial and final consonants.

1. grind	2. fair	3. put	4. nuisance	5. cushion
6. bush	7. fruit	8. kind	9. pair	10. wind
11. butcher	12. air	13. behind	14. mind	15. find
16. bull	17. pull	18. suit	19. chair	20. blind

Record scores in the space provided on the front cover of the Student Assessment Record and calculate the Percentage of Mastery Score as indicated.

Word Recognition and Word Comprehension*

Name _____

1 behind (grind) blind	2 air hair (fair)	3 (put) pull push	4 (nuisance) suitcase cruise	5 pudding bullet (cushion)
6 butcher (bush) bull	7 suit (fruit) juice	8 (kind) find full	9 chair stair (pair)	10 mind bind (wind)
11 pudding nuisance (butcher)	12 put (air) stair	13 (behind) bullet suitcase	14 push (mind) bush	15 (find) fruit fair
16 bind (bull) pair	17 (kind) (pull) cruise	18 full hair (suit)	19 cushion (chair) juice	20 (blind) wind grind

Word Recognition _____   Word Comprehension _____
Number Correct   Number Correct

p.1

Word Comprehension: ī as in find, u as in o͞o, air, ui=o͞o

Directions: Tell your student to put his/her finger on box #1 again and listen to what you say:

Instructor: *Underline the word that (is)...*

1. means not able to see. blind
2. what you breathe. air
3. means to shove. push
4. a vacation on a ship. cruise
5. a kind of dessert. pudding
6. a person whose job is to cut meat. butcher
7. a set of clothes, usually a jacket and pants. suit
8. the opposite of empty. full
9. a place to sit. chair
10. means to obey. mind
11. someone or something that bothers people. nuisance
12. a part of a set of steps. stair
13. something you put your clothes in when traveling. suitcase
14. a kind of a big plant. bush
15. a sweet juicy food. fruit
16. means a set of two things that are alike. pair
17. can be used to describe a nice person. kind
18. something that grows on the top of your head. hair
19. something to drink. juice
20. to crush into small pieces. grind

Record scores in the space provided on the front cover of the Student Assessment Record and calculate the Percentage of Mastery Score as indicated.

Raceway Step 30A

Book End Assessment
Phonetic Storybook Reader 15

Word Recognition: or=er, Contractions

Instructor: Direct student to "Put your finger on box #1. Now circle the word in the box that I call... 'worm.' Put your finger on box #2. Now circle the word 'didn't,' etc." The words the instructor should call are listed below. Say each word distinctly with emphasis upon initial and final consonants.

1. worm	2. didn't	3. favor	4. mirror	5. color
6. actor	7. aren't	8. worry	9. humor	10. word
11. we're	12. worth	13. world	14. can't	15. author
16. janitor	17. tractor	18. motor	19. flavor	20. they're

Record scores in the space provided on the front cover of the Student Assessment Record and calculate the Percentage of Mastery Score as indicated.

p.2

Word Comprehension: or=er, Contractions

Directions: Tell your student to put his/her finger on box #1 again and listen to what you say:

Instructor: *Underline the word that (is)...*

1. a person that comes to see you. visitor
2. means cannot. can't
3. the way food tastes. flavor
4. a person that cleans the building. janitor
5. what a person uses to shave. razor
6. another word for engine. motor
7. means "have not". haven't
8. another name for the planet Earth. world
9. means "they are". they're
10. a person who writes a book. author
11. means "did not". didn't
12. a person that takes care of you when you are sick. doctor
13. the person who is in charge of a city or town. mayor
14. means "do not". don't
15. a person you may see on television or in the movies. actor
16. means "are not". aren't
17. a person that works on a ship. sailor
18. a thing that shows you how you look. mirror
19. the name of things like red, blue and yellow. color
20. what you put on a hook to catch a fish. worm

Record scores in the space provided on the front cover of the Student Assessment Record and calculate the Percentage of Mastery Score as indicated.

Raceway Step 30B

Book End Assessment
Phonetic Storybook Reader 15

Word Recognition: āre=air, ä, c=s

Instructor: Direct student to "Put your finger on box #1. Now circle the word in the box that I call... 'dare.' Put your finger on box #2. Now circle the word 'circle,' etc." The words the instructor should call are listed below. Say each word distinctly with emphasis upon initial and final consonants.

1. dare	2. circle	3. wand	4. prince	5. flare
6. choice	7. swamp	8. share	9. concert	10. wad
11. since	12. stare	13. voice	14. rare	15. cent
16. care	17. wasp	18. spare	19. wash	20. office

Record scores in the space provided on the front cover of the Student Assessment Record and calculate the Percentage of Mastery Score as indicated.

Word Recognition and Word Comprehension
Name _____

1 bare	2 circus	3 wand	4 police	5 rare
dare	circle	wash	prince	hare
fare	cent	want	princess	flare

6 choice	7 swamp	8 spare	9 groceries	10 wad
voice	watch	share	concert	wasp
city	watt	care	office	swap

11 race	12 stare	13 circle	14 bare	15 cent
face	father	choice	rare	concert
since	peace	voice	race	flare

16 circus	17 groceries	18 spare	19 wash	20 office
city	wasp	swamp	watt	police
care	dare	swap	since	share

Word Recognition _____ | Word Comprehension _____
Number Correct | Number Correct

p.3

Word Comprehension: āre=air, ä, c=s

Directions: Tell your student to put his/her finger on box #1 again and listen to what you say:

Instructor: *Underline the word that (is)...*

1. the money paid for a ticket for a bus, train or plane trip. fare
2. another name for a penny. cent
3. means to be in need. want
4. people that protect and help you. police
5. a kind of rabbit. hare
6. a large town. city
7. something used to tell time. watch
8. means extra. spare
9. a place where people work. office
10. a stinging insect. wasp
11. a part of the body. face
12. a person who is a parent. father
13. a round shape. circle
14. a speed contest. race
15. a place you might go to hear music. concert
16. a place to go to see animals, clowns and acrobats. circus
17. things that can be bought at a store. groceries
18. an area of wetland. swamp
19. a measure of electricity. watt
20. means a part of something or to give a part to someone. share

Record scores in the space provided on the front cover of the Student Assessment Record and calculate the Percentage of Mastery Score as indicated.

Sentence Comprehension

"Bubble" Format Directions pp. 69-70

1. C	5. B	9. E	13. D	17. C
2. A	6. B	10. A	14. E	18. A
3. D	7. C	11. B	15. C	19. B
4. E	8. D	12. A	16. E	20. D

Story Comprehension

"Bubble" Format Directions pp. 69-70

1. jobs when you grow up
2. enjoy
3. Author
4. to be nice
5. happy
6. just after paying the toll
7. at the side of the road
8. so the other cars could see them
9. in the trunk
10. Yes

Vocabulary and Reading

Silent k̶ and Silent w̶ Words and Related Stories in Storybook Reader 16

Goals
To read, write, and spell words with
silent k̶ and **silent w̶**
To read words with **silent k̶** and **silent w̶** in context
To practice Grammar Skills

Suggested Pacing
2 days

Materials
1. *Raceway Book*, pp. 177-178
2. Phonetic Storybook Reader 16,
   The Knight Book, pp. 3-29

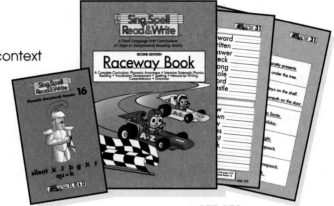

pp. 177-178

PROCEDURE

Have student:

- Open **Raceway Book** to p. 177 and mark the words as indicated in #1.
- Read, write, and spell all words on p. 177.

Instructor: Initial and date boxes at bottom of p. 177.

Have student:

- Read pp. 3-29 in **Storybook Reader 16**.
- Read each story two or three times for fluency.
- Complete **Raceway Book** p. 178.

Instructor: Teach **Grammar Chalkboard Lessons**/Manual p. 195.

Phonics Song(s)/Games

Each day's lesson should begin with one or two previously learned phonics songs and end with a phonics game.

Written Spelling Tests and Homework

Each day dictate the previous day's 10 spelling "homework" words for a written spelling test. Following the test, have your student circle the next 10 words in the Raceway Book. These 10 spelling words will be for today's homework (writing sentences or a story) and tomorrow's test. See pp. 97 and 143 in this Manual for directions.

Phonetic Storybook Reader 16

Comprehension Questions

Did You Write to Santa?

Story 1 • pp. 3-15

Have student read orally the designated pages. Ask the following questions:

After reading pp. 4-15:

- What makes this story a poem? *(Analyzing)* Rhyming words; rhyme

- Why are the elves taking toys from the shelf? *(Inference/Drawing Conclusion)* They are going to wrap them and get them ready for Christmas.

- What do they do next? Next? And next? *(Story Detail)* Hang a wreath; trim the tree; put trains out

- What do you think is the name of the elf who wrote the letter to Santa? *(Predicting)* William/Willie/Wilbur

- What did the elf want for himself? *(Story Detail)* A truck

- What did he want for Wrinkles? *(Story Detail)* A box of Woofy Dog Chow

- Look at the pictures on pages 12-13. Let's identify the ones that would meet Santa's approval and the ones that would not. *(Classification)* Numbers 1 and 4 do not; all others do

Read the poem in unison with your student.

Comprehension Questions

The Brave Knight

Story 2 • pp. 16-29

Have student read orally the designated pages. Ask the following questions:

After reading p. 17:

- What is one word that describes Tom? *(Story Detail)* Brave

- What does the king want Tom to do? *(Story Detail)* Fight a dragon

After reading pp. 18-21:

- Name the four things Tom put in his knapsack. *(Story Detail)* Knife; socks; club; book of Dragon Knowledge

- Where did Tom find the dragon? *(Story Detail)* In the king's cornfield

After reading pp. 22-23:

- What is the first thing Tom does to capture the dragon? *(Context Clue)* Waved the socks on his knife

- What do you think Tom is hoping will happen? *(Predicting)* The dragon will be distracted by the yellow waving sock.

After reading pp. 24-25:

- What do you think Tom was planning to do with his club? *(Predicting)* Hit the dragon

- Why did the dragon fall on his knees? *(Context Clue)* He didn't want to be hit or banged; he gave up.

- What did Tom do to the dragon? *(Story Detail)* Tied a knot in his tail

(Continued on next page)

After reading pp. 26-27:

- When did Tom know the dragon had given up the fight? *(Story Detail)* After he got on his knees and said, "I know you have won."

- What does the dragon promise to do? *(Story Detail)* Work for the king

- What kind of work do you think a dragon could do for a king? *(Predicting)* Answers will vary.

After reading pp. 28-29:

- What kind of work will the dragon do first? *(Story Detail)* Pop popcorn

- Why could a dragon pop corn? *(Analyzing)* There are hot flames coming from its mouth.

- How does the king feel about Tom? *(Context Clue)* Proud and thankful

- Could this story be true? Why couldn't it be true? *(Reality/Fantasy)* No; there are no real dragons.

Complete pp. 38-44 in Raceway Book. See directions below.

Raceway Book: Comprehension

Choose the Correct Sentence, *p. 178*
Student will underline the sentence that goes with each picture.

p. 178

Grammar Chalkboard Lessons

CONTRACTIONS

Write the sentences shown below. Student will write the sentence using a contraction for the underlined words.

Contractions
1. Mom <u>did not</u> bake cookies. didn't
2. We <u>are not</u> on time. aren't
3. Gus <u>is not</u> big. isn't
4. They <u>do not</u> live here. don't
5. <u>We are</u> going to the store. We're

Write the sentences shown below. Student will write the sentences using the two words the contraction stands for.

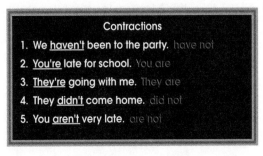

Contractions
1. We <u>haven't</u> been to the party. have not
2. <u>You're</u> late for school. You are
3. <u>They're</u> going with me. They are
4. They <u>didn't</u> come home. did not
5. You <u>aren't</u> very late. are not

Move Raceway Car to Step **32**

Vocabulary and Reading

Silent ʃ and Silent ø Words and Related Stories in Storybook Reader 16

pp. 179-180

Goals

To read, write, and spell words with **silent ʃ** and **silent ø**

To read words with **silent ʃ** and **silent ø** in context

To practice Grammar Skills

Suggested Pacing

2 days

Materials

1. *Raceway Book,* pp. 179-180
2. Phonetic Storybook Reader 16,
   The Knight Book, pp. 30-63

PROCEDURE

Have student:

- Open **Raceway Book** to p. 179 and cross out the **silent ʃ** and **silent ø** in each word.
- Read, write, and spell all words on p. 179.

Instructor: Initial and date boxes at bottom of p.179.

Have student:

- Read pp. 30-63 in **Storybook Reader 16**.
- Read each story two or three times for fluency.
- Complete **Raceway Book** p. 180.

Instructor: Teach **Grammar Chalkboard Lessons**/Manual p. 199.

Phonics Song(s)/Games

Each day's lesson should begin with one or two previously learned phonics songs and end with a phonics game.

Written Spelling Tests and Homework

Each day dictate the previous day's 10 spelling "homework" words for a written spelling test. Following the test, have your student circle the next 10 words in the Raceway Book. These 10 spelling words will be for today's homework (writing sentences or a story) and tomorrow's test. See pp. 97 and 143 in this Manual for directions.

Phonetic Storybook Reader 16

Comprehension Questions

Sam and His Folks

Story 3 • pp. 30-44

Sam went with his folks. They drove in the car for half the day. They drove to the country. 31

Have student read orally the designated pages. Ask the following questions:

After reading pp. 31-33:

- Where do Sam and his folks live? *(Inference/Drawing Conclusion)* In the city

- How long did it take to drive there? *(Story Detail)* Half the day

- How does Dad feel about where they are camping? *(Context Clue)* He likes it because it's peaceful.

- What will they sleep in? *(Picture Clue)* A tent, sleeping bags

After reading pp. 34-35:

- Do you think Sam is paying attention to the surroundings when he goes for a walk? Why? *(Context Clue)* Yes, because he spotted a caterpillar.

After reading pp. 36-37:

- How do you know Sam is not afraid of the caterpillar? *(Context Clue)* Because he picked it up

- How did it feel to have the caterpillar crawl on him? *(Picture Clue/Person Experience)* It tickled.

- What will it soon become? *(Story Detail)* A butterfly

- Why didn't Sam take the butterfly home with him? *(Context Clue)* It should be free.

- Do you know anything about poison ivy? *(Personal Experience)* Answers will vary.

After reading pp. 38-39:

- How did Mom know Sam had poison ivy? *(Context Clue)* She saw the leaves of poison ivy.

- What did it mean when Mom said, "Leaflets three, let them be." *(Interpretation)* If a plant has three leaves together, it's poison ivy.

- What will Mom do for Sam's poison ivy? How will the salve help? *(Story Detail)* Put salve on it. It stops the itching.

Comprehension Questions

Red Robin's Numb Toes
Story 4 • pp. 45-63

Red Robin sat on his limb. He was getting cold.
46

Red was tired. Tired of digging worms. Tired of hunting for crumbs.
47

Have student read orally the designated pages. Ask the following questions:

After reading pp. 46-47:

• What did we find out about Red Robin? *(Summarizing)* He was cold and tired.

• How do you feel about Red Robin? *(Personal Experience)* Answers will vary.

After reading pp. 48-51:

• Why will Red Robin go south? *(Context Clue)* Red doesn't like cold.

• What did Red pack in his bag? *(Picture Clue/Story Detail)* Comb, brush, toy lamb, crumbs

• What are his "last few crumbs"? *(Interpretation)* Probably bread crumbs

After reading pp. 52-53:

• How do you think Red Robin caused his problems? *(Analyzing)* He waited too long before going south.

• What is the weather in the south like in the wintertime? *(Context Clue)* Warmer than in the north

• What happened just as Red Robin flew off? *(Story Detail)* The first snow began to fall.

• Read the sign on Red Robin's house. What does R.R. stand for? *(Analyzing)* Red Robin

After reading pp. 54-55:

• What happened to Red Robin? *(Summarizing)* A big wind smacked him.

• What does "doubted" mean? *(Context Clue)* He didn't believe he could get to the south.

After reading pp. 56-57:

• Describe Red Robin's situation. *(Summarizing)* He was cold, hungry, and had a long way to go.

• What do you think will happen to Red Robin? *(Predicting)* Answers will vary.

After reading pp. 58-59:

• How is Red trying to solve his problem? *(Story Detail)* He waved and a truck stopped for him.

After reading pp. 60-63:

• How is this part of the story written? *(Poem)* As a poem

• What is the occupation of this man? *(Story Detail)* A plumber

• What did the man say he would make for Red to ride on? *(Story Detail)* A limb

• Is this what you think of as a limb? *(Personal Experience)* No

• What is this limb made of? *(Picture Clue)* A plunger and pipes

• Why would he use these items for a limb? *(Analyzing)* That's what he had in his truck.

• How did Red show his appreciation? *(Context Clue)* He sang sweet songs.

• When Red got to the south, how did he feel? *(Context Clue)* Great

• What does "He had weathered the storm" mean? *(Interpretation/Context Clue)* He made it through difficulties.

• Turn back to page 60 and find rhyming words on pages 61, 62, and 63. *(Decoding/Rhyming Words)* See-me; met- debt; warm - storm

• Could this be a true story? *(Reality/Fantasy)* No

Complete p. 180 in Raceway Book. See directions on next page.

Raceway Book: Comprehension

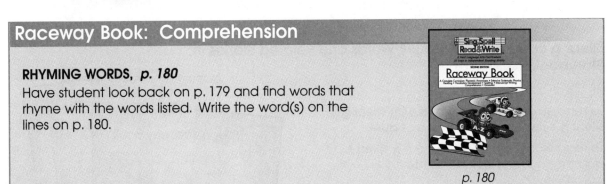

RHYMING WORDS, *p. 180*
Have student look back on p. 179 and find words that
rhyme with the words listed. Write the word(s) on the
lines on p. 180.

p. 180

Grammar Chalkboard Lessons

COMPOUND WORDS

Write words shown below on the board. Select a word from each circle and write
compound words.

Choose one compound word and write a sentence.

Example: some one = someone; I see someone.

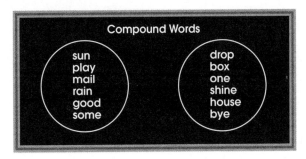

Compound Words

sun	drop
play	box
mail	one
rain	shine
good	house
some	bye

COMPOUND WORDS

Write words shown below on the board. Have student draw a line from the words in Group 1
to the words in Group 2 to make compound words.
Choose one compound word and write a sentence.

Compound Words

Group 1	Group 2
1. rain	1. shell
2. sea	2. brush
3. pocket	3. coat
4. school	4. book
5. paint	5. house

Move
Raceway Car
to Step **33**

Sing Spell
Read & Write.

RACEWAY STEP 33

Vocabulary and Reading

Silent g̸, Silent h̸, Silent l̸, qu=k Words and Related Stories in Storybook Reader 16

Goals

To read, write, and spell words with **silent g̸ silent h̸ silent l̸**, and the sound of **qu=k**

To read words with **silent g̸ silent h̸ silent l̸**, and the sound of **qu=k** in context

To practice Grammar Skills

To take Book End Assessment

Suggested Pacing

3 days

pp. 181-182

Materials

1. *Raceway Book,* pp. 181-182
2. Phonetic Storybook Reader 16,
   The Knight Book, pp. 64-80
3. Assessment Book: Assessment for Phonetic Storybook Reader 16

PROCEDURE

Have student:

- Open **Raceway Book** to p. 181 and mark the words as indicated in #1.
- Read, write, and spell all words on p. 181.

Instructor: Initial and date boxes at bottom of p. 181.

Have student:

- Read pp. 64-80 in **Storybook Reader 16.**
- Read each story two or three times for fluency.
- Complete **Raceway Book**, p. 182.

Instructor:

- Teach **Grammar Lessons**/Manual p. 202.
- Teach **Creative Writing Lesson**/Manual p. 203.
- Administer **Assessment**/Manual p. 204.

Phonics Song(s)/Games

Each day's lesson should begin with one or two previously learned phonics songs and end with a phonics game.

Written Spelling Tests and Homework

Each day dictate the previous day's 10 spelling "homework" words for a written spelling test. Following the test, have your student circle the next 10 words in the Raceway Book. These 10 spelling words will be for today's homework (writing sentences or a story), and tomorrow's test. See pp. 97 and 143 in this Manual for directions.

200

Phonetic Storybook Reader 16

Comprehension Questions

Can a Gnat Gnaw?

Story 5 • pp. 64-67

Have student read orally the designated pages.
Ask the following questions:

After reading pp. 65-67:

• What does the sign advertise for? *(Story Detail)*
Strong gnats

• How much will this job pay? *(Story Detail)*
Good pay

• Are there gnats interested in this job? How do
you know? *(Inference/Drawing Conclusion)*
Yes; they're talking about it.

• Where should they go to apply for this job?
(Story Detail) The Acorn Forest

• Which animal on pp. 66-67 could probably do
this job? *(Inference/Drawing Conclusion)*
The squirrel or mouse.

• Do you want me to tell you what a gnu is?
It's an African wild beast.

Comprehension Questions

Listen! Your Honor, The Ant Queen

Story 6 • pp. 68-80

Have student read orally the designated pages.
Ask the following questions:

After reading p. 69:

• What does the queen do to get everyone's
attention? *(Inference/Drawing Conclusion)*
She blows her whistle.

• After she gets their attention, what does she begin
to do? *(Context Clue)* She shouts out orders.

• What is the first order? *(Story Detail)*
Get a brush with good bristles.

After reading pp. 70-71:

• Where does the queen live? *(Context Clue)*
In a castle

• What do you think the queen is preparing for?
(Inference/Drawing Conclusion)
Somebody's arrival

• Name the jobs the queen has ordered to be
done. *(Story Detail)* Moisten the stamps, send
invitations, put a bouquet on the table, make a
cookie tray, and light the antique lamps.

After reading pp. 72-73:

• What else has the queen ordered to be done?
(Story Detail) Take out her jewels

• Do you think the queen has trained her workers
well? *(Inference/Drawing Conclusion)* Yes

• What are the workers to do about her jewels?
Curtains? *(Story Detail)* Polish them;Fasten them
with new golden chains

After reading pp. 74-77:

• Who is all the preparation for?
(Context Clue) The king

• Where has King John been?
(Story Detail) Camping

After reading pp. 78-80:

• Why does the ant queen work so hard?
(Inference/Drawing Conclusion) She's happy
her husband, King John, is coming home.

(Continued on next page)

- How did King John arrive? *(Story Detail)*
  On a big golden horse
- What do you think of all the hustle and bustle taking place in the castle?
  (Opinion) **Answers will vary.**
- Could this story be true? Why not?
  (Realism/Fantasy) **No; ants don't do those things.**

Reference Skills

1) How many stories are in this book? **6**
2) What page does **Red Robin's Numb Toes** begin on? End on? **p. 45, p. 63**
3) Who is the author of all the stories?
   Lynda MacDonald

Complete p. 182 in Raceway Book. See directions below.

Raceway Book: Grammar

FILL IN THE BLANK, *p. 182*
Have student circle the correct word and write it on the blank.

p. 182

Grammar Lesson

COMPOUND WORD REVIEW

The instructor will say the first part of the compound words listed below. Next, the student will say a word to add the second part of the compound word. Some words have several answers.

Example: rain (bow, coat, drop)

Words to be called:

1. snow	6. sun	11. any
2. school	7. mail	12. good
3. fire	8. play	13. tree
4. paint	9. some	14. every
5. sea	10. rain	15. grand

Grammar Chalkboard Lesson

WRITING SENTENCES

Write the compound words shown below. Student will write one asking and one telling sentence for each compound word.

Example: rainbow - Do you see the rainbow? I see the rainbow.

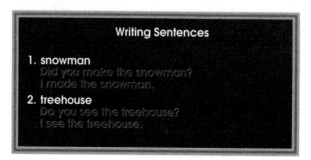

Writing Sentences

1. snowman
   Did you make the snowman?
   I made the snowman.
2. treehouse
   Do you see the treehouse?
   I see the treehouse.

Creative Writing Lesson

This *Creative Writing Lesson* follows the reading of the story, **Listen! Her Honor, the Ant Queen**, Phonetic Storybook Reader 16, *The Knight Book*, pp. 68-80.

Your student will write a description of the dining room in the castle. First, ask student to recall where the story took place. Next, have him/her turn to p. 71 in the storybook. Ask student to name some items pictured in the dining room and instructor will write the responses to build a word bank:

dining table	vase
chairs	stairs
lighted antique lamps	window
cookies	ladder
gold tray	table
flowers	

Have student use the words generated for the word bank to write a description of the dining room in the castle. Illustrate the story.

Administer Book End Assessment
for Phonetic Storybook Reader 16.
Directions and Answer Key on next page.

Assessment Book

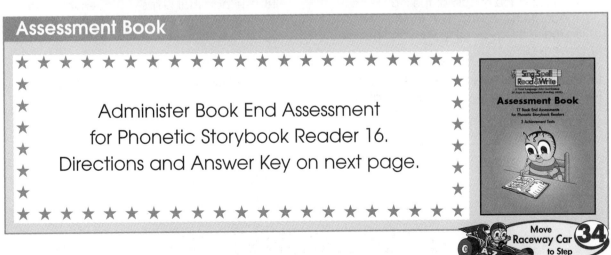

Move Raceway Car to Step **34**

Directions and Answer Key

for Book End Assessment
Phonetic Storybook Reader 16

Word Recognition: Silent w̶, k̶

Instructor: Direct student to "Put your finger on box #1. Now circle the word in the box that I call... 'wrapper.' Put your finger on box #2. Now circle the word 'knock,' etc." The words the instructor should call are listed below. Say each word distinctly with emphasis upon initial and final consonants.

1. wrapper	2. knock	3. wreck	4. knowledge	5. wrestle
6. known	7. answer	8. knob	9. wrote	10. kneel
11. wrench	12. wrinkles	13. knit	14. wrestle	15. knot
16. write	17. know	18. wren	19. wrist	20. sword

Record scores in the space provided on the front cover of the Student Assessment Record and calculate the Percentage of Mastery Score as indicated.

Word Recognition and Word Comprehension

write	knot	wreck	knapsack	wrestle
wren	knight	wreath	knowledge	wrench
wrapper	knock	wrinkles	knuckles	written
knife	answer	knob	toward	know
known	sword	knee	wrote	kneel
knew	wrong	knives	wring	knit
wrench	wrinkles	wrist	wrench	knot
whole	written	knit	knapsack	wrong
known	knowledge	wrap	wrestle	wreath
knight	toward	knit	knee	knife
write	answer	wren	wrist	sword
whole	know	knob	knock	wrench

p.1

Word Comprehension: Silent w̶, k̶

Directions: Tell your student to put his/her finger on box #1 again and listen to what you say:

Instructor: *Underline the word that (is)...*

1. to use pencil and paper. write
2. what you may get in your shoelace. knot
3. lines you get in your skin when you get older. wrinkles
4. a part of a finger. knuckles
5. a pen or pencil was used to put the words on paper. written
6. something you use when eating. knife
7. the opposite of correct. wrong
8. the joint in the middle of the leg. knee
9. means to twist. wring
10. to make things by using yarn and needles. knit
11. means all. whole
12. something you get from learning. knowledge
13. the place where the hand attaches to the arm. wrist
14. something that can be used to carry things when camping. knapsack
15. a decoration for a wall or door. wreath
16. a person who wears armor. knight
17. what you give when you are asked a question. answer
18. the part that helps you open the door. knob
19. means to hit something. knock
20. a tool. wrench

Record scores in the space provided on the front cover of the Student Assessment Record and calculate the Percentage of Mastery Score as indicated.

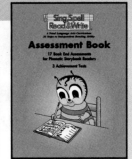

for Book End Assessment
Phonetic Storybook Reader 16

Word Recognition: ͭ, ͭ

Instructor: Direct student to "Put your finger on box #1. Now circle the word in the box that I call... 'salve.' Put your finger on box #2. Now circle the word 'crumb,' etc." The words the instructor should call are listed below. Say each word distinctly with emphasis upon initial and final consonants.

1. salve	2. crumb	3. talk	4. doubt	5. calf
6. half	7. climb	8. should	9. dumb	10. stalk
11. debt	12. thumb	13. limb	14. walk	15. would
16. folk	17. doubted	18. salmon	19. debt	20. could

Record scores in the space provided on the front cover of the Student Assessment Record and calculate the Percentage of Mastery Score as indicated.

p.2

Word Comprehension: ͭ, ͭ

Directions: Tell your student to put his/her finger on box #1 again and listen to what you say:

Instructor: *Underline the word that (is)...*

1. to go by moving your feet and legs. walk
2. a part of your hand. thumb
3. a kind of fish. salmon
4. a baby sheep. lamb
5. the yellow center of an egg. yolk
6. means to be quiet and restful. calm
7. a person that fixes broken pipes. plumber
8. means you possibly can. could
9. money that is owed. debt
10. something that you use to arrange your hair. comb
11. a part of your hand. palm
12. a small piece of bread, cookie or cracker. crumb
13. a baby cow. calf
14. to have no feeling. numb
15. means to not be sure. doubt
16. what you do when you say words. talk
17. something that might explode. bomb
18. a medicine that you put on a rash to help it get better. salve
19. means to go up. climb
20. something that can be used for writing. chalk

Record scores in the space provided on the front cover of the Student Assessment Record and calculate the Percentage of Mastery Score as indicated.

Directions and Answer Key

Raceway Step 33

for Book End Assessment
Phonetic Storybook Reader 16

Word Recognition: Silent g, k, t, qu=k

Instructor: Direct student to "Put your finger on box #1. Now circle the word in the box that I call... 'sign.' Put your finger on box #2. Now circle the word 'bustle,' etc." The words the instructor should call are listed below. Say each word distinctly with emphasis upon initial and final consonants.

1. sign	2. bustle	3. antique	4. bristle	5. gnash
6. honor	7. rustle	8. croquet	9. whistle	10. often
11. glisten	12. John	13. hour	14. mosquito	15. honest
16. thistle	17. gnaw	18. fasten	19. bouquet	20. moisten

Record scores in the space provided on the front cover of the Student Assessment Record and calculate the Percentage of Mastery Score as indicated.

p.3

Word Comprehension: Silent g, k, t, qu=k

Directions: Tell your student to put his/her finger on box #1 again and listen to what you say:

Instructor: *Underline the word that (is)...*

1. to chew on a bone. gnaw
2. means to join together. fasten
3. an insect that bites. mosquito
4. means to shine. glisten
5. a boy's name. John
6. a measure of time. hour
7. a place where the king and queen live. castle
8. a bunch of flowers. bouquet
9. to make wet. moisten
10. what you do with your ears. listen
11. means to write your name. sign
12. a game that is played on the lawn. croquet
13. means to be truthful. honest
14. a very tiny insect. gnat
15. to busily move back and forth. bustle
16. means happening many times. often
17. a small shop or store. boutique
18. a piece of meat that is very hard to chew. gristle
19. means to give up. resign
20. a thorny weed. thistle

Record scores in the space provided on the front cover of the Student Assessment Record and calculate the Percentage of Mastery Score as indicated.

Raceway Steps 31-32-33

Sentence Comprehension

"Bubble" Format Directions pp. 69-70

1. C	5. D	9. E	13. D	17. A
2. E	6. B	10. C	14. B	18. B
3. A	7. A	11. C	15. E	19. C
4. B	8. D	12. A	16. D	20. E

Story Comprehension

"Bubble" Format Directions pp. 69-70

1. He was a knight
2. Could you fight a dragon?
3. No
4. Yes
5. sock
6. his big knife
7. club with knob on top
8. a knob
9. Dragon Knowledge
10. a knight getting ready to fight a dragon

206

Vocabulary and Reading

ph=f and Related Stories in Storybook Reader 17

pp. 183-184

Goals

To read, write, and spell words with the sound of **ph=f**

To read **ph=f** words in context

To practice Grammar Skills

Suggested Pacing

1 day

Materials

1. *Raceway Book*, pp. 183-184
2. Phonetic Storybook Reader 17, *The Trophy Book*, pp. 3-13

PROCEDURE

Have student:

- Open **Raceway Book** to p.183 and circle the letters **ph** in each word.
- Read, write, and spell all words on p. 183.

Instructor: Initial and date boxes at bottom of p. 183.

Have student:

- Read pp. 3-13 in **Storybook Reader 17**.
- Read each story two or three times for fluency.
- Complete **Raceway Book** p. 184.

Instructor: Teach **Grammar Chalkboard Lesson**/Manual p. 209.

Phonics Song(s)/Games

Each day's lesson should begin with one or two previously learned phonics songs and end with a phonics game.

Written Spelling Tests and Homework

Each day dictate the previous day's 10 spelling "homework" words for a written spelling test. Following the test, have your student circle the next 10 words in the Raceway Book. These 10 spelling words will be for today's homework (writing sentences or a story), and tomorrow's test. See pp. 97 and 143 in this Manual for directions.

Phonetic Storybook Reader 17

Comprehension Questions

Baseball in Philadelphia
Story 1 • pp. 3-13

Have student read orally the designated pages.
Ask the following questions:

No ball game today. Ducks and dolphins like rain, but not gophers !

It was a rainy day.
"Phooey !" said Joseph.
"Phooey !" said Ralph.

After reading pp. 4-6:

- Who do you think the main characters are going to be? *(Context Clue)*
  Joseph and Ralph

- What kind of day is it? *(Story Detail)* Rainy

- How are they feeling? Why? *(Context Clue)*
  Sad; there would be no ball game.

- Who would like rain? *(Story Detail)*
  Ducks and dolphins

After reading pp. 6-7:

- What is happening on p. 6? *(Interpretation)*
  Ralph and Joseph are not really on the train but thinking how they would like to be.

- How are Ralph and Joseph feeling?
  (Story Detail) Sad and mad

After reading pp. 8-11:

- What did Mom tell the gophers to do that you learned a long time ago? *(Story Detail)*
  Write the alphabet and sing the
  A to Z Phonics Song

- What makes us think the gophers are polite and will do what Mom says? *(Context Clue)*
  They did what Mom suggested.

- Who called on the telephone?
  (Story Detail) Dad

- Why do you think he called? *(Predicting)*
  He had some news for them.

After reading pp. 12-13:

- What is Dad's good news? *(Context Clue)*
  They're going to the game.

- Why is Dad especially eager to go to the game in Philadelphia? *(Context Clue)*
  Their team is on top (winning).

- How do we know Ralph and Joseph are happy now? *(Picture Clue/Context Clue)*
  They say "hurray" and are jumping up and down, clicking their heels.

- Can you read where Dad works? Why is it written backwards? *(Personal Experience)*
  Yes, because the sign is for people who are outside the building.

- What is a pharmacy? What is another name for a pharmacy? *(Expanding Vocabulary)*
  A place to buy medicine; a drug store

- What do Ralph and Joseph expect their team to win? *(Story Detail)* A trophy

- Have you ever won a trophy? Maybe at the end of this book you will win one.
  You will deserve it! *(Personal Experience)*
  Answers will vary.

*Complete p. 184 in Raceway Book.
See directions on next page.*

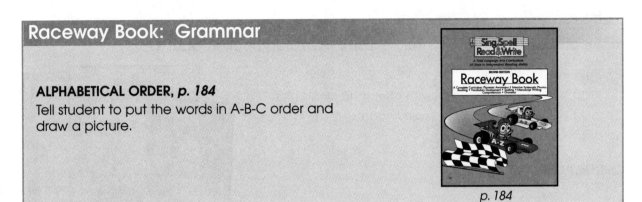
Raceway Book: Grammar

ALPHABETICAL ORDER, p. 184
Tell student to put the words in A-B-C order and
draw a picture.

p. 184

Grammar Chalkboard Lesson

SUFFIX REVIEW

Draw balloons and write words that end in **ed** on them. Ask student to read the words and tell
how they are alike. (They all end in **ed**.)

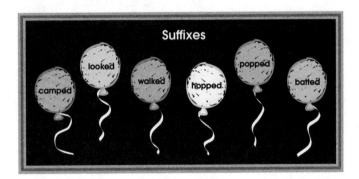

Use the root word in each balloon in a sentence and have your student change each
sentence to the past tense.

       Example: Instructor: Today I camp.

                  Student: Yesterday I camped.

Continue with words in the balloons and these additional words: **played, rained, scrubbed,
pulled, baked, cooked, hunted, fished.**

Vocabulary and Reading

ch=k and ss=sh Words and Related Stories in Storybook Reader 17

Goals
To read, write, and spell words with **ch=k** and **ss=sh**

To read words with **ch=k** and **ss=sh** in context

To practice Grammar Skills

Suggested Pacing
1 day

Materials
1. *Raceway Book*, pp. 185-186
2. Phonetic Storybook Reader 17, *The Trophy Book*, pp. 14-35

pp. 185-186

PROCEDURE

Have student:

- Open **Raceway Book** p.185 and circle the **ch** and **sh** in each word.
- Read, write, and spell all words on p. 185.

Instructor: Initial and date boxes at bottom of p. 185.

Have student:

- Read pp. 14-35 in **Storybook Reader 17**.
- Read each story two or three times for fluency.
- Complete **Raceway Book** p. 186.

Instructor: Teach **Grammar Chalkboard Lesson**/Manual p. 212.

Phonics Song(s)/Games

Each day's lesson should begin with one or two previously learned phonics songs and end with a phonics game.

Written Spelling Tests and Homework

Each day dictate the previous day's 10 spelling "homework" words for a written spelling test. Following the test, have your student circle the next 10 words in the Raceway Book. These 10 spelling words will be for today's homework (writing sentences or a story), and tomorrow's test. See pp. 97 and 143 in this Manual for directions.

RACEWAY STEP 34ᴮ

Phonetic Storybook Reader 17

Comprehension Questions

Christopher's Trip
Story 2 • pp. 14-35

Have student read orally the designated pages. Ask the following questions:

After reading p. 15:

- What does the title tell us about Christopher? *(Context Clue)* He's going on a trip.
- What time of year is it? *(Story Detail)* Winter/Christmas

After reading pp. 16-17:

- How is Chris going to travel? *(Story Detail)* By ship
- Does anyone know what it means to christen a ship? *(Personal Experience)* Answers will vary.
- Why did this ship need to be christened? *(Context Clue)* It was a new ship.
- What was the name of the ship? *(Story Detail)* The Christy Breeze

After reading pp. 18-21:

- Why did Chris stand at attention when they sang the *Star Spangled Banner? (Personal Experience)* It's our national anthem.
- Why was it important for the ship to leave on schedule? *(Inference/Drawing Conclusion)* The tide is going out.
- Why does the anchor have to be pulled up for the ship to leave the dock? *(Personal Experience)* The anchor is like a brake for a boat.

After reading pp. 22-23:

- What happened as the ship pulled out into the harbor and then out to sea? *(Context Clue/Picture Clue)* The whistle blew.
- How much did it cost to see a movie on the ship? *(Context Clue)* It's free.

After reading pp. 24-27:

- How many dining rooms were there? *(Story Detail)* Three
- What does it mean when it says "Chris gave himself a mission"? *(Interpretation)* He gave himself a job or task.

- Where did he go first and what did he have? *(Story Detail)* He went to the snack bar and had a lemon soda.
- What did Chris do next? *(Story Detail)* He played Ping-Pong with his dad.
- Why did Chris want a root beer? *(Context Clue)* He was thirsty after playing Ping-Pong.
- Write the following sentences and have your student arrange them in sequence. *(Sequence)*
  - (4) Chris played shuffleboard.
  - (2) Chris played Ping-Pong.
  - (1) Chris had a lemon soda.
  - (3) Chris had a root beer.

After reading pp. 28-29:

- What do you think is happening to Chris? *(Prediction)* He's getting seasick.

After reading pp. 30-31:

- Tell me what happened on these two pages. *(Summarizing)* They put Chris to bed and called the doctor who gave him some medicine.
- Talk about car sickness or motion sickness with the students. Why did the author write these pages in wavy lines? *(Interpretation)* To show how Chris was feeling

After reading pp. 32-33:

- When did Chris feel better? *(Story Detail)* Soon
- What did they have on the ship to celebrate Christmas? *(Context Clue)* A Christmas tree and wreath, and a chorus to sing carols.
- What did the children do for others? *(Context Clue)* They sang songs.

(Continued on next page)

After reading pp. 34-35:

- What present did each child receive from Captain Hank? *(Story Detail)* He let each child come up to the bridge of the ship.

- What is the *bridge* of the ship? *(Context Clue)* Where the captain steers the ship.

- What do you think Chris liked best about his vacation? *(Predicting)* Answers will vary.

- Could this story be true? *(Realism/Fantasy)* Yes

- What big problem did Chris have in this story? *(Analyzing)* He got seasick.

- How was it solved? *(Analyzing)* The doctor gave him medicine.

- Which of these sentences is the main idea of this story? *(Main Idea)*
  Chris steers the Christy Breeze.
  Chris gets sick on the ship.
  Chris takes a vacation on a ship.

Complete p. 186 in Raceway Book. See directions below.

Raceway Book: Grammar

PRONOUNS, *p. 186*
Pronouns are words that stand for the names of people, places, or things. Examples: *you, he, we, me, I, they, him, her,* etc. Students will write the names the underlined pronouns stand for on p. 186.

p. 186

Grammar Chalkboard Lesson

SENTENCE REVIEW

Write the words shown below. Student will write a sentence with each pair of action words.

Example: walk - walked Today I walk to school. Yesterday I walked to school.

> **Sentences**
> 1. play - played
> 2. look - looked
> 3. cook - cooked

Move Raceway Car to Step **35**

Sing Spell Read & Write

Vocabulary and Reading

Rulebreaker and Wacky Words, ch=sh Words, and Related Stories in Storybook Reader 17

Goals
To read, write, and spell **rulebreaker** and **wacky words**, and **ch=sh words**

To read **rulebreaker** and **wacky words**, and **ch=sh words** in context

To practice Grammar Skills

Suggested Pacing
2 days

Materials
1. *Raceway Book,* pp. 187-190

2. Phonetic Storybook Reader 17, *The Trophy Book,* pp. 36-67

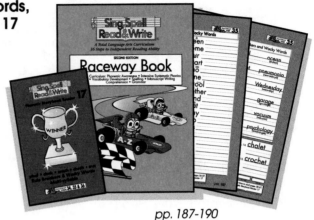

pp. 187-190

PROCEDURE

Instructor:

- Have student open **Raceway Book** to pp. 187-188.
- Introduce these rulebreaker words using pronunciation markings.
- Have student read, write, and spell each word on pp. 187-188.
- Initial and date boxes at bottom of pp. 187-188.

Have student:

- Read pp. 36-67 in **Storybook Reader 17**.
- Read each story two or three times for fluency.
- Complete **Raceway Book** pp. 189-190.

Instructor:

- Teach **Grammar Chalkboard Lessons**/Manual p. 216.
- Teach **Creative Writing Lesson**/Manual p. 216.

Phonics Song(s)/Games

Each day's lesson should begin with one or two previously learned phonics songs and end with a phonics game.

Written Spelling Tests and Homework

Each day dictate the previous day's 10 spelling "homework" words for a written spelling test. Following the test, have your student circle the next 10 words in the Raceway Book. These 10 spelling words will be for today's homework (writing sentences or a story), and tomorrow's test. See pp. 97 and 143 in this Manual for directions.

Brave Heart is an Indian boy. He lives near the ocean.

37

Phonetic Storybook Reader 17

Comprehension Questions
Brave Heart
Story 3 • pp. 36-49

Have student read orally the designated pages. Ask the following questions:

After reading p. 37:
- Who is the story going to be about? *(Main Character)* Brave Heart
- Where does he live? *(Story Detail)* Near the ocean

After reading pp. 38-39:
- Why don't his shoes make noise when he walks in the woods? *(Context Clue)* They are very soft leather.

After reading pp. 40-43:
- Let's try to find all the living things in the picture on pp. 40-41. 18 besides Brave Heart
- How do we know Brave Heart spends lots of time in the woods? *(Inference/Drawing Conclusion)* He knows all the paths.
- Think of some words to describe Brave Heart. Kind, smart, loves animals, likes outdoors
- Let's try to find the eleven creatures in the picture on pp. 42-43. Raccoon, rabbit, squirrel, bear, turtle, 2 birds, a bee, caterpillar, worm, and butterfly

After reading pp. 44-45:
- What happened one Wednesday? *(Story Detail)* Two deer came to Brave Heart.

- Why did Brave Heart think the deer had come to him? *(Story Detail)* One deer did not look well and perhaps needed his help.

After reading pp. 46-47:
- How did Brave Heart help the deer? *(Story Detail)* He took the deer to see his friend who knew about healthy plants.
- How do we know the medicine was good for the deer? *(Inference/Drawing Conclusion)* It seemed to make the deer feel well again.
- How long did it take for the deer to get well? *(Context Clue)* Until the next Wednesday
- What does the deer want to do for Brave Heart? *(Story Detail)* Give him a reward
- What do you think the reward will be? *(Predicting)* Something from the forest

After reading pp. 48-49:
- What was the reward? *(Story Detail)* Sweet sap from the maple tree
- What will Brave Heart make from the maple sap? *(Story Detail)* Maple syrup and sugar
- What was the problem in this story? *(Analyzing)* A deer was sick and needed help.

Four friends can have fun. They can play together.

Tim, Ed, Sally and Ann are friends. They like to play Secret Spy.

51

Comprehension Questions
Friends
Story 4• pp. 50-57

Have student read orally the designated pages. Ask the following questions:

After reading p. 51:
- What are the boys' names? *(Story Detail)* Tim and Ed

- What are the girls' names? *(Story Detail)* Ann and Sally

(Continued on next page)

- What do they like to play?
  (Story Detail) Secret Spy

After reading pp. 52-53:

- Why was Tim chosen to be the colonel?
  (Inference/Drawing Conclusion)
  He's the biggest.
- What will Ed and Sally be?
  (Story Detail) Sergeants
- Where do you think they are playing?
  (Inference/Drawing Conclusion)
  In the backyard
- What did they have for lunch?
  (Story Detail) Soup
- What makes work easy?
  (Context Clue) When everyone works together

After reading pp. 54-55:

- What did the friends do after lunch?
  (Story Detail) They went on a hike in the woods.

Comprehension Questions
The Move to Chicago
Story 5• pp. 58-67

Have student read orally the designated pages. Ask the following questions:

After reading p. 59:

- How many children are in this family?
  (Context Clue) Three
- What city is this family moving to?
  (Story Detail) Chicago

After reading pp. 60-61:

- Where is this family moving from?
  (Context Clue) Michigan
- How will the family get to Chicago?
  (Story Detail) They'll drive.

After reading pp. 62-65:

- Put these items in the order they went into the van. *(Sequence)*
  2 dining room chandelier
  4 toy parachute
  1 chaise lounge
  3 chef hat
- Who loaded the furniture in the van?
  (Story Detail) The movers

- What did they see? *(Story Detail)* Some tracks
- What game did they play?
  (Story Detail) Secret Spy
- Why did they become frightened?
  (Context Clue) They heard noises.
- What do you think is making the noise?
  (Predicting) An animal

After reading pp. 56-57:

- Who was making the noise? *(Story Detail)* Rex
- How did they feel when they realized it was Rex making the noise? *(Context Clue)*
  Relieved
- Which sentence is the main idea? *(Main Idea)*
  1. Mom had pizza for the children when they got home.
  2. Tim was the colonel.
  3. Four friends had fun together in the woods.

Charlotte, Michelle, and Cheryl Chalfonte are so happy. They are moving to Chicago ! 59

- What do you think they packed in their car?
  (Predicting) Clothes and delicate, breakable things
- Why would they need to take some clothes in the car? *(Analyzing)* They'll need a change of clothes before the van is unloaded.

After reading pp. 66-67:

- What did Mom say they will listen to as they ride? *(Story Detail)* Chopin tapes
- How did this family feel about their move?
  (Context Clue) They were very happy.
- What was the problem in this story?
  (Analyzing) Moving
- How did they solve it? *(Analyzing)*
  They hired a moving van and everybody helped.
- Tell me in a few words the main idea of this story.
  (Main Idea) The Chalfonte family is moving to Chicago.

Raceway Book: Grammar/Comprehension

PLURALS, p. 189
Remind the student to add **es** to words ending in **ch, sh, s, x,** or **z.** Choose the correct word to fill in the blank.

SEQUENCE, p. 190
Tell the student to think about what happened *first, next* and *last* to understand a story. The pictures on p. 190 should be numbered 1, 2, and 3, etc., to show what happened *first, next* and *last.*

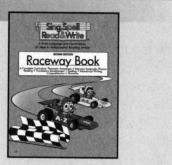

pp. 189-190

Grammar Chalkboard Lessons

COMPOUND WORD REVIEW

Write the words and pictures shown below. Student will draw pictures to illustrate the two words in a compound word.

Example: mailbox

Compound Words

1. fireman
2. pocketbook
3. basketball
4. seashell

CONTRACTION REVIEW

Write the words shown below . Have student write the contraction for the two words.

Example: do not=don't

Contractions

1. did not didn't
2. are not aren't
3. is not isn't
4. have not haven't

1. were not weren't
2. we are we're
3. you are you're
4. they are they're

Creative Writing Lesson

This *Creative Writing Lesson* follows the reading of the story **Friends**, pp. 50-57 in Storybook Reader 17, *The Trophy Book.*

Your student will make a cartoon showing a different ending for the story. (Tell student to refer back to ending on pp. 55-57.) Student will write a sentence for each page and illustrate it.

I hear scary noises!

A bear! Run for your life!

We're safe at home. The bear stopped to eat our soup.

(Sample Cartoon)

The cartoon may be taped together as a fold-out, or stapled together in book form with a cover page.

Move Raceway Car to Step **36**

Vocabulary and Reading

ous Words, Multi-Syllable Words, and Related Stories in Storybook Reader 17

Goals

To read, write, and spell **ous** and **multi-syllable words**

To read **ous** and **multi-syllable words** in context

To practice Grammar Skills

To take Book End Assessment

Suggested Pacing

2 days

Materials

1. *Raceway Book*, pp. 191-192
2. Phonetic Storybook Reader 17,
   The Trophy Book, pp. 68-80
3. Assessment Book: Assessment for Phonetic Storybook Reader 17
   Achievement Test 3

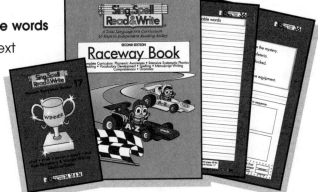

pp. 191-192

PROCEDURE

Have student:

- Open **Raceway Book** to p. 191 and circle the letters **ous** in each word #1 to #12.
- Read, write, and spell all words on p. 191.

Instructor: Initial and date at bottom of p. 191.

Have student:

- Read pp. 68-80 in **Storybook Reader 17**.
- Read each story two or three times for fluency.
- Complete **Raceway Book** p. 192.

Instructor:

- Teach **Grammar Chalkboard Lessons**/Manual p. 219.
- Administer **Assessment**/Manual p. 220.
- Administer **Achievement Test 3**/Manual p. 223.

Phonics Song(s)/Games

Each day's lesson should begin with one or two previously learned phonics songs and end with a phonics game.

Written Spelling Tests and Homework

Each day dictate the previous day's 10 spelling "homework" words for a written spelling test. Following the test, have your student circle the next 10 words in the Raceway Book. These 10 spelling words will be for today's homework (writing sentences or a story), and tomorrow's test. See pp. 97 and 143 in this Manual for directions.

Comprehension Questions
The Enormous Surprise
Story 6 • pp. 68-80

Have student read orally the designated pages.
Ask the following questions:

After reading p. 69:

* What made Bob curious? *(Story Detail)*
  The locked cafeteria door; a fabulous smell

* What is the setting for this part of the story?
  (Analyzing) The school

* Think of some words besides "fabulous" to
  describe the smell. *(Expanding Vocabulary)*
  Wonderful, delicious, good

After reading pp. 70-71:

* Why did Bob want Rick to help him find an
  explanation? *(Inference/Drawing Conclusion)*
  Rick's a detective.

* Where does Rick live? *(Story Detail)*
  In the Maple Grove Apartments

* How do you know Rick lives upstairs?
  (Context Clue) Because Bob takes the
  elevator there

* What was Rick doing when Bob arrived?
  (Story Detail) Subtraction homework

After reading pp. 72-73:

* What did Rick need to take with him?
  (Story Detail) His detective equipment

* Why did they climb the tree? *(Story Detail)*
  To try to see in the window

After reading pp. 74-75:

* What did they find out when Rick looked in
  the window from the tree he was in?
  (Story Detail) He saw smoke.

* What is Bob going to do? *(Story Detail)*
  Call the fire department

* What do you think the smoke is from?
  (Predicting) Something cooking

* Why would the chef tell them to call off the
  fire engines? *(Inference/Drawing Conclusion)*
  He knows what it's all about and they won't
  need the fire engines.

After reading pp. 76-77:

* What was the surprise?
  (Story Detail) A cake

* Why do you think this class is getting a
  Raceway cake? *(Predicting)*
  Because they finished the 36 steps

After reading pp. 78-80:

* What was the cake for? *(Story Detail)*
  To celebrate finishing the Raceway Book

* What will each child receive for finishing the
  Raceway Book? *(Story Detail)* A trophy

* Your class is like Bob and Rick's class. You have
  also finished the Raceway Book and can now
  read almost anything you want. What a
  fabulous thing you have done!
  Congratulations!

Complete p. 192 in Raceway Book.
See directions below.

Raceway Book: Phonetic Analysis

Raceway Book, *p. 192*
The student will number the five sentences to sequence the
story. Next, student will choose a favorite fairy tale, write the
title on the line, and illustrate it.

p. 192

Grammar Chalkboard Lessons

PUNCTUATION REVIEW

Write the sentences shown below. Student will write the sentences correctly.

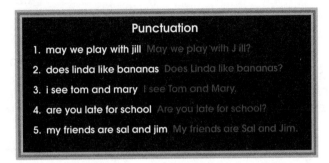

Punctuation

1. may we play with jill   May we play with Jill?
2. does linda like bananas   Does Linda like bananas?
3. i see tom and mary   I see Tom and Mary.
4. are you late for school   Are you late for school?
5. my friends are sal and jim   My friends are Sal and Jim.

CLASSIFICATION REVIEW

Write the list of words shown below. Have your student choose a heading for each group of words, and write it on the lines.

Example: <u>buildings</u>
　　　　house
　　　　school
　　　　store

Classification

1. _____	2. _____	3. _____	4. _____
banana	ball	Mom	cat
apple	bat	Dad	dog
beans	skates	Bill	rabbit

Assessment Book

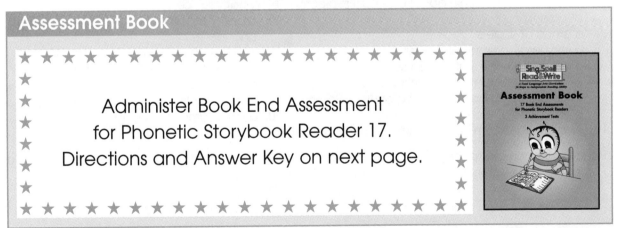

Administer Book End Assessment
for Phonetic Storybook Reader 17.
Directions and Answer Key on next page.

Sing Spell Read & Write
Assessment Book
17 Book End Assessments
for Phonetic Storybook Readers
3 Achievement Tests

You've finished the race! Award a prize from the Treasure Chest to your student as he/she crosses the Finish Line! Hold up his/her arm standing and give three cheers! Write the student's name on a "Winning Trophy Certificate" (found in back of Assessment Book). Compliment the student and pin a blue ribbon on the child's chest!

Instructor, congratulations! Take yourself out to dinner! You have taught someone to read, write and spell!!

Sing Spell Read & Write

Directions and Answer Key

Book End Assessment
Phonetic Storybook Reader 17

Word Recognition: ph=f, ch=k, ss=sh, ch=sh

Instructor: Direct student to "Put your finger on box #1. Now circle the word in the box that I call... 'photo.' Put your finger on box #2. Now circle the word 'chaise,' etc." The words the instructor should call are listed below. Say each word distinctly with emphasis upon initial and final consonants.

1. photo	2. chaise	3. mission	4. school	5. dolphin
6. chandelier	7. chord	8. orphan	9. admission	10. autograph
11. christen	12. gopher	13. Christy	14. telephone	15. phonics
16. anchor	17. Philadelphia	18. alphabet	19. discussion	20. schedule

Record scores in the space provided on the front cover of the Student Assessment Record and calculate the Percentage of Mastery Score as indicated.

p.1

Word Comprehension: ph=f, ch=k, ss=sh, ch=sh

Directions: Tell your student to put his/her finger on box #1 again and listen to what you say:

Instructor: *Underline the word that (is)...*

1. the study of the sounds of a language. phonics
2. what you must wear when you jump from and airplane. parachute
3. to talk to other people about a certain subject. discussion
4. a group of singers. chorus
5. a very large animal. elephant
6. a large city in the state of Illinois. Chicago
7. what keeps a boat from floating away. anchor
8. what you might get if you win a contest. trophy
9. a kind of pain. ache
10. what you get from using a camera. photograph
11. a part of the body. stomach
12. a boy child of your brother or sister. nephew
13. a plan for when things will happen. schedule
14. what you use when you spell words. alphabet
15. a pretty light that hangs from the ceiling. chandelier
16. a place where you go to learn. school
17. a place to buy medicine. pharmacy
18. something used to talk to people. telephone
19. means to allow you to do something. permission
20. a girl's name. Charlotte

Record scores in the space provided on the front cover of the Student Assessment Record and calculate the Percentage of Mastery Score as indicated.

Book End Assessment
Phonetic Storybook Reader 17

Word Recognition: Rulebreakers and Wacky Words

Instructor: Direct student to "Put your finger on box #1. Now circle the word in the box that I call...'of.' Put your finger on box #2. Now circle the word 'has,' etc." The words the instructor should call are listed below. Say each word distinctly with emphasis upon initial and final consonants.

1. of	2. has	3. your	4. door	5. any
6. who	7. been	8. is	9. does	10. said
11. they	12. some	13. one	14. was	15. four
16. says	17. very	18. once	19. the	20. as

Record scores in the space provided on the front cover of the Student Assessment Record and calculate the Percentage of Mastery Score as indicated.

p.2

Word Comprehension: Rulebreakers and Wacky Words

Directions: Tell your student to put his/her finger on box #1 again and listen to what you say:

Instructor: *Underline the word that (is)...*

1. means to work. do
2. what you use to see. eyes
3. a number. four
4. the opposite of difficult. easy
5. means to have made something. built
6. a number. two
7. someone you like to be with. friend
8. means someone uses their voice. says
9. something to eat. soup
10. something sweet. sugar
11. a part of the body. heart
12. means a lot. many
13. means it happened one time. once
14. means someone has spoken. said
15. means someone owns it. has
16. a question word you answer with a person's name. who
17. a question word you answer with the name of a thing. what
18. means to go in the direction of. to
19. more than one person. they
20. a number. one

Record scores in the space provided on the front cover of the Student Assessment Record and calculate the Percentage of Mastery Score as indicated.

Directions and Answer Key

Book End Assessment
Phonetic Storybook Reader 17

Word Recognition: Multi-Syllable and ous Words

Instructor: Direct student to "Put your finger on box #1. Now circle the word in the box that I call... 'explanation.' Put your finger on box #2. Now circle the word 'fabulous,' etc." The words the instructor should call are listed below. Say each word distinctly with emphasis upon initial and final consonants.

1. explanation
2. fabulous
3. spaghetti
4. serious
5. sergeant
6. dangerous
7. together
8. generous
9. vacuum
10. lieutenant
11. colonel
12. elevator
13. enormous
14. scissors
15. jealous
16. pneumonia
17. department
18. location
19. garage
20. ocean

Record scores in the space provided on the front cover of the Student Assessment Record and calculate the Percentage of Mastery Score as indicated.

p. 3

Word Comprehension: Multi-Syllable and ous Words

Directions: Tell your student to put his/her finger on box #1 again and listen to what you say:

Instructor: *Underline the word that (is)...*

1. means very, very large. enormous
2. the day after today. tomorrow
3. a kind of sickness. pneumonia
4. a machine that moves up and down. elevator
5. a day of the week. Wednesday
6. the day before today. yesterday
7. a place to go and eat. cafeteria
8. means very beautiful. gorgeous
9. a large body of water. ocean
10. means the place where someone or something is. location
11. means to be interested in something. curious
12. something to eat that has a crust. pizza
13. means to look for information and facts. investigation
14. means to be very well known. famous
15. a rank in the army. sergeant
16. you must be very careful when you see this word on a sign. dangerous
17. means it is terrific. fabulous
18. used to clean the rug. vacuum
19. taking one number away from another. subtraction
20. means to be with one another. together

Record scores in the space provided on the front cover of the Student Assessment Record and calculate the Percentage of Mastery Score as indicated.

Sentence Comprehension

"Bubble" Format Directions pp. 69-70

1. C	6. B	11. A	16. B	21. D
2. B	7. C	12. D	17. A	22. C
3. E	8. A	13. B	18. D	23. E
4. A	9. D	14. E	19. E	24. A
5. D	10. E	15. C	20. C	25. B

Story Comprehension

"Bubble" Format Directions pp. 69-70

1. hot
2. Secret Spy
3. they worked together
4. after they climbed on some rocks
5. to the woods
6. It was time to go.
7. Yes
8. a thermos
9. Tim
10. "Four Friends Have Fun"

DIRECTIONS FOR ACHIEVEMENT TEST 3

Achievement Test 3 may be used:

- As a post assessment to measure growth
- To determine mastery of skills

TO BEGIN

- Remove Achievement Test 3 from back of student's Assessment Book.

ADMINISTERING

SECTION A: Spelling

- Call the words below. Tell student to circle the correct spelling.

1. glue	7. knee
2. bread	8. calf
3. often	9. might
4. word	10. lamb
5. color	11. half
6. wrong	12. sign

SECTION B: Compound Words

- Tell student compound words are two words put together to make one word. Student will draw a line to divide the compound word into two words.
- Use this example: some/one
- Stop when you complete #6 and see the .

SECTION C: Contractions

- Tell student a contraction is a short way to write two words.
  Example: doesn't = does not
- Student will write the two words for each contraction.
- Stop when you complete #6 and see the .

SECTION D: Word Recognition

- Tell student to look at the picture in the box and circle the word that names the picture.
- Remind him/her to read all four words before circling a word.
- Stop when you complete #10 and see the STOP.

SECTION E: Sentence Comprehension

- Tell student to look at the four pictures in each box.
- Read the sentence. Put an X on the correct picture.
- Stop when you are finished and see the .

SECTION F: Story Comprehension

- Tell student to read the story. Next, read each question and fill in the correct answer.
- Remind student that he/she may go back and reread the story to find answers.

SCORING ACHIEVEMENT TEST 3

- There are 50 items on Achievement Test 3. Score each Section, total the number of items correct, and multiply by 2. This will give you the student's Percentage of Mastery Score.
- 40 items correct x 2 = 80%.
- A score of 80% or above indicates mastery level.

Answer Key

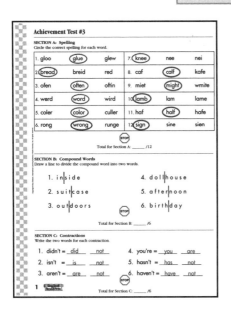

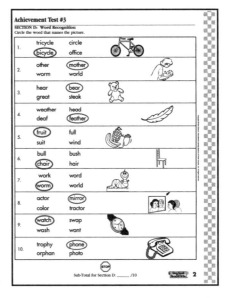

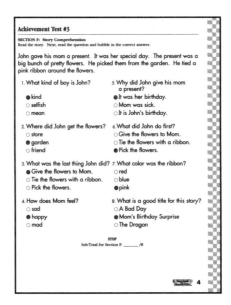

36 Steps to Independent Reading Ability

RACEWAY
STEP **16**

DUCK POND